Cloud Native Architectures

Design high-availability and cost-effective applications
for the cloud

Tom Laszewski
Kamal Arora
Erik Farr
Piyum Zonooz

BIRMINGHAM - MUMBAI

Cloud Native Architectures

Commissioning Editor: Aaron Lazar
Acquisition Editor: Chaitanya Nair
Content Development Editor: Rohit Singh
Technical Editor: Ketan Kamble
Copy Editor: Safis Editing
Project Coordinator: Vaidehi Sawant
Proofreader: Safis Editing
Indexer: Aishwarya Gangawane
Graphics: Jason Monteiro
Production Coordinator: Shantanu Zagade

First published: August 2018

Production reference: 2031018

Published by Packt Publishing Ltd.
Livery Place
35 Livery Street
Birmingham
B3 2PB, UK.

ISBN 978-1-78728-054-0

www.packtpub.com

`mapt.io`

Mapt is an online digital library that gives you full access to over 5,000 books and videos, as well as industry leading tools to help you plan your personal development and advance your career. For more information, please visit our website.

Why subscribe?

- Spend less time learning and more time coding with practical eBooks and Videos from over 4,000 industry professionals

- Improve your learning with Skill Plans built especially for you

- Get a free eBook or video every month

- Mapt is fully searchable

- Copy and paste, print, and bookmark content

PacktPub.com

Did you know that Packt offers eBook versions of every book published, with PDF and ePub files available? You can upgrade to the eBook version at `www.PacktPub.com` and as a print book customer, you are entitled to a discount on the eBook copy. Get in touch with us at `service@packtpub.com` for more details.

At `www.PacktPub.com`, you can also read a collection of free technical articles, sign up for a range of free newsletters, and receive exclusive discounts and offers on Packt books and eBooks.

Foreword

The purpose of this book is to find the intersection between practicality and cloud native. It's an exploration of what's possible, and includes the whys and the hows. This book is the jumping-off point for the next generation of cloud computing, nothing less.

The goal is to turbocharge the power of cloud computing, and have applications be all that they can be on the platform. Everyone related to cloud computing can benefit from this book, including developers, end users, and thus the business as a whole. Remember, it should always be the objective of IT to meet and exceed the needs of the business. This book will help IT make effective plans to meet those goals.

The pros of going to cloud-native features include the following:

- **Performance**: You typically access native features of the public cloud services to provide better performance than is possible with non-native features. For example, you can deal with an I/O system that works with auto-scaling and load-balancing features.
- **Efficiency**: Cloud-native applications' use of cloud-native features and APIs should provide more efficient use of underlying resources. That translates to better performance and/or lower operating costs.
- **Cost**: Applications that are more efficient typically cost less to run. Cloud providers send you a monthly bill based upon the amount of resources consumed, so if you can do more with less, you save on dollars spent.
- **Scalability**: Because you write the application to the native cloud interfaces, you also have direct access to the auto-scaling and load-balancing features of the cloud platform.

To take proper advantage of a cloud platform, including IaaS platforms such as AWS, you have to design the applications so that they're decoupled from any specific physical resource. For example, if you access I/O directly from a platform such as Linux, you need to access the cloud's abstraction layer, or their native APIs.

Clouds *can* provide an abstraction or virtualization layer between the application and the underlying physical (or virtual) resources, whether they're designed for cloud or not. But that's not good enough. If you're going truly cloud native, you need to directly control the native resources.

When this architecture is considered in the design, development, and deployment of an application, the utilization of the underlying cloud resources can be as much as 70 percent more efficient. This cloud computing efficiency equals money. You're paying for the resources you use, so applications that work more efficiently with those resources run faster and generate smaller cloud services bills at the end of the month.

Cloud native is not only about changing the code to follow the features of a specific cloud; it's also about changing your approach to architecture design. These cloud-aligned architectures can auto-scale, and are also distributed, stateless, and loosely coupled, just to name a few features. If you want to make applications truly cloud native, the architecture must be rethought before you begin refactoring the code.

Does this new approach to application architecture suck resources and money, as well as add a great deal of risk? Yes. However, the risk-reward typically leans to the reward side, if the life of an application is 10 to 15 years (which it is for most enterprises). **The effort of both re-architecture and refactoring for an application with long-term use will pay for itself many times over.**

When migrating applications to the cloud, the evidence is compelling for the cloud-native applications path. The benefits outweigh the costs for most applications that are picked to move to the cloud, but given that refactoring costs 30 times that of simple re-hosting, enterprises are reluctant to dive in with both feet.

So, this will be another learning process similar to what users saw when we made applications platform-native, Unix/Linux-native APIs. We had to fail before we succeeded. Here I suspect we'll follow the same patterns. Meaning, in a few years, cloud native will become the best practice. However, that won't happen until we fall on our faces a few more times. Some things never change.

So, cloud native that leverages cloud native architectures—is it the way to go? Judging by the fact that you're reading the foreword of this book, I suspect you're already convinced that it is. Reading the rest of the book will only seal the deal. When you deploy your first or second cloud-native architecture, you will have truly seen the light.

David Linthicum

Chief Cloud Strategy Officer, Deloitte Consulting LLP

As I write this, in the summer of 2018, cloud computing has become an accepted part of most corporate and enterprise computing strategies. By hosting applications in the cloud, companies can reduce spend and dependence on non-value-adding costs such as brick and mortar/physical facilities, servers, and networks. It's no wonder that nearly 90 percent of companies are tapping into cloud resources in some way, according to RightScale.

However, using the cloud simply as a cheap outsourced or virtualized data center leaves much of the value of cloud computing on the table. By adopting a *cloud-native* approach to systems and application architectures, companies can take advantage of the elastic and near-limitless compute, storage, and networking capacity of the modern public cloud, and by doing so, provide much better value to their customers.

What are *cloud-native* applications? Cloud-native apps, first and foremost, are defined by their ability to scale automatically as load increases and decreases. Today, most companies provision the maximum number of servers in their data centers in anticipation of a heavy load—and then watch as, most days, their CPU utilization remains in the single digits. By leveraging automated scale-out features in the cloud, applications can grow—and shrink—as needed without human intervention. If you need capacity, it's available; if you don't, that capacity is returned, and you are not charged for it.

A cloud-native application is also resilient in the face of errors or failures. If, for some reason, a piece of hardware, such as a server or a router, fails, or if a database experiences a catastrophic error, a cloud-native application should detect the error and heal itself, perhaps by creating a new instance of itself on another rack or even in another cloud data center in another region.

Cloud-native computing accelerates both IT and the business it serves, allowing IT to adopt Agile and DevOps-based development approaches faster and with less effort. This enables them to deploy new code more frequently—perhaps many times a day—and use automated testing pipelines for greater reliability. They can experiment with cloud capabilities such as machine learning and advanced analytics without having to make expensive procurement decisions. And, because of the acceleration in IT, businesses can provide better, faster responses to their customers, reach new customers through the cloud's global reach, and perhaps even change their core business models.

There are many new technologies—containers, API gateways, event managers, serverless—that, if properly implemented, can give you the benefits of cloud-native computing as envisioned. However, the shift to cloud native implies not only technological changes but also organizational and cultural changes: moving from a waterfall development model to Agile and lean approaches, implementing a continuous integration/continuous delivery automation, and building a culture of experimentation can help shift to a cloud-native mindset.

The rewards of adopting cloud-native methodologies and architectures include improved IT capability and, more importantly, potentially exponential new innovative opportunities for your business. These benefits make cloud-native computing imperative and a leading driver of modern cloud adoption.

I highly recommend you read *Cloud Native Architectures*. In it, you'll find recipes for creating applications that use the cloud as intended, opening a new world of intelligent innovative solutions.

Miha Kralj

Managing Director, Cloud Native Architecture, Accenture LLP

Contributors

About the authors

Tom Laszewski is a leader and cloud technologist who has helped ISVs, SIs, start-ups, and enterprise customers modernize IT systems and develop innovative software solutions. He currently leads a team of Enterprise Technologists responsible for the business and IT transformation strategy with key AWS customers. Many of these customers are pursuing cloud modernization and digital transformation initiatives utilizing cloud native architectures. He enjoys traveling the world with his teenage sons Slade and Logan.

Kamal Arora is an inventor, author, and technology leader with more than 15 years of IT experience. He currently works at Amazon Web Services and leads a diverse team of highly experienced solutions architects who enable global consulting partners and enterprise customers on their journey to cloud. Kamal has also led the creation of biggest global technical partnerships, set his team's vision and execution model, and incubated multiple new strategic initiatives. He's passionate about the latest innovations in the cloud and the AI/ML space, and their impact on our society and daily-life.

> *My special thanks to my wife Poonam Arora for unconditional support and my family Kiran, Rajiv, Nisha, Aarini, and Rian for their care and support all the time. Last, but not the least, we miss you dad!*

Erik Farr is a technology leader with over 18 years in the IT industry. He has been on the leading edge of cloud technology and enterprise architecture, working with some of the largest companies and system integrators in the world. In his current role at Amazon Web Services, he leads a team of experienced solution architects to help global system integrator partners design enterprise scale cloud native architectures. Before AWS, he has experience with Capgemini and The Walt Disney Company, always working to create highly valuable outcomes for customers.

I wanted to especially thank my wonderful family, Stacey, Faith and Sydney for all of your support along this journey.

Piyum Zonooz is a Global Partner Solution Architect at Amazon Web Services, where he works with companies across all industries to help drive cloud adoption and re-architect products to cloud native. He's led projects in TCO analysis, infrastructure design, DevOps adoption, and complete business transformation. Prior to AWS, Piyum was a Lead Architect as part of the Accenture Cloud Practice where he led large-scale cloud adoption projects. Piyum holds a BSc and MSc. degree in Engineering from the University of Illinois at Urbana-Champaign.

About the reviewer

Sanjeev Jaiswal is a Computer Graduate from CUSAT with 9 years of industrial experience. He basically uses Perl, Python, AWS, and GNU/Linux for his day-to-day activities. He is currently working on projects involving penetration testing, source code review, security design, and implementations in AWS and cloud security projects. He is learning DevSecOps and security automation currently as well. Sanjeev loves teaching engineering students and IT professionals. He has been teaching for the last 8 years in his leisure time.

He wrote *Instant PageSpeed Optimization*, and co-authored *Learning Django Web Development* with Packt Publishing.

> *My special thanks to my wife, Shalini Jaiswal, for her unconditional support, and my friends Ranjan, Ritesh, Mickey, Shankar, and Santosh for their care and support all the time.*

Packt is searching for authors like you

If you're interested in becoming an author for Packt, please visit `authors.packtpub.com` and apply today. We have worked with thousands of developers and tech professionals, just like you, to help them share their insight with the global tech community. You can make a general application, apply for a specific hot topic that we are recruiting an author for, or submit your own idea.

Table of Contents

Preface

This book will help you understand the core design elements required to build scalable systems. You will learn how to plan resources and technology stacks effectively to achieve high security and fault tolerance. While doing so, you will also explore core architectural principles using real-world examples. This book adopts a hands-on approach with real-world examples and use cases, which will cater to your need to architect cloud applications and migrate your business to cloud efficiently

Who this book is for

This book is for software architects who are keen on designing resilient, scalable, and highly available applications that are native to the cloud.

What this book covers

Chapter 1, *Introducing Cloud Native Architecture*, set the tone of the book and be used as a base to define and explain what cloud native architecture is and is not. Various points will be discussed, including the pros, cons, myths, challenges and impacts.

Chapter 2, *The Cloud Adoption Journey*, explores what it means to adopt the cloud. This will be looked at from various angles, including how to migrate from an on-premises or existing environment to a cloud environment.

Chapter 3, *Cloud Native Application Design*, dives deep into the development of cloud native architectures, using microservices and serverless computing as a design principle.

Chapter 4, *How to Choose Technology Stacks*, explores the common technology that is used to create cloud native architectures, from open source to licensed software. It will explore marketplaces that can be used to consume resources in the cloud. Finally, it will discuss the procurement process and licensing models that are common in the cloud.

Chapter 5, *Scalable and Available*, talks about available tools/features and strategies to employ when designing cloud native systems for scale and HA. The chapter will explore how these tools/features work, how they enable cloud native applications and how to deploy them.

Chapter 6, *Secure and Reliable,* discusses security models, features available in the cloud, pitfalls, and best practices related to security of IT systems. It will also explore how these security features work and how they can help enable cloud users to deploy better secured environments.

Chapter 7, *Optimizing Cost,* covers the pricing model for Cloud environments. We will then discuss how to approach costing exercises as well as the differences between the old and cloud models.

Chapter 8, *Cloud Native Operations,* talks about tools, procedures, and models to ensure environments that are deployed in the cloud stay running. The chapter will outline organizational models, governance strategies, and deployment patterns that support operationally healthy systems.

Chapter 9, *Amazon Web Services,* focuses on providing a perspective on Amazon WebServices' cloud native application development capabilities, strengths, ecosystem maturity and overall approach.

Chapter 10, *Microsoft Azure,* focuses on providing a perspective on Microsoft Azure's cloud native application development capabilities, strengths, ecosystem maturity and overall approach.

Chapter 11, *Google Cloud Platform,* focus on providing a perspective on Google Cloud Platform's cloud native application development capabilities, strengths, ecosystem maturity and overall approach.

Chapter 12, *What's Next? Cloud Native Application Architecture Trends,* looks at future trends and what to expect from various cloud providers in this space.

To get the most out of this book

1. A prior experience with software architecture will be helpful to follow this book.
2. All the examples and instructions are given at the relevant instances.

Download the example code files

You can download the example code files for this book from your account at www.packtpub.com. If you purchased this book elsewhere, you can visit www.packtpub.com/support and register to have the files emailed directly to you.

You can download the code files by following these steps:

1. Log in or register at www.packtpub.com.
2. Select the **SUPPORT** tab.
3. Click on **Code Downloads & Errata**.
4. Enter the name of the book in the **Search** box and follow the onscreen instructions.

Once the file is downloaded, please make sure that you unzip or extract the folder using the latest version of:

- WinRAR/7-Zip for Windows
- Zipeg/iZip/UnRarX for Mac
- 7-Zip/PeaZip for Linux

The code bundle for the book is also hosted on GitHub at https://github.com/PacktPublishing/Cloud-Native-Architectures. We also have other code bundles from our rich catalog of books and videos available at https://github.com/PacktPublishing/. Check them out!

Conventions used

There are a number of text conventions used throughout this book.

CodeInText: Indicates code words in text, database table names, folder names, filenames, file extensions, pathnames, dummy URLs, user input, and Twitter handles. Here is an example: "For the handler, specify the value as lambda_function.lambda_handler."

A block of code is set as follows:

```
print('Loading function') def respond(err, res=None): return {
'statusCode': '400' if err else '200', 'body': err if err else res,
'headers': { 'Content-Type': 'application/json', }, }
```

When we wish to draw your attention to a particular part of a code block, the relevant lines or items are set in bold:

```
print('Loading function')

def respond(err, res=None):
    return {
        'statusCode': '400' if err else '200',
        'body': err if err else res,
        'headers': {
            'Content-Type': 'application/json',
        },
    }
```

Bold: Indicates a new term, an important word, or words that you see onscreen. For example, words in menus or dialog boxes appear in the text like this. Here is an example: "Click on the API's name, **Serverless Weather Service**, to drill down into its configuration."

Warnings or important notes appear like this.

Tips and tricks appear like this.

Get in touch

Feedback from our readers is always welcome.

General feedback: Email `feedback@packtpub.com` and mention the book title in the subject of your message. If you have questions about any aspect of this book, please email us at `questions@packtpub.com`. Alternatively, you can also share feedback/comments with the authors by emailing them at `cloudnativearchitectures@gmail.com`.

Errata: Although we have taken every care to ensure the accuracy of our content, mistakes do happen. If you have found a mistake in this book, we would be grateful if you would report this to us. Please visit `www.packtpub.com/submit-errata`, selecting your book, clicking on the Errata Submission Form link, and entering the details.

Piracy: If you come across any illegal copies of our works in any form on the Internet, we would be grateful if you would provide us with the location address or website name. Please contact us at `copyright@packtpub.com` with a link to the material.

If you are interested in becoming an author: If there is a topic that you have expertise in and you are interested in either writing or contributing to a book, please visit `authors.packtpub.com`.

Reviews

Please leave a review. Once you have read and used this book, why not leave a review on the site that you purchased it from? Potential readers can then see and use your unbiased opinion to make purchase decisions, we at Packt can understand what you think about our products, and our authors can see your feedback on their book. Thank you!

For more information about Packt, please visit `packtpub.com`.

1

Introducing Cloud Native Architecture

The advent of the cloud has led to a new paradigm in designing, implementing, and ongoing maintenance of computer systems. While there are many different names for this new paradigm, the one most commonly used is **cloud native architectures**. In this book, we will explore what exactly cloud native architectures are, why they are new and different, and how they are being implemented across a wide range of global companies. As the name suggests, it's all about the cloud and using cloud vendor services to design these architectures to solve business problems in new, robust, and secure ways. The purpose of this chapter is to explain and define what cloud native architectures are, and provide some insights into the pros, cons, and myths of cloud native architectures. We will explore what it means to be cloud native, understand the spectrum and components that are required for this type of architecture, and appreciate the journey that a company would need to undertake to move up in maturity on the model.

What are cloud native architectures?

If you asked 100 people what the definition of *cloud native* was, you just might get 100 different answers. Why are there so many different answers? To start with, cloud computing itself is still evolving every day, so the definitions offered a few years ago are quite possibly not fully up to date with the current state of the cloud. Secondly, cloud native architectures are a completely new paradigm that use new methods to solve business problems that can typically only be achieved at the scale of cloud computing. Finally, depending on the role of the person being asked, the definition is very different, whether they be an architect, developer, administrator, or decision maker. So, what exactly is the definition of cloud native?

Let's start with a generally accepted definition of what cloud computing is according to AWS:

> *"Cloud computing is the on-demand delivery of compute power, database storage, applications, and other IT resources through a cloud services platform via the internet with pay-as-you-go pricing."*

Therefore, at its most basic form, **cloud native** means to embrace cloud computing services to design the solution; however, that only covers part of what is required to become cloud native. There is a lot more than just using the underlying cloud infrastructure, even if it's the most mature service available.

Automation and application design play significant roles in this process as well. The cloud, with its API-driven design, allows for extreme automation at scale to not only create instances or specific systems, but to also completely roll out an entire corporate landscape with no human interaction. Finally, a critical component in creating a cloud native architecture is the approach used to design a specific application. Systems designed with the best cloud services, and deployed with extreme automation, can still fail to achieve desired results if the logic of the application does not take into consideration the new scale at which it can operate.

Defining the cloud native maturity model

There is no one right answer to what a cloud native architecture is; many types of architectures could fall into the cloud native category. Using the three design principles or axes—cloud native services, application centric design, and automation—most systems can be evaluated for their level of cloud native maturity. In addition, since these principles are ever expanding as new technologies, techniques or design patterns are developed, and so the maturity of cloud native architectures will continue to mature. We, the authors of this book, believe that cloud native architectures are formed by evolution and fall into a maturity model. For the remainder of this book, cloud native architectures will be described using the **Cloud Native Maturity Model** (**CNMM**), following the design principles outlined, so that architecture patterns can be mapped to their point of evolution:

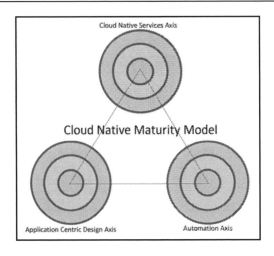

Axis 1 – Cloud native services

To understand where a system will fall on the CNMM, it's important to understand what the components of cloud native architecture are. By definition, being cloud native requires the adoption of cloud services. Each cloud vendor will have its own set of services, with the most mature having the richest set of features. The incorporation of these services, from basic building blocks to the most advanced, cutting-edge technologies, will define how sophisticated a cloud native architecture is on the cloud services axis:

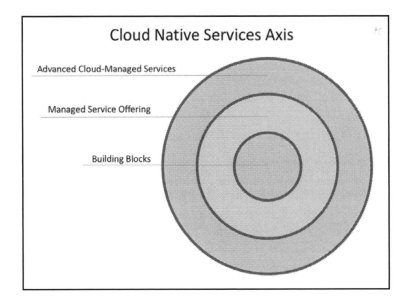

A mature cloud vendor's services

Amazon Web Services (AWS) is often cited as the most advanced cloud platform (at the time of writing). The following diagram shows all the services that AWS has to offer, from basic building blocks, to managed service offerings, to advanced platform services:

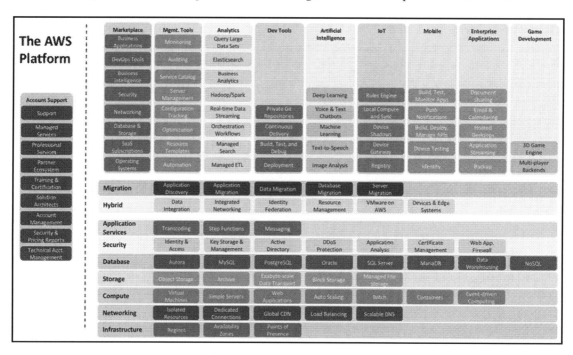

Cloud native services building blocks

Regardless of the level of maturity of the cloud vendor, they will have the building blocks of infrastructure, which include compute, storage, networking, and monitoring. Depending on the cloud maturity level of an organization and the team designing a system, it might be common to begin the cloud native journey by leveraging these baseline infrastructure building blocks. Virtual server instances, block disk storage, object storage, fiber lines and VPNs, load balancers, cloud API monitoring, and instance monitoring are all types of building blocks that a customer would use to start consuming the cloud. Similar to what would be available in an existing on-premises data center, these services would allow for a familiar look and feel for design teams to start creating applications in the cloud. The adoption of these services would be considered the bare minimum required to develop a cloud native architecture, and would result in a relatively low level on the cloud native services axis.

Often, a company will choose to migrate an existing application to the cloud and perform the migration in a lift-and-shift model. This approach would literally move the application stack and surrounding components to the cloud with no changes to the design, technology, or component architecture. Therefore, these migrations only use the basic building blocks that the cloud offers, since that is what is also in place at the customer-on-premises locations. While this is a low level of maturity, it allows for something critical to happen: gaining experience with how the cloud works. Even when using the cloud services building blocks, the design team will quickly add their own guard rails, policies, and naming conventions to learn more efficient techniques to deal with security, deployments, networking, and other core requirements for an early-stage cloud native system.

One of the key outcomes that a company will gain from this maturity stage is the basic premise of the cloud and how that impacts their design patterns: for example, horizontal scaling versus vertical scaling, and the price implications of these designs and how to implement them efficiently. In addition, learning how the chosen cloud vendor operates and groups their services in specific locations and the interactions between these groupings to design high availability and disaster recovery through architecture. Finally, learning the cloud approach to storage and the ability to offload processing to cloud services that scale efficiently and natively on the platform is a critical approach to designing architectures. Even though the adoption of cloud services building blocks is a relatively low level of maturity, it is critical for companies that are beginning their cloud journey.

Cloud vendor managed service offerings

Undifferentiated heavy lifting is often used to describe when time, effort, resources, or money are deployed to perform tasks that will not add to the bottom line of a company. *Undifferentiated* simply means that there is nothing to distinguish the activity from the way others do it. *Heavy lifting* refers to the difficult task of technology innovation and operations which, if done correctly, nobody ever recognizes, and if done wrong, can cause catastrophic consequences to business operations. These phrases combined mean that when a company does difficult tasks—that if done wrong will cause business impact, but that company doesn't have a core competency to distinguish itself in doing these tasks—it not only doesn't add business value, but can easily detract from the business.

Unfortunately, this describes a large majority of the IT operations for enterprise companies, and is a critical selling point to using the cloud. Cloud vendors do have a core competency in technology innovation and operations at a scale that most companies could never dream of. Therefore, it only makes sense that cloud vendors have matured their services to include managed offerings, where they own the management of all aspects of the service and the consumer only needs to develop the business logic or data being deployed to the service. This will allow the undifferentiated heavy lifting to be shifted from the company to the cloud vendor, and allow that company to dedicate significantly more resources to creating business value (their differentiators).

As we have seen, there are lots of combinations of cloud services that can be used to design cloud native architectures using only the basic building blocks and patterns; however, as a design team grows in their understanding of the chosen cloud vendor's services and becomes more mature in their approach, they will undoubtedly want to use more advanced cloud services. Mature cloud vendors will have managed service offerings that are often able to replace components that require undifferentiated heavy lifting. Managed service offerings from cloud vendors would include the following:

- Databases
- Hadoop
- Directory services
- Load balancers
- Caching systems
- Data warehouses
- Code repositories
- Automation tools
- Elastic searching tools

Another area of importance for these services is the agility they bring to a solution. If a system were designed to use these tools but managed by the company operations team, often the process to provision the virtual instance, configure, tune, and secure the package will significantly slow the progress being made by the design team. Using cloud vendor managed service offerings in place of those self-managed components will allow the teams to implement the architecture quickly, and begin the process of testing the applications that will run in that environment.

Using managed service offerings from a cloud vendor doesn't necessarily lead to more advanced architecture patterns; however, it does lead to the ability to think bigger and not be constrained by undifferentiated heavy lifting. This concept of not being constrained by limitations that are normally found on-premises, like finite physical resources, is a critical design attribute when creating cloud native architectures, which will enable systems to reach a scale hard to achieve elsewhere. For example, some areas where using a cloud vendor managed service offering would allow for a more scalable and native cloud architecture are as follows:

- Using managed load balancers to decouple components in an architecture
- Leveraging managed data warehouse systems to provision only the storage required and letting it scale automatically as more data is imported
- Using managed RDBMS database engines to enable quick and efficient transactional processing with durability and high availability built in

Advanced cloud native managed services

Cloud vendors are on their journey and continue to mature service offerings to ever more sophisticated levels. The current wave of innovation among the top cloud vendors suggests a continued move into more and more services that are managed by the vendor at scale and security, and reduces the cost, complexity, and risk to the customer. One way they are achieving this is by re-engineering existing technology platforms to not only deal with a specific technical problem, but by also doing it with the cloud value proposition in mind. For example, AWS has a managed database service, Amazon Aurora, built on a fully distributed and self-healing storage service deigned to keep data safe and distributed across multiple availability zones. This service increases the usefulness of the managed service offerings specific to databases, as described in the previous section, by also allowing for a storage array that grows on demand and is tuned for the cloud to provide performance of up to five times better than a similar database engine.

Not all advanced managed services are re-engineered ideas of existing technology; with the introduction of serverless computing, cloud vendors are removing undifferentiated heavy lifting away from not only operations, but also the development cycle. With the virtually limitless resources the cloud can offer, decoupling large applications into individual functions is the next big wave of distributed systems design, and leads directly into the formation of cloud native architectures.

According to AWS:

> *"Serverless computing allows you to build and run applications and services without thinking about servers. Serverless applications don't require you to provision, scale, and manage any servers. You can build them for virtually any type of application or backend service, and everything required to run and scale your application with high availability is handled for you."*

There are many types of serverless services, including compute, API proxies, storage, databases, message processing, orchestration, analytics, and developer tools. One key attribute to define whether a cloud service is serverless or only a managed offering is the way that licensing and usage are priced. Serverless leaves behind the old-world model of core-based pricing, which would imply it is tied directly to a server instance, and relies more on consumption-based pricing. The length of time a function runs, the amount of transactions per second required, or a combination of these, are common metrics that are used for consumption-based pricing with serverless offerings.

Using these existing advanced cloud native managed services, and continuing to adopt the new ones as they are released, represents a high level of maturity on the CNMM, and will enable companies to develop some of the most advanced cloud native architectures. With these services and an experienced design team, a company will be able to push the boundaries of what is possible when old-world constraints are removed and truly limitless capacity and sophistication are leveraged. For example, instead of a traditional three-tier distributed computing stack consisting of a front end web, an application, or middleware tier and an OLTP database for storage, a new approach to this design pattern would be an API gateway that uses an event-driven computing container as an endpoint, and a managed and scalable NoSQL database for persistence. All these components could fall into a serverless model, therefore allowing the design team to focus on the business logic, and not how to achieve the scale required.

Beyond serverless and other advanced managed services lies the future. Currently, the cutting edge of cloud computing is the offerings being released in the artificial intelligence, machine learning, and deep learning space. Mature cloud vendors have services that fall into these categories with continued innovation happening on a hyperscale. It is still very early in the cycle for artificial intelligence, and design teams should expect more to come.

Cloud native services axis recap

The *Cloud native services axis* section described the components that could make up a cloud native architecture, and showed ever more mature approaches to creating applications using them. As with all of the design principles on the CNMM, the journey will begin with a baseline understanding of the principle and mature as the design team becomes more and more knowledgeable of how to implement at scale; however, cloud computing components are only one part of the design principles that are required to make up a mature cloud native architecture. These are used in conjunction with the other two principles, automation and application centricity, to create systems that can take advantage of the cloud in a secure and robust way.

Axis 2 – Application centric design

The second cloud native principle is about how the application itself will be designed and architected. This section will focus on the actual application design process, and will identify architecture patterns that are mature and lead to cloud native architectures. Similar to the other design principles of the CNMM, developing and architecting cloud native applications is an evolution with different patterns that are typically followed along the way. Ultimately, used in conjunction with the other CNMM principles, the outcome will be a mature, sophisticated, and robust cloud native architecture that is ready to continue evolving as the world of cloud computing expands:

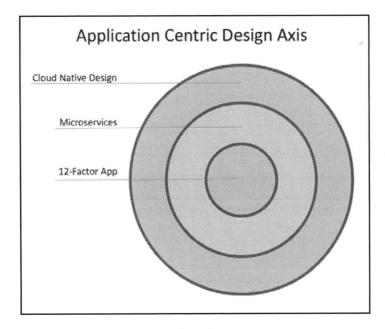

Twelve-factor app design principles

The **twelve-factor app** is a methodology for building software-as-a-service applications (`https://12factor.net/`). This methodology was written in late 2011, and is often cited as the base building blocks for designing scalable and robust cloud native applications. Its principles apply to applications written in any programming language, and which use any combination of backing services (database, queue, memory cache, and so on), and is increasingly useful on any cloud vendor platform. The idea behind the twelve-factor app is that there are twelve important factors to consider when designing applications that minimize the time and cost of adding new developers, cleanly interoperate with the environment, can be deployed to cloud vendors, minimize divergence between environment, and allow for scaling of the application. The twelve factors (`https://12factor.net/`) are as follows:

Factor No.	Factors	Description
1	Code base	One code base tracked in revision control, many deploys.
2	Dependencies	Explicitly declare and isolate dependencies.
3	Config	Store config in the environment.
4	Backing services	Treat backing services as attached resources.
5	Build, release, run	Strictly separate build and run stages.
6	Processes	Execute the app as one (or more) stateless process(es).
7	Port binding	Export services through port binding.
8	Concurrency	Scale-out through the process model.
9	Disposability	Maximize robustness with fast startup and graceful shutdown.
10	Dev/prod parity	Keep development, staging, and production as similar as possible.
11	Logs	Treat logs as event streams.
12	Admin processes	Run admin/management tasks as one-off processes.

Previous sections of this chapter have already discussed how the CNMM takes into consideration multiple factors from this methodology. For example, *factor 1* is all about keeping the code base in a repository, which is standard best practice. *Factors 3, 10, and 12* are all about keeping your environments separate, but making sure they do not drift apart from each other from a code and configuration perspective. *Factor 5* ensures that you have a clean and repeatable CICD pipeline with a separation of functions. And *factor 11* is about treating logs as event streams so they can be analyzed and acted upon in near real time. The remaining factors align well to cloud native design for the simple reason that they focus on being self-contained (*factor 2*), treat everything as a service (*factors 4 and 7*), allow efficient scale-out (*factors 6 and 8*), and handle faults gracefully (*factor 9*). Designing an application using the 12 factor methodology is not the only way to develop cloud native architectures; however, it does offer a standardized set of guidelines that, if followed, will allow an application to be more mature on the CNMM.

Monolithic, SOA, and microservices architectures

Architecture design patterns are always evolving to take advantage of the newest technology innovations. For a long time, **monolithic architectures** were popular, often due to the cost of physical resources and the slow velocity in which applications were developed and deployed. These patterns fit well with the workhorse of computing and mainframes, and even today there are plenty of legacy applications running as a monolithic architecture. As IT operations and business requirements became more complex, and speed to market was gaining importance, additional monolithic applications were deployed to support these requirements. Eventually, these monolithic applications needed to communicate with each other to share data or execute functions that the other systems contained. This intercommunication was the precursor to **service-oriented architectures** (**SOA**), which allowed design teams to create smaller application components (as compared to monolithic), implement middleware components to mediate the communication, and isolate the ability to access the components, except through specific endpoints. SOA designs increasingly gained popularity during the virtualization boom, since deploying services became easier and less expensive on virtualized hardware.

Service-oriented architectures consist of two or more components which provide their services to other services through specific communication protocols. The communication protocols are often referred to as *web services*, and consist of a few different common ones: WSDL, SOAP, and RESTful HTTP, in addition to messaging protocols like JMS. As the complexity of these different protocols and services grew, using an **enterprise service bus** (**ESB**) became increasingly common as a mediation layer between services. This allowed for services to abstract their endpoints, and the ESB could take care of the message translations from various sources to get a correctly formatted call to the desired system. While this ESB approach reduced the complexity of communicating between services, it also introduced new complexity in the middleware logic required to translate service calls and handle workflows. This often resulted in very complex SOA applications where application code for each of the components needed to be deployed at the same time, resulting in a big bang and risky major deployment across the composite application. The SOA approach had a positive impact on the blast radius issues that monolithic architectures inherently had by separating core components into their own discrete applications; however, it also introduced a new challenge in the complexity of deployment. This complexity manifested itself in a way that caused so many interdependencies that a single large deployment across all SOA applications was often required. As a result of these risky *big bang* deployments, they were often only undertaken a few times a year, and drastically reduced velocity slowed the pace of the business requirements. As cloud computing became more common and the constraints of the on-premises environments began to fade a way, a new architecture pattern evolved: **microservices**. With the cloud, application teams no longer needed to wait months to have compute capacity to test their code, nor were they constrained by a limited number of physical resources, either.

The microservices architecture style takes the distributed nature of SOA and breaks those services up into even more discrete and loosely coupled application functions. Microservices not only reduce blast radius by even further isolating functions, but they also dramatically increase the velocity of application deployments by treating each microservice function as its own component. Using a small DevOps team accountable for a specific microservice will allow for the continuous integration and continuous delivery of the code in small chunks, which increases velocity and also allow for quick rollbacks in the event of unintended issues being introduced to the service.

Microservices and cloud computing fit well together, and often microservices are considered the most mature type of cloud native architecture at this point in time. The reason why they fit so well together is due to the way cloud vendors develop their services, often as individual building blocks that can be used in many ways to achieve a business result. This building block approach gives the application design teams the creativity to mix and match services to solve their problems, rather then being forced into using a specific type of data store or programming language. This has led to increased innovation and design patterns that take advantage of the cloud, like serverless computing services to further obfuscate the management of resources from the development teams, allowing them to focus on business logic.

Cloud native design considerations

Regardless of the methodology used or the final cloud native design pattern implemented, there are specific design considerations that all cloud native architectures should attempt to implement. While not all of these are required to be considered a cloud native architecture, as these considerations are implemented, the maturity of the system increases, and will fall on a higher level of the CNMM. These considerations include instrumentation, security, parallelization, resiliency, event-driven, and future-proofed:

- **Instrumentation**: Including application instrumentation is about more than just log stream analysis; it requires the ability to monitor and measure the performance of the application in real time. Adding instrumentation will directly lead to the ability of the application to be self-aware of latency conditions, component failures due to system faults, and other characteristics that are important to a specific business application. Instrumentation is critical to many of the other design considerations, so including it as a first-class citizen in the application will enable long-term benefits.

- **Security**: All applications need security built in; however, designing for a cloud native security architecture is critical to ensure the application takes advantage of cloud vendor security services, third-party security services, and design-level security in layers, all of which will harden the posture of the application and reduce the blast radius in the event of an attack or breach.
- **Parallelization**: Designing an application that can execute distinct processes in parallel with other parts of the application will directly impact its ability to have the performance required as it scales up. This includes allowing the same set of functions to execute many times in parallel, or having many distinct functions in the application execute in parallel.
- **Resiliency**: Considering how the application will handle faults and still perform at scale is important. Using cloud vendor innovations, like deployment across multiple physical data centers, using multiple decoupled tiers of the application, and automating the startup, shutdown, and migration of application components between cloud vendor locations are all ways to ensure resiliency for the application.
- **Event-driven**: Applications that are event-driven are able to employ techniques that analyze the events to perform actions, whether those be business logic, resiliency modification, security assessments, or auto scaling of application components. All events are logged and analyzed by advanced machine learning techniques to enable additional automation to be employed as more events are identified.
- **Future-proofed**: Thinking about the future is a critical way to ensure that an application will continue to evolve along the CNMM as time and innovation moves on. Implementing these considerations will help with future-proofing; however, all applications must be optimized through automation and code enhancements constantly to always be able to deliver the business results required.

Application centric design axis recap

There are many different methodologies that can be employed to create a cloud native application, including microservices, twelve-factor app design patterns, and cloud native design considerations. There is no one correct path for designing cloud native applications, and as with all parts of the CNMM, maturity will increase as more robust considerations are applied. The application will reach the peak maturity for this axis once most of these designs are implemented.

Axis 3 – Automation

The third and final cloud native principle is about automation. Throughout this chapter, the other CNMM principles have been discussed in detail and explained, particularly why using cloud native services and application centric design enable cloud native architectures to achieve scale. However, these alone do not allow a system to really take advantage of the cloud. If a system were designed using the most advanced services available, but the operational aspects of the application were done manually, it would have a hard time realizing its intended purpose. This type of operational automation is often referred to as **Infrastructure as Code**, and there is an evolution in maturity to achieve a sophisticated cloud native architecture. Cloud vendors typically develop all of their services to be API endpoints, which allows for programmatic calls to create, modify, or destroy services. This approach is the driver behind Infrastructure as Code, where previously an operations team would be responsible for the physical setup and deployment of components in addition to the infrastructure design and configuration.

With Infrastructure as Code automation, operations teams can now focus on the application-specific design and rely on the cloud vendor to handle the undifferentiated heavy lifting of resource deployment. This Infrastructure as Code is then treated like any other deployment artifact for the application, and is stored in source code repositories, versioned and maintained for long-term consistency of environment buildouts. The degree of automation still evolves on a spectrum with the early phases being focused on environment buildout, resource configuration, and application deployments. As a solution matures, the automation will evolve to include more advanced monitoring, scaling, and performance activities, and ultimately include auditing, compliance, governance, and optimization of the full solution. From there, automation of the most advanced designs use artificial intelligence and machine and deep learning techniques to self-heal and self-direct the system to change its structure based on the current conditions.

Automation is the key to achieving the scale and security required by cloud native architectures:

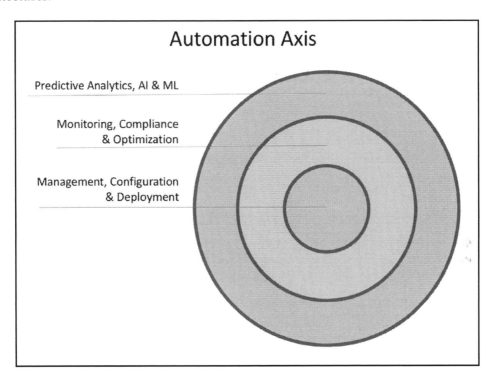

Environment management, configuration, and deployment

Designing, deploying, and managing an application in the cloud is complicated, but all systems need to be set up and configured. In the cloud, this process can become more streamlined and consistent by developing the environment and configuration process with code. There are potentially lots of cloud services and resources involved that go well beyond traditional servers, subnets, and physical equipment being managed on-premises. This phase of the automation axis focuses on API-driven environment provisioning, system configuration, and application deployments, which allows customers to use code to handle these repeatable tasks.

Whether the solution is a large and complex implementation for an enterprise company or a relatively straightforward system deployment, the use of automation to manage consistency is critical to enabling a cloud native architecture. For large and complex solutions, or where regulatory requirements demand the separation of duties, companies can use Infrastructure as Code to isolate the different operations teams to focus only on their area—for example, core infrastructure, networking, security, and monitoring. In other cases, all components could be handled by a single team, possibly even the development team if a DevOps model is being used. Regardless of how the development of the Infrastructure as Code happens, it is important to ensure that agility and consistency are a constant in the process, allowing systems to be deployed often, and following the design requirements exactly.

There are multiple schools of thought on how to handle the operations of a system using Infrastructure as Code. In some cases, every time an environment change occurs, the full suite of Infrastructure as Code automation is executed to replace the existing environment. This is referred to as **immutable infrastructure**, since the system components are never updated, but replaced with the new version or configuration every time. This allows a company to reduce environment or configuration drift, and also ensures a strict way to prove governance and reduce security issues that could be manually implemented.

While the immutable infrastructure approach has its advantages, it might not be feasible to replace the full environment every time, and so changes must be made at a more specific component level. Automation is still critical with this approach to ensure everything is implemented with consistency; however, it would make the cloud resources mutable, or give them the ability to change over time. There are numerous vendors that have products to achieve instance-level automation, and most cloud vendors have managed offerings to perform this type of automation. These tools will allow for code or scripts to be run in the environment to make the changes. These scripts would be a part of the Infrastructure as Code deployment artifacts, and would be developed and maintained in the same way as the set of immutable scripts.

Environment management and configuration is not the only way automation is required at this baseline level. Code deployments and elasticity are also very important components to ensuring a fully automated cloud native architecture. There are numerous tools on the market that allow for the full deployment pipeline being automated, often referred to as **continuous integration, continuous deployment (CICD)**. A code deployment pipeline often includes all aspects of the process, from code check-in, automated compiling with code analysis, packaging, and deployment, to specific environments with different hooks or approval stops to ensure a clean deployment. Used in conjunction with Infrastructure as Code for environment and operations management, CICD pipelines allow for extreme agility and consistency for a cloud native architecture.

Monitoring, compliance, and optimization through automation

Cloud native architectures that use complex services and span across multiple geographic locations require the ability to change often based on usage patterns and other factors. Using automation to monitor the full span of the solution, ensure compliance with company or regulatory standards, and continuously optimize resource usage shows an increasing level of maturity. As with any evolution, building on the previous stages of maturity enables the use of advanced techniques that allow for increased scale to be introduced to a solution.

One of the most important data points that can be collected is the monitoring data that cloud vendors will have built into their offerings. Mature cloud vendors have monitoring services natively integrated to their other services that can capture metrics, events, and logs of those services that would otherwise be unobtainable. Using these monitoring services to trigger basic events that are happening is a type of automation that will ensure overall system health. For example, a system using a fleet of compute virtual machines as the logic tier of a services component normally expects a certain amount of requests, but at periodic times a spike in requests causes the CPU and network traffic on these instances to quickly increase. If properly configured, the cloud monitoring service will detect this increase and launch additional instances to even out the load to more acceptable levels and ensure proper system performance. The process of launching additional resources is a design configuration of the system that requires Infrastructure as Code automation, to ensure that the new instances are deployed using the same exact configuration and code as all the others in the cluster. This type of activity is often called auto scaling, and it also works in reverse, removing instances once the spike in requests has subsided.

Automated compliance of environment and system configurations is becoming increasingly critical for large enterprise customers. Incorporating automation to perform constant compliance audit checks across system components shows a high level of maturity on the automation axis. These configuration snapshot services allow a complete picture in time of the full environmental makeup, and are stored as text for long-term analysis. Using automation, these snapshots can be compared against previous views of the environment to ensure that configuration drift has not happened. In addition to previous views of the environment, the current snapshot can be compared against desired and compliant configurations that will support audit requirements in regulated industries.

Optimization of cloud resources is an area that can easily be overlooked. Before the cloud, a system was designed and an estimation was used to determine the capacity required for that system to run at peak requirements. This led to the procurement of expensive and complex hardware and software before the system had even been created. Due to that, it was common for a significant amount of over-provisioned capacity to sit idle and waiting for an increase in requests to happen. With the cloud, those challenges all but disappear; however, system designers still run into situations where they don't know what capacity is needed. To resolve this, automated optimization can be used to constantly check all system components and, using historical trends, understand if those resources are over-or under-utilized. Auto scaling is a way to achieve this; however, there are much more sophisticated ways that will provide additional optimization if implemented correctly; for example, using an automated process to check running instances across all environments for under-used capacity and turning them off, or performing a similar check to shut down all development environments on nights and weekends, could save lots of money for a company.

One of the key ways to achieve maturity for a cloud native architecture with regards to monitoring, compliance, and optimization is to leverage an extensive logging framework. Loading data into this framework and analyzing that data to make decisions is a complex task, and requires the design team to fully understand the various components and make sure that all required data is being captured at all times. These types of frameworks help to remove the thinking that logs are files to be gathered and stored, and instead focus on logs as streams of events that should be analyzed in real time for anomalies of any kind. For example, a relatively quick way to implement a logging framework would be to use ElastiCache, Logstash, and Kibana, often referred to as an *ELK stack*, to capture all types of the system log events, cloud vendor services log events, and other third-party log events.

Predictive analytics, artificial intelligence, machine learning, and beyond

As a system evolves and moves further up the automation maturity model, it will rely more and more on the data it generates to analyze and act upon. Similar to the monitoring, compliance, and optimization design from the previous part of the axis, a mature cloud native architecture will constantly be analyzing log event streams to detect anomalies and inefficiencies; however, the most advanced maturity is demonstrated by using **artificial intelligence** (**AI**) and **machine learning** (**ML**) to predict how events could impact the system and make proactive adjustments before they cause performance, security, or other business degradation. The longer the event data collected is stored and the amount of disparate sources the data comes from will allow these techniques to have ever-increasing data points to take action upon.

Using the automation building blocks already discussed from this axis in combination with the AI and ML, the system has many options to deal with a potential business impacting event.

Data is king when it comes to predictive analytics and machine learning. The never-ending process of teaching a system how to categorize events takes time, data, and automation. Being able to correlate seemingly unrelated data events to each other to form a hypothesis is the basis of AI and ML techniques. These hypotheses will have a set of actions that can be taken if they occur, which, in the past, has resulted in anomaly correction. Automated responses to an event that matches an anomaly hypothesis and taking corrective action is an example of using predictive analytics based on ML to resolve an issue before it becomes business-impacting. In addition, there will always be situations where a new event is captured and historical data cannot accurately correlate that to a previously known anomaly. Even still, this lack of correlation is actually an indicator in itself and will enable the cross-connection of data events, anomalies, and responses to gain more intelligence.

There are many examples of how using ML on datasets will show correlation that could not be seen by a human reviewing the same datasets—like how often a failed user login resulted in a lockout versus a retry over millions of different attempts, and if those lockouts were the result of a harmless user forgetting a password, or a brute-force attack to gain system entry. Because the algorithm can search all required datasets and correlate the results, it will be able to identify patterns of when an event is harmless or malicious. Using the output from these patterns, predictive actions can be taken to prevent potential security issues by quickly isolating frontend resources or blocking requests from users deemed to be malicious due to where they come from (IP or country specific), the type of traffic being transmitted (Distributed Denial of Service), or another scenario.

This type of automation, if implemented correctly across a system, will result in some of the most advanced architectures that are possible today. With the current state of the cloud services available, using predictive analytics, artificial intelligence, and machine learning is the cutting edge of how a mature cloud native architecture can be designed; however, as the services become more mature, additional techniques will be available and innovative people will continue to use these in ever-increasing maturity to ensure their systems are resilient to business damage.

Automation axis recap

Automation unlocks significant value when implemented for a cloud native architecture. The maturity level of automation will evolve from simply setting up environments and configuring components to performing advanced monitoring, compliance, and optimization across the solution. Combined with increased innovation of cloud vendor services, the maturity of automation and using artificial intelligence and machine learning will allow for predictive actions to be taken to resolve common, known, and increasingly unknown anomalies in a system. This combination of cloud vendor services adoption and automation form two of the three critical design principles for the CNMM, with the application design and architecture principle being the final requirement.

The cloud native journey

Companies large and small, new and mature, are seeing the benefits of cloud computing. There are many paths to get to the cloud, and that often depends on the maturity of the organization and the willingness of senior management to enact the change required. Regardless of the type of organization, the shift to cloud computing is a journey that will take time, effort, and persistence to be successful. It is easy for a company to say they want to be cloud native; however, for most companies, getting there is a complex and difficult prospect. For organizations that are mature and have lots of legacy workloads and manage data centers, they will have to not only identify a roadmap and plan for migration, but also manage the people and process aspect of the journey. For companies that are newer and don't have a lot of technical debt in the form of traditional workloads, their journey will accelerate with the cloud being the place of early experimentation; however, maturing to a cloud native enterprise will still take time.

The decision to be cloud-first

Cloud computing is here to stay. Years ago there were many discussions on whether a company should declare a cloud-first model, or not chase the latest and greatest technologies; however, at this point in time, just about every company has taken the first step towards cloud computing, and many have made the decision to be a cloud-first organization. At its most basic level, making this decision simply means that all new workloads will be deployed to the chosen cloud vendor unless it is proven that this will not be sufficient for the business requirements. Sometimes this happens due to information security (that is, government-classified or regulatory conditions), and sometimes it's because of a specific technical issue or limitation that the cloud vendor has, which is difficult to overcome in a short time. Regardless, the vast majority of new projects will end up in the cloud with various stages of maturity, as described in the CNMM earlier.

Even though this decision is common in today's IT environment, there are still challenges that need to be addressed for it to be successful. IT and business leaders need to ensure that their people and processes are aligned to a cloud-first model. In addition, developing a DevOps and agile methodology will help the organization overcome the slow and rigid nature of waterfall projects with siloed development and operations teams.

People and process changes in the cloud

Organizations with large IT departments or long-term outsourced contracts will inherently have a workforce that is skilled at the technologies that have been running in the company up until that point. Making the shift to any new technology, especially cloud computing, will require a significant amount of retooling, personnel shifting, and a change in the thought pattern of the workforce. Organizations can overcome these people challenges by splitting their IT workforce into two distinct sections: those who maintain the legacy workloads and keep the original methodologies, and those who work on the cloud-first model and adopt the new technologies and process to be successful. This approach can work for a while; however, over time, and as workloads are moved to the target cloud platform, more and more people will shift to the new operating model. The benefits of this approach allow a select few people who are passionate and excited to learn new technologies and techniques to be the trail-blazers, while the rest of the workforce can retool their skills at a more methodical pace.

One specific area that can often be difficult for experienced IT professionals to overcome, especially if they have gained their experience with data center deployments and lots of large legacy workloads, is the concept of unlimited resources. Since most cloud vendors have effectively unlimited resources to be consumed, removing that constraint on application design will open up a lot of unique and innovative ways to solve problems that were impossible when designing applications before. For example, being bound to a specific set of CPU processors to complete a batch job will cause developers to design less parallelization, whereas with unlimited CPUs, the entire job could be designed to be run in parallel, potentially faster and cheaper than with lots of serial executions. Those people who can think big and remove constraints should be considered for the trail-blazers team.

Processes are also a big hurdle for being a cloud-first organization. Lots of companies that are transitioning to the cloud phase are also in transitioning from the SOA to microservices phase. Therefore, it would be common for the processes in place to be supportive of SOA architectures and deployments, which are most likely there to slow things down and ensure that the *big bang* deployments to the composite application are done correctly and with significant testing. Being cloud-first and using microservices, the goal is to deploy as fast as possible and as many times as possible, to support quickly changing business requirements. Therefore, modifying processes to support this agility is critical. For example, if an organization is strictly following ITIL, they might require a strict approval chain with checks and balances before any modification or code deployment can be made to production. This process is probably in place because of the complex interconnected nature of the composite applications, and one minor change could impact the entire set of systems; however, with microservices architectures, since they are fully self-contained and only publish an API (usually), as long as the API is not changing, the code itself would not impact other services. Changing processes to allow for lots of smaller deployments or rollbacks will ensure speed and business agility.

Agile and DevOps

The cloud is not a magic place where problems go away. It is a place where some of the traditional challenges go away; however, new challenges will come up. Legacy enterprise companies have been making the switch from waterfall project management to agile for a while now. That is good news for a company intending to be cloud native, since iteration, failing fast, and innovation are critical to long-term success, and *agile* projects allow for that type of project delivery. A large part of the reason this methodology is popular with cloud native companies is the fast pace of innovation that cloud vendors are going through. For example, AWS launched 1,430 new services and features in 2017, which is almost four per day, and it is set to eclipse that again in 2018. With this level of innovation happening, cloud services are changing, and using an agile methodology to manage cloud native projects will enable companies to take advantage of these as they come out.

DevOps (or the merging of development teams and operations teams) is a new IT operating model that helps bridge the gap between how code is developed and how it is operated once deployed to production. Making a single team accountable for the code logic, testing, deployment artifacts, and the operations of the system will ensure that nothing is lost in the life cycle of a code development process. This model fits well with the cloud and microservices, since it enables a small team to own the full service, write in whatever code they are most suited to, deploy to the cloud platform chosen by the company, and then operate that application and be in the best position to resolve any issues the application might have once it's in production.

Together, agile methodologies and DevOps are a critical change needed by companies that are considering the move to becoming a cloud native organization.

Cloud operating environment

The journey to the cloud will take time and lots of trial and error. Typically, a company will have identified a primary cloud vendor for their requirements and, in some cases, they will have a second cloud vendor for specific requirements. In addition, almost all companies begin with a hybrid architecture approach, which allows them to leverage their existing investments and applications while moving workloads into their chosen cloud. Often, the cloud native journey begins with a single workload being either migrated or designed for the cloud, which gives critical experience to the design team and helps create the operating foundation the organization will use for the cloud.

Cloud operating foundation

The cloud is a vast set of resources that can be used to solve all kinds of business problems; however, it is also a complex set of technologies that requires not only skillful people to use it, but also a strict operating foundation to ensure it is being done securely and with cost and scale in mind. Even before a single workload is deployed to the cloud, it is important for a company to fully identify their expected foundational design. This would include everything from account structures, virtual network design, regional/geographic requirements, security structure in terms of areas such as identity and access management and compliance, or governance considerations with regards to specific services to be used for different types of workloads. Understanding how to leverage Infrastructure as Code, as pointed out in the axis automation earlier, is also a critical element that should be identified early.

Once all of the decisions are made and the cloud operating foundation is in place, that is the time for the initial projects to begin. Between the decision-making process and the first few projects being deployed, the DevOps teams will gain lots of experience with both the agile pace of working, the target cloud vendor platform, and the company's set of guidelines and approaches to their cloud native environment.

Hybrid cloud

In addition to the foundation of the cloud platform, a company must decide how to leverage its existing assets. While the value proposition of cloud computing is not debated much anymore, the pace of migration and how fast to deprecate existing assets is. Using a hybrid cloud approach for the beginning of the cloud native journey is very common, and lets the company easily operate with its two existing groups (the legacy group and the cloud-first group). This approach will also enable a cheaper pathway to success, since it doesn't require a 'big bang' migration from existing data centers to the cloud, but allows for individual projects, business units, or other segregated areas to move faster than others.

All cloud vendors have a hybrid architecture option that can be leveraged when a company wants to keep some workloads in their data centers and have others in the cloud. This hybrid architecture approach typically involves setting up some type of network connectivity from one or more data center(s) to one or more cloud vendor geographical region(s). This network connectivity can take place in the form of a VPN over public internet paths, or various dedicated fiber options. Regardless of the type of connectivity, the outcome should be a single network that makes all company resources and workloads visible to each other (within security and governance constraints). Typical patterns for a hybrid cloud architecture are:

- Legacy workloads on-premises and new projects in the cloud
- Production workloads on-premises and non-production in the cloud
- Disaster recovery environment in the cloud
- Storage or archival in the cloud
- On-premises workloads bursting into the cloud for additional capacity

Over time, as more workloads are migrated into the cloud or retired from the on-premises environments, the center of gravity will shift to the cloud and an organization will have more resources in the cloud than on-premises. This progress is natural, and will signify the tipping point of a company that is well into its cloud native journey. Eventually, a cloud native company would expect to have all of its workloads in the cloud and remove just about all hybrid connectivity options since they are no longer in use. At that point, the organization would be considered a mature cloud native company.

Multi-cloud

Enterprise companies need to ensure their risk is spread out so that they reduce the blast radius in the event of an issue, whether this be a natural disaster, security event, or just making sure that they are covering their customers in all of the locations they operate in. Therefore, the allure of a multi-cloud environment is strong, and some larger organizations are starting to go down this path for their cloud journey. In the right circumstances, this approach does make sense and gives the additional assurance that their business can withstand specific types of challenges; however, for most companies this type of architecture is going to add significant complexity and possibly slow down adoption of the cloud.

The myth of multi-cloud deployments and architectures is often spread around by system integrators that thrive on complexity and change management. They want to promote the most complex and design-heavy architecture possible, so that a company feels compelled to leverage them more to ensure their IT operations are running smoothly. **Multi-cloud** is the most recent way of going about this, since taking this route will require twice the amount of cloud-specific knowledge and twice the amount of hybrid or intercloud connectivity. Often, there is a promise of a cloud broker, where a single platform can manage resources in multiple clouds and on-premises to make the cloud operations easier. The challenge with this school of thought is that these cloud brokers are really just exposing the lowest common denominator of the cloud vendors, typically instances, storage, load balancers, and so on, and do not have the ability to allow use of the most innovative services from the chosen cloud vendors. This will stifle cloud native architecture innovation and force the company into a similar operating model as they used before the cloud, often paying another company to manage the environments for them and not gaining much from their cloud journey.

Another common approach to multi-cloud is the use of containers for moving workloads between clouds. In theory, this approach works and solves a lot of the challenges that multi-cloud poses. There is currently a lot of innovation going on with this approach and the ability to be successful with moving containers between clouds is still in its infancy. As additional frameworks, tools, and maturity level appear, this is an area that could promise a new way to create cutting edge cloud native architectures.

Companies that are in their cloud native journey and are considering a multi-cloud approach should ask themselves the reasons why this is being considered. The authors of this book would argue that organizations would gain more speed and efficiency in the early and middle parts of their journey if they choose a single cloud vendor and focus all of their re-tooling, efforts, and people on that, versus trying to add a second cloud into the design. Ultimately, choose the path that will best serve the needs of the business and that will fit culturally into the organization.

Application migration at scale

Companies will start off the journey with the decision to be a cloud-first organization and the creation of a DevOps team, and will then continue with choosing a cloud vendor and setting up the target cloud-operating foundation. Soon after these activities are complete, the time to scale-out and ramp up migrations begins. A cloud native company will have the goal of reducing their self-managed data centers and workloads and shifting those as much as possible to the cloud. There are three main paths this can present:

- Lift-and-shift migration of legacy workloads to the cloud
- Re-engineering of legacy workloads to optimize in the cloud
- Greenfield cloud native development

For most large enterprise companies, all three of these options will take place with different parts of the legacy workloads. For smaller companies, any mix of the three could be employed, depending on the outcomes being sought.

Lift-and-shift migration

Lift-and-shift migration is the act of moving existing workloads, as is, to the target cloud-operating foundation already implemented. This type of exercise is usually done against a grouping of applications, by business unit, technology stack, or complexity level of some other type of metric. A lift-and-shift migration in its purest form is literally bit-by-bit copies of existing instances, databases, storage, and so on, and is actually rare, since the cost benefits of doing this to the cloud would be negligible. For example, moving 100 instances from an on-premises data center to the cloud, with no changes to size or taking into consideration scaling options, would most likely result in a higher cost to the company.

The more common derivative of a lift-and-shift is a **lift-tinker-shift migration**, where the majority of the workloads are moved; however, specific components are upgraded or swapped out for cloud services. For example, moving 100 instances from an on-premises data center to the cloud, but standardizing on a specific operating system (for example, Red Hat Enterprise Edition), moving all databases into a cloud vendor managed service (for example, Amazon Relational Database Service), and storing backup or archive files in a cloud storage blog storage (for example, Amazon Simple Storage Service) would constitute a lift-tinker-shift migration. This type of migration would most likely save the company a lot of money for the business case, take advantage of some of the most mature services in the cloud, and allow for significant long-term advantages with future deployments.

Re-engineer migration

Companies that are truly moving to be a cloud native organization will most likely choose to re-engineer most of their legacy workloads so that they can take advantage of the scale and innovation that the cloud has to offer. Workloads that are chosen to be migrated to the cloud but re-engineered in the process might take longer to move, but once completed they will fall on some part of the CNMM and be considered cloud native. These types of migrations are not quite greenfield development projects, but are also not lift-and-shift migrations either; they are designed to have significant portions of the application workloads rewritten or replatformed, so they fit the cloud native standards. For example, a composite application contains 100 instances using a traditional SOA architecture, containing five different distinct workloads with an ESB to mediate traffic. To re-engineer this composite application, the company would decide to remove the ESB, break the distinct workloads into more function-based microservices, remove as many instances as possible by leveraging serverless cloud services, and reformat the database to be NoSQL instead of relational.

Migrating workloads using a re-engineering approach is a good way for the trail blazers of a company's DevOps team to create a significant project, dive deep into the designing of the architecture, and employ all new skills and techniques for their cloud native journey. We believe that, over time, the majority of migration projects will be re-engineering existing workloads to take advantage of cloud computing.

Cloud native companies

While technically not a migration, cloud native companies that are creating new applications will choose to go through the entire development cycle with a cloud native architecture in mind. Even workloads that are re-engineered might not be able to fully change their underlying technologies for whatever reason. When a company chooses to go full cloud native development, all legacy approaches to development, scale constraints, slow deployments, and process and legacy-skilled workers are removed, and only the latest and greatest cloud services, architectures, and techniques are employed. Companies that have gotten to this phase of the journey are truly cloud native, and are set up for long-term success with how they develop and deploy business applications.

Cloud native architecture case study – Netflix

Netflix is often the first company that is brought up when people talk about a visionary cloud native company, but why? This section will break up the journey that Netflix has undertaken to get to the point it is at today. Using the CNMM, each of the axis will be discussed and key points taken into account to demonstrate their maturity along the cloud native journey.

The journey

As with all major migrations to the cloud, Netflix's journey was not something that happened overnight. As early as May 2010, Netflix had been publicly touting AWS as its chosen cloud computing partner. The following quote has been extracted from the press release that both companies published at that time (`http://phx.corporate-ir.net/ phoenix.zhtml?c=176060p=irol-newsArticleID=1423977`):

> *"Amazon Web Services today announced that Netflix, Inc., has chosen AWS to run a variety of mission-critical, customer-facing and backend applications. While letting Amazon Web Services do the worrying about the technology infrastructure, Netflix continues to improve its members' overall experience of instantly watching TV episodes and movies on the TV and computer, and receiving DVDs by mail."*

That press release goes on to say that Netflix had actually been using AWS for the experimentation of workload development for over a year, meaning that since 2009, Netflix has been on their cloud native journey. Since AWS released its first service in 2006, it is evident that Netflix saw the benefits from the very beginning and aggressively moved to take advantage of the new style of computing.

They phased the migration of components over time to reduce risk, gain experience, and leverage the newest innovations that AWS was delivering. Here's a quick timeline of their migration [2009 - 2010] `http://www.sfisaca.org/images/FC12Presentations/D1_2.pdf`, [2011 - 2013] `https://www.slideshare.net/AmazonWebServices/ent209-netflix-cloud-migration-devops-and-distributed-systems-aws-reinvent-2014` (Slide 11), and [2016] `https://medium.com/netflix-techblog/netflix-billing-migration-to-aws-451fba085a4`:

- 2009: Migrating video master content system logs into AWS S3
- 2010: DRM, CDN Routing, Web Signup, Search, Moving Choosing, Metadata, Device Management, and more were migrated into AWS

- 2011: Customer Service, International Lookup, Call Logs, and Customer Service analytics
- 2012: Search Pages, E-C, and Your Account
- 2013: Big Data and Analytics
- 2016: Billing and Payments

You can read more about this at `https://media.netflix.com/en/company-blog/completing-the-netflix-cloud-migration`. This seven-year journey enabled Netflix to completely shut down their own data centers in January 2016, and so they are now a completely cloud native company. Admittedly, this journey for Netflix was not easy, and a lot of tough decisions and trade-offs had to be made along the way, which will be true for any cloud native journey; however, the long-term benefits of re-engineering a system with a cloud native architecture, instead of just moving the current state to the cloud, means that all of the technical debt and other limitations are left behind. Therefore, in the words of Yury Izrailevsky (Vice President, Cloud and Platform Engineering at Netflix):

"We chose the cloud native approach, rebuilding virtually all of our technology and fundamentally changing the way we operate the company. Architecturally, we migrated from a monolithic app to hundreds of micro-services, and denormalized and our data model, using NoSQL databases. Budget approvals, centralized release coordination and multi-week hardware provisioning cycles made way to continuous delivery, engineering teams making independent decisions using self-service tools in a loosely coupled DevOps environment, helping accelerate innovation."

This amazing journey for Netflix continues to this day. Since the cloud native maturity model doesn't have an ending point, as cloud native architectures mature, so too will the CNMM and those companies that are pushing the boundaries of how to develop these architectures.

The benefits

The journey to becoming a cloud native company at Netflix was impressive, and continues to yield benefits for Netflix and its customers. The growth Netflix was enjoying around 2010 and beyond made it difficult for them to logistically keep up with the demand for additional hardware and the capacity to run and scale their systems. They quickly realized that they were an entertainment creation and distribution company, and not a data center operations company. Knowing that managing an ever-growing number of data centers around the world would continue to cause huge capital outflows and require a focus that was not core to their customers, they made their cloud-first decision.

Elasticity of the cloud is possibly the key benefit for Netflix, as it allows them to add thousands of instances and petabytes of storage, on demand, as their customer base grows and usage increases. This reliance on the cloud's ability to provide resources as required also includes their big data and analytics processing engines, video transcoding, billing, payments, and many other services that make their business run. In addition to the scale and elasticity that the cloud brings, Netflix also cites the cloud as away to significantly increase their services availability. They were able to use the cloud to distribute their workloads across zones and geographies that use fundamentally unreliable but redundant components to achieve their desired 99.99% availability of services.

Finally, while cost was not a key driver for their decision to move to the cloud, their *costs per streaming start* ended up being a fraction of what it was when they managed their own data centers. This was a very beneficial side effect of the scale they were able to achieve, and the benefit was only possible due to the elasticity of the cloud. Specifically, this enabled them to *continuously optimize instance type mix and to grow and shrink our footprint near-instantaneously without the need to maintain large capacity buffers. We can also benefit from the economies of scale that are only possible in a large cloud ecosystem.* These benefits have enabled Netflix to have a laser focus on their customer and business requirements, and not spend resources on areas that do not directly impact that business mission.

CNMM

Now that we understand what the Netflix journey was about and how they benefited from that journey, this section will use the CNMM to evaluate how that journey unfolded and where they stand on the maturity model. Since they have been most vocal about the work they did to migrate their billing and payment system to AWS, that is the workload that will be used for this evaluation. That system consisted of batch jobs, billing APIs, and integrations, with other services in their composite application stack, including an on-premises data center at the time. Full details about that migration can be found at their blog, `https://medium.com/netflix-techblog/netflix-billing-migration-to-aws-451fba085a4`, on this topic.

Cloud native services axis

The focus of the cloud native services adoption spectrum is to demonstrate the amount of cloud vendor services that are in use for the architecture. While the full extent of the services that Netflix uses is unknown, they have publicly disclosed numerous AWS services that help them achieve their architecture. Referring to the mature cloud vendor services diagram in the beginning of this chapter, they certainly use most of the foundational services that fall into the infrastructure: networking, compute, storage, and database tiers. They also use most of the services from the security and application services tier. Finally, they have discussed their usage of lots of services in the management tools, analytics, dev tools, and artificial intelligence tiers. This amount of services usage would classify Netflix as a very mature user of cloud native services, and therefore they have a high maturity on the cloud native services axis.

It is also important to note that Netflix also uses services that are not in the cloud. They are very vocal that their usage of **content delivery networks (CDNs)** are considered a core competency for their business to be successful, and therefore they set up and manage their own global content network. This point is made in a blog post at `https://media.netflix.com/en/company-blog/how-netflix-works-with-isps-around-the-globe-to-deliver-a-great-viewing-experience` by the company in 2016, where they articulated their usage of AWS and CDNs and why they made their decisions:

> *"Essentially everything before you hit "play" happens in AWS, including all of the logic of the application interface, the content discovery and selection experience, recommendation algorithms, transcoding, etc.; we use AWS for these applications because the need for this type of computing is not unique to Netflix and we can take advantage of the ease of use and growing commoditization of the "cloud" market. Everything after you hit "play" is unique to Netflix, and our growing need for scale in this area presented the opportunity to create greater efficiency for our content delivery and for the internet in general."*

In addition, there are cases where they choose to use open source tools running on cloud building blocks, like Cassandra for their NoSQL database, or Kafka for their event streams. These architecture decisions are the trade-offs they made to ensure that they are using the best tools for their individual needs, not just what a cloud vendor offers.

Application centric design axis

Designing an application for the cloud is arguably the most complicated part of the journey, and having a high level of maturity on the application centric design axis will require specific approaches. Netflix faced some big challenges during its billing and payment system migration to the cloud; specifically, they wanted near-zero downtime, massive scalability, SOX compliance, and global rollout. At the point of time where they begin this project, they already had many other systems running in the cloud as decoupled services. Therefore, they used the same decoupling approach by designing microservices for their billing and payment systems.

To quote their blog on this topic:

> *"We started chipping away existing code into smaller, efficient modules and first moved some critical dependencies to run from the Cloud. We moved our tax solution to the Cloud first. Next, we retired serving member billing history from giant tables that were part of many different code paths. We built a new application to capture billing events, migrated only necessary data into our new Cassandra data store and started serving billing history, globally, from the Cloud. We spent a good amount of time writing a data migration tool that would transform member billing attributes spread across many tables in Oracle into a much simpler Cassandra data structure. We worked with our DVD engineering counterparts to further simplify our integration and got rid of obsolete code."*

The other major redesign during this process was the move from an Oracle database's heavy relational design to a more flexible and scalable NoSQL data structure for subscription processing, and a regionally distributed MySQL relational database for user-transactional processing. These changes required other Netflix services to modify their design to take advantage of the decoupling of data storage and retry the ability for data input to their NoSQL database solution. This enabled Netflix to migrate millions of rows from their on-premises Oracle database to Cassandra in AWS without any obvious user impact.

During this billing and payment system migration to the cloud, Netflix made many significant decisions that would impact its architecture. These decisions were made with long-term impact in mind, which caused a longer migration time, but ensured a future-proofed architecture that could scale as they grew internationally. The cleaning up of code to remove technical debt is a prime example of this, and allowed them to ensure the new code base was designed using microservices, and had other cloud native design principles included. Netflix has demonstrated a high level of maturity on the application-centric design axis.

Automation axis

The **automation axis** demonstrates a company's ability to manage, operate, optimize, secure, and predict how their systems are behaving to ensure a positive customer experience. Netflix understood early on in their cloud journey that they had to develop new ways to verify that their systems were operating at the highest level of performance, and almost more importantly, that their systems were resilient to service faults of all kinds. They created a suite of tools called the Simian Army (`https://medium.com/netflix-techblog/the-netflix-simian-army-16e57fbab116`), which includes all kinds of automation that is used to identify bottlenecks, break points, and many other types of issues that would disrupt their operations for customers. One of the original tools and the inspiration for the entire Simian Army suite is their Chaos Monkey; in their words:

> "...our philosophy when we built Chaos Monkey, a tool that randomly disables our production instances to make sure we can survive this common type of failure without any customer impact. The name comes from the idea of unleashing a wild monkey with a weapon in your data center (or cloud region) to randomly shoot down instances and chew through cables—all the while we continue serving our customers without interruption. By running Chaos Monkey in the middle of a business day, in a carefully monitored environment with engineers standing by to address any problems, we can still learn the lessons about the weaknesses of our system, and build automatic recovery mechanisms to deal with them. So next time an instance fails at 3 am on a Sunday, we won't even notice."

Having systems that can survive randomly shutting down critical services is the definition of high levels of automation. This means that the entire landscape of systems must follow strict automated processes, including environment management, configuration, deployments, monitoring, compliance, optimization, and even predictive analytics. Chaos Monkey went on to inspire many other tools that all fall into the Simian Army toolset. The full suite of the Simian Army is:

- **Latency Monkey**: Induces artificial delays into RESTful calls to similar service degradation
- **Conformity Monkey**: Finds instances that do not adhere to predefined best practices and shuts them down
- **Doctor Monkey**: Taps into health checks that run on an instance to monitor external signs of health
- **Janitor Monkey**: Searches for unused resources and disposes of them

- **Security Monkey**: Finds security violations and vulnerabilities and terminates offending instances
- **10-18 Monkey**: Detects configuration and runtime problems in specific geographic regions
- **Chaos Gorilla**: Similar to Chaos Monkey, but simulates an entire outage of AWS available zones

However, they didn't stop there. They also created a cloud wide telemetry and monitoring platform known as Atlas (`https://medium.com/netflix-techblog/introducing-atlas-netflixs-primary-telemetry-platform-bd31f4d8ed9a`), which is responsible of capturing all-time series data. The primary goal for Atlas is to support queries over dimensional time series data so they can drill down into problems as quickly as possible. This tool satisfies the logging aspect of the twelve-factor app design, and allows them to have enormous amounts of data and events to analyze and take action on before they become customer-impacting. In addition to Atlas, in 2015 Netflix released a tool called Spinnaker (`https://www.spinnaker.io/`), which is an open source, multi-cloud, continuous delivery platform for releasing software changes with high velocity and confidence. Netflix is constantly updating and releasing additional automation tools that help them manage, deploy, and monitor all their services, using globally distributed AWS regions and, in some cases, using other cloud vendor services.

Netflix has been automating everything in their environment for almost as long as they have been migrating workloads to the cloud. Today, they rely on those tools to ensure their global network is functioning properly and serving their customers. Therefore, they would fall on the highly mature level of the automation axis.

Summary

In this chapter, we defined exactly what a cloud native is and what areas of focus are required to develop a mature cloud native architecture. Using a CNMM, we identified that all architectures will have three design principles: cloud services adoption, degree of automation, and application-centric design. These principles are used to gauge the maturity of the components of the architecture, as it relates to them and where they fall on their own spectrum. Finally, we broke down what a cloud native journey is for a company, how they make the cloud-first decision, how they change their people, process, and technology, how they create a cloud-operating environment, and finally, how a company would migrate or redesign their workloads to be in the cloud-first world they have created.

In the next chapter, we will start out with a deep dive into the cloud adoption framework, and understand the cloud journey that a company undertakes in more detail by looking into the seven pillars of the framework. We will understand migrations and the greenfield development of the journey, and we will finish with the security and risk that come along with the adoption of the cloud.

The Cloud Adoption Journey 2

Becoming a cloud native company is undeniably a journey, and one that is not only focused on technology. As demonstrated by the Netflix case study, this journey can take a very long time to do correctly and will often be full of tough decisions, including those relating to technology and business trade-offs. In addition, this journey is never-ending. The cloud is still in its infancy and the innovations being delivered by major cloud vendors are accelerating, not slowing down. This chapter will identify the drivers that are often used to make a cloud adoption decision. It will examine the frameworks that are commonly used as organizations start down the cloud adoption path and will explain what components and approaches are taken with a cloud migration. Finally, it will describe how to build a comprehensive cloud operating model that takes into consideration the challenges of risk, security, and QA in the cloud.

Cloud adoption drivers

Adopting the cloud is not an accident, but a decision that has to be made. That decision, however, is the starting point of a long journey that will involve lots of manpower, processes, and technology changes. There are many reasons why an organization will make this decision, with agility and cost factors often being very high on the list. However, there are other important factors that are considered along with those, including security and governance of company assets, the regional or international expansion of operations, and a desire to attract top technical talent or to take advantage of the technical innovations being developed. Companies of all sizes are using these drivers to determine their journey to the cloud, and this section will explain why these drivers are important and how they impact the decision-making process.

Moving fast and constraining costs

Before the advent of cloud computing, when a system was being designed, the team would have to estimate the performance requirements and then procure hardware resources to match those estimations, an expensive and slow process often undertaken with limited data. Not only is this a bad pricing decision, but it also means that unused capacity is sitting idle in data centers. Furthermore, performing these estimations could be impossible if the idea is to design a completely new business channel. Therefore, starting out with the smallest investment possible and aiming for exponential growth is a potential path to success for a company trying to innovate using the cloud. Buying or leasing hardware from a longstanding vendor is not cloud computing. Cloud computing is being able to provision resources on demand and remove those resources when they're no longer required.

Agility

Often cited as the top driver for cloud adoption is agility. A common issue facing companies for decades has been long lead times in deploying hardware to their data centers, causing all kinds of issues, including the expansion of project timelines. Removing this constraint by having virtually limitless capacity and providing the ability to use that capacity within minutes is critical for an organization with high business velocity requirements. As the world moves toward an even faster flow of ideas due to the internet and social media, companies will be chasing those ideas and trying to monetize them for their business models. Since an idea or fad can often come and go in a few months, having to wait that long just for the physical resources means the opportunity could easily be missed. In the case of cloud computing, this is not an issue and allows the organization to develop a market strategy based on their core competencies, while allowing the cloud vendor to focus on commodity IT resources.

Failing fast is another area where cloud agility and experimentation is important. The disruption of ideas and companies is happening at record speeds these days and, for a company to be able to withstand that disruption, they need to be constantly iterating on their business model to match their customers' demands. To quote Jeff Bezos on the concept of an experiment – *"It's not an experiment if you know it's going to work"*. This means that continuously trying new ideas, designing new products or services, and doing it quickly, is important. It also means that some of these ideas, probably a lot of them, will fail to fulfill the objectives of the business, and that has to be OK, since, every once in a while, they will succeed.

Cloud computing allows for this agility by enabling resources to be created and destroyed exactly when needed, or when no longer needed. It means that a minimally deployable system of resources, if properly designed, will grow exponentially along with demand and never put the company in a position where hardware is idle, or otherwise underutilized.

Cost

Failing fast is important, and so is the ability to constrain costs in so doing. If the cost of experimentation is high, then failure becomes something that will have an impact on the company. As soon as a project or system has a meaningful impact on the company, checks and balances will be implemented that are designed to slow it down to prevent an expensive decision from being made with little chance of a good return on investment, such as procuring expensive hardware. It's not as if this concept of business agility is new, owing to the cloud; it has been around for decades. However, what cloud computing provides is the cost benefits of being agile, coupled with minimal upfront costs. The full life cycle of a new business idea could be measured in weeks or months and, in the beginning, it is important to only use very limited cloud resources. If that idea becomes popular, then a cloud native architecture will enable that system to scale up as the system is increasingly used. If the idea doesn't achieve its desired results, then it can be easily stopped, with only the minimal resources invested being regarded as sunk costs. This is the power of failing fast while using the cloud to innovate.

Cost drivers don't only stop with using minimal deployable resources for a new system. Most cloud vendors have innovated in the way the resources are billed to the customer. It's common for the largest vendors to have very fine-grained billing mechanisms, sometimes charging by the second or even faster, with aggregated monthly bills. Gone are the days of a vendor requiring the company to buy the resources and then charging a substantial fee for ongoing maintenance. The costs of cloud resources are fully contained for those resources and have the added benefit of being automatically enhanced as the cloud vendor performs their upgrade cycles. These monthly bills have a huge benefit to most organizations of allowing them to be recognized as operational expenses and not having to request approval for long-term capital expense. While this is mostly an accounting issue, it is an important aspect of the agility that a company gains by using the cloud, since new concepts or systems don't have to wait for approval or a capital request cycle to occur.

Being secure and maintaining proper governance

For a long time, organizations of all sizes had to run their own data centers to be able to control the security and governance of their data and workloads. Cloud computing, however, has finally delivered an option that provides higher security and governance than most organizations can achieve on their own. This is because the major cloud vendors make it their business to offer secure and compliant services to solve business problems for all of their customers. Since these cloud vendors are constantly iterating on their offerings, whenever a new security pattern, government compliance requirement, or other important aspect is identified, they quickly work to incorporate that into their cloud. Therefore, just by being a customer and using the cloud, companies will automatically benefit from the scale and focus these vendors bring to security and governance, usually at little or no additional cost.

Security

Every organization is different, with different security requirements, different governance needs, and different ways they believe their company assets should be managed and secured. Cloud vendors have staked their business and reputation on the fact that they provide their services in the most secure way possible. While there are still companies that believe they can run their workloads more securely in a self-managed data center using a private cloud architecture, the cloud is undeniably incredibly secure when properly configured. This security trend is going to continue as vendors mature and implement more and more innovations in terms of how to secure their services. Every day, the major cloud vendors employ hundreds or even thousands of people whose sole job is to think about how to more securely manage their environment, design new ways to scale out encryption, secure data management, or any number of ways to run workloads on their platforms in a more secure manner. As artificial intelligence and machine learning techniques mature, cloud security will grow exponentially and allow for not only proactive monitoring, but also for self-discovery of potential security compromises, the automated resolution of misconfigured controls, and all sorts of ways to protect data and systems.

While there are probably companies or organizations that can claim a similar level of focus on this important topic, the vast majority cannot deploy the resources required to continuously innovate their security like cloud vendors can. Furthermore, the same argument for using the cloud applies to the security sub-topic as well, and that is, even if you could match the innovations of a cloud vendor, is that really the best use of an organizations resources, or should they be focused on business results? The case for leveraging the cloud for security is almost as compelling as the cost and agility benefits, and it is important for any organization to perform a very detailed review of what their requirements are before a decision is made to invest in on-premises hardware or a private cloud. This will often require a hard look at the teams who control those reviews and it must be ensured that they are not trying to cling to what they know using security or governance as an excuse and putting everyone in jeopardy in the process.

Governance

Operating on the premise that the cloud is secure is one thing, but being able to actually take advantage of security to ensure a robust posture is another. Cloud vendors have lots of services designed to meet just about every security requirement. However, it is up to the individual systems to implement those services according to their design specifications. The follow-up challenge is making sure that the security that was implemented is adequately being followed and maintained, which requires a significant amount of governance. The cloud offers services that interact with the other services to form an overlay of monitoring, auditing, configuration controls, and other governance activities. Using the cloud will enable the workloads that are deployed by the company to all have the same governance model, not skipping out due to complexities or cost, which can sometimes occur when deploying on premises.

Company expansion

Company growth is commonly a top priority for most organizations, in addition to serving existing customers, gaining market share, and exploring new business channels. This expansion can quickly become a major expense to the company if the need to deploy more data centers arises. Setting up a data center is not something that a company will do unless they have a strong business case for their return on that investment, and, even then, a significant capital outlay will be required. The time expended, capital costs, and the risks associated with deploying a new data center are all significant and, increasingly, companies are reconsidering whether this is a viable option. Those risks increase even more when expansion occurs outside of traditional markets, either in a new location within their geographical area or internationally.

Using the cloud for this expansion is the ideal way to achieve the desired goals and to do it with much less upfront capital expenditure. Whether this expansion is on the other side of the country or the world, most major cloud vendors have operations in locations that can serve concentrations of consumers. If the company puts enough thought into the automation of workloads upfront, then deploying those workloads to additional regional cloud locations is relatively easy. Going global in minutes is a big selling point of major cloud vendors and one that any company should consider strongly when deploying their workloads.

Attracting and retaining talent

Companies that are moving to the cloud require talented people who understand the technology and the new processes that accompany that change. In a lot of cases, a company will seek to retain their existing workforce and focus on re-tooling them to be successful on their cloud journey. This process is advantageous for many reasons, the main one of which is the fact that all of the institutional knowledge that these individuals possess stays within the company. Business processes and approaches will often be similar as workloads are moved to the cloud, so having a long-term background in why certain decisions were made during a legacy workload implementation is critical to making sure that it is designed correctly as it is moved to the cloud.

In addition to retention, the attraction of external talent will be important for the long-term success of the cloud journey. There are significant benefits associated with hiring cloud computing experts that will help realign the company to think beyond the limitations that were faced in their data centers. This external talent is not just technical, and business professionals who understand the challenges associated with this change, and can help navigate companies through this journey, have very important roles. The global battle for top-tier cloud talent is already high and demand will only increase as more and more companies begin their journey. This is a critical area that must be part of the decision-making process for any company making the move to the cloud.

Cloud innovation and economies of scale

Allowing major cloud vendors to innovate as fast as possible and then taking advantage of that innovation while focusing resources on the core competencies of a company is the best path to success for a cloud journey. There are very few companies that can claim managing data centers as their core competency and, therefore, any decision made to go cloud native must consider this as a driving principle. This driver is a catch-all that will reinforce the other cloud adoption drivers and should be viewed as a major benefit to any organization. Cloud innovation will help companies be more agile, drive down costs, secure their workloads, expand to new markets, and attract or retain the best talent available for their needs.

In addition to the rapid pace of innovation that the cloud is experiencing, these cloud vendors have tremendous scale and can leverage that scale to negotiate prices with their vendors that most companies, regardless of their size, cannot do. This is true for compute, power, storage, networking costs, land for data center expansion, and even the talent to help drive this innovation in the first place. Companies considering their cloud options need to think through this economies of scale situation and, unless they have significant pricing power, the cloud will offer a better option.

The cloud operating model

Once an organization evaluates the cloud adoption drivers and makes the decision to begin a cloud journey, this is when the work begins, but how? According to Amazon Web Services' Cloud Adoption Framework (`https://d0.awsstatic.com/whitepapers/aws_cloud_adoption_framework.pdf`), *"Cloud adoption requires that fundamental changes are discussed and considered across the entire organization, and that stakeholders across all organizational units—both outside and within IT—support these changes"*. Furthermore, the three typical areas of focus – people, processes, and technology – still apply to the cloud journey, but that is too simple for the scale of the change being made. This journey will involve business owners, human resource considerations, and procurement changes, and will require strong governance and have project management requirements. In addition, the technology will have a wide variety of impacts on all parties and specific decisions relating to the target platform, security, and operations are critical.

There are many organizational change theories that can be applied to how the cloud journey is approached, and, similar to any large transformational undertaking, it will take stakeholders across the whole organization to participate. One organizational change pattern that aligns well to the cloud journey is Dr. Kotter's theory (`https://www.kotterinternational.com/8-steps-process-for-leading-change/`). Kotter has identified eight steps that lead to successful, top-down change management across enterprises. These steps are as follows:

1. Create a sense of urgency
2. Build a guiding coalition
3. Form a strategic vision and initiatives
4. Enlist a volunteer army
5. Enable action by removing barriers
6. Generate short-term wins
7. Sustain acceleration
8. Institute change

Using this methodology for the cloud journey works well because typically, the change is so large and transformational that it must start at the very top, often with the Board of Directors and CEO. At those levels, the idea of simple cost savings or agility are too narrow, but a targeted business change must be the desired outcome, one that will set the company on a new course to increased revenues and shareholder value. Therefore, aligning this journey to this business change is the sense of urgency often required and, from there, a coalition is established of believers who will drive this vision forward. The people who are actually involved in the work will form the initial volunteer army; these people are risk takers and high performers that see this change as a way to increase their knowledge of a new technology, advance their own career, or be a part of something big, and removing barriers will enable them to move fast and stay focused. Long-term success will require buy-in from the less adventurous and, to do that, there must be a significant number of minor gains to prove that this is a successful strategy, ultimately leading to the acceleration of new cloud native projects or migrations that will then be finalized as the new normal.

Stakeholders

The journey to the cloud is not just about what new technology will be implemented; it's about business change agility and all of the other drivers outlined in the beginning of this chapter. Therefore, the list of stakeholders that will be impacted, and who should therefore be included in all aspects of the journey, can be long. In almost all cases, the full C-suite will be involved in some way, since this change is transformative to the entire company. In addition, the lines of business heads and their respective organizations will have a major role to play, since the typical focus area of applications is designed to support the sales or delivery needs of these business units. Finally, IT cannot be discounted as a key participant, and this department will be integrating itself throughout the company to champion the cloud and the changes associated with it.

In many organizations, the IT department is made up of a few important functions, most notably, the CIO or VP of corporate systems, the CTO or VP of business applications, the VP of end user computing or support, the VP of infrastructure, and a CISO, whose remit encompasses all existing functions. The cloud doesn't remove these roles, although, in some cases, it does change their functions. For example, the VP of infrastructure is often transformed into the VP of DevOps or something similar, since the requirement to manage infrastructure shifts from the physical to code. This change alone can free up significant resources that were dedicated to keeping the lights on at data centers, or to the procurement of hardware, and realigning them to the development of business applications. In addition to this major change, each of the other IT groups will need to realign their skills to the chosen cloud platform, which often requires significant training, enabling, and top-down messaging.

The business is frequently talked about as a key participant in this journey, but what exactly does that mean? In this case, the business is the part of the organization that drives revenue and owns the product or services on behalf of the company. For large multinational corporations, the business may actually be separate subsidiaries with many sub-business groups that work toward their specific requirements. In other smaller companies, the business would represent the specific product that is being produced. Regardless, the business drives the revenues of the company, and is constantly innovating new ideas and trying to bring those ideas to market faster than their competitors, which is exactly what is meant by the term **business agility**. The goal of any company should be to focus as many resources on this business agility as possible in order to give them a competitive advantage. Therefore, when the IT department can realign people away from undifferentiated heavy lifting tasks toward the designing or implementing of business applications, it will have a direct impact on company revenues.

Change and project management

As an organization undertakes its journey to the cloud, it must consider the processes that will be impacted, specifically change management and project management. These two important aspects to an IT operating model must be considered with the journey, and changes are usually required to existing policies on how they will be achieved in the cloud. A careful examination of the change management of many organizations will show that while extensive and mature, there are actually many processes in place to slow down the deployment of IT resources, impacting business velocity for the sake of risk mitigation. These processes were not created as a way to slow things down, but, over time, additional bureaucracy is added due to one-off situations or gaps that are identified. These incremental steps accumulate to cause additional approval requirements, lengthier rollback plans, and other activities that impede business agility. This slowdown also had a side effect of ensuring that, before significant capital expenditure was undertaken, lots of analysis was done to ensure proper alignment with project requirements and budgets.

The cloud doesn't remove the need to have strict change management processes. What it does, however, is change how these are implemented in ways that can actually increase their effectiveness, while removing a lot of the bureaucracy that caused the slowdowns to begin with. Cloud native architectures, by their very nature, are less tightly coupled and more services-based, thus removing large big-bang deployments and speeding up the delivery process. Moving to the cloud can remove not only technical debt in the form of obsolete code, but also in removing obsolete processes. For example, ITIL is a common governance and change management style used across lots of enterprise companies, designed to align IT services with the needs of the business. ITIL has strict processes for how changes get implemented, which include documentation, approval chains, rollback plans, and other such activities. These will still exist in the cloud. However, the velocity of change will increase because the size of deployments are often reduced and the risk of these changes is much smaller. This usually is the result of new views of the change management and project management processes of an organization.

Change management

Cloud native application design patterns, specifically those made up of many smaller services, are not the only reason why change management is happening faster; automation and containerization are also key contributors. This is not something that is unique to the cloud. However, due to the API-driven nature of the cloud and the almost unlimited ability to collect, store, and analyze data, it is causing a revolution in the way change management is happening. Automated deployments using DevOps philosophies and **continuous integration, continuous deployment (CICD)** pipelines make the process of code deployment, and rollback, seamless and, most importantly, consistent. Cloud vendors have tools that natively solve a lot of the challenges involving code storage, code building, code deployments, and code testing. In addition, there are ways to achieve advanced CICD pipelines using custom development methods as well.

Project management

In addition to the change management processes, the approach to project management will need to evolve with the shift to the cloud. The waterfall methodology, where the full requirements are identified in advance, and these requirements are then developed in sequence, with testing cycles happening at the end, is too slow for the business agility required. In the past, with the time associated with the provisioning of hardware, or the lack of team communication, slowing things down, the waterfall method worked to produce high-quality systems. With these barriers removed, the agile methodology is often used in the cloud. This style allows for parallel activities to occur, including requirement gathering, development, testing, and deployment. The cloud's ability to provision resources instantaneously and scale up when needed makes this project management style work really well. The speed with which the business needs to change requirements due to market conditions can be high, and managing projects with agility allows for quickly modifying requirements without a significant amount of rework.

When changing the project management processes to account for *cloud first* design principles, one important impact would be to include best practices for cloud native development. Including quality assurance checks in the design processes that identify best practices for designing scalable, secure, and cloud native architectures will ensure that workloads are deployed cloud-scale ready, and will need less remediation once they are in production. By incorporating these cloud native design practices into the project management processes, a company will start to develop cloud native architectures earlier, focus on automation and innovation from cloud vendors, and be in a position to change direction quickly, based on the needs of the business. These changes not only increase business velocity, but reduce risk.

Risk, compliance, and quality assurance

The risk profile of a company is higher as it moves to the cloud, at least initially. This is not because the cloud is a risky place, quite the opposite; it's because there are new ways for problems to occur that a company must understand. Once company assets (data, and code, for example) are migrated to compute resources located outside of its direct control, there must be additional considerations regarding how to keep those resources secure. Following industry compliance standards is a critical first step to ensuring that the basics are met for the data collected by the company. In addition, the governance of processes and auditing these processes will ensure that nothing slips by that could cause data leaks or result in a backdoor to company assets being found. Finally, quality assurance testing, not just of system code and functionality, but of the infrastructure provisioning, security controls, and other high availability procedures and business continuity plans, is a must-have for cloud native companies.

All of these technical aspects are often very different when comparing on-premises with the cloud and it is critical for companies to not only adjust their approach in the cloud, but also to adjust their on-premises approach to better align to the cloud. As with any journey, the cloud native goal is to transform the way the company consumes IT resources and remove on-premises limitations as to how applications are designed. This means that even for operations happening on-premises, these ideas must be used so that, as those legacy workloads are transferred to the cloud, they are already following the approved design principles. Over time, as the company's center of gravity shifts to the cloud through migration and new development, the approach to risk, compliance, and quality assurance will also shift. The technology considerations are actually among the most straightforward part of the operating model. While complicated and often new, it also follows predictable patterns and there are lots of opportunities to learn and acquire skills.

Risk and compliance

Risk is inevitable, whenever a company stores data, processes transactions, or interacts with their customers. They are dealing with risky situations since there will always be bad actors that want to steal or manipulate the data, transactions, or interactions. But bad actors are not the only risk that a company faces; compute resource faults or software bugs are also a very real possibility that must be managed appropriately by any company. The cloud offers a shift in risk, but not a reduction in risk. Most major cloud providers operate under a shared responsibility model for implementation of security and controls. Typically, this means that the cloud provider owns and operates (and assumes the risk for) the concrete to the hypervisor, while customers are responsible for the operating system up to the application stack. It is also typical that cloud providers often are very aggressive in achieving various industry and governmental compliance certifications (the Payment Card Industry Data Security Standard, or PCI-DSS, ISO 27001, for example) for their individual services. The risk with this is that a company must understand that, under the shared responsibility model, the cloud provider's services might be certified for a specific type of workload, but unless the workload is designed by the company to implement these same controls, it will not pass audits.

Compliance is not only an external concern; often, a company will have a strict internal governance model that requires specific controls to be in place for certain types of data and workloads. In these cases, the cloud provider will not be able to implement those requirements since they are specific to that organization. However, there are often ways to map these internal controls to other certifications with similar requirements to show compliance. The mapping of these controls, both external and internal, are critical to success in the cloud to ensure that the data and workloads are using services that are in scope for the classification of a specific application. Large and complex organizations often have hundreds or thousands of applications and each will have specific characteristics of data and processing types, so completing this compliance exercise is an important component of the cloud operating model.

One important consideration to be discussed here is that the pace of innovation of the cloud vendors will likely outpace a company's ability to analyze and approve services for use in new workloads. While it's critical that a company is diligent in ensuring that services being used in their systems are secure and can pass external and internal audits, it is also important that they not use that as a way to slow down their own business requirements. It is possible to leverage new service innovation in a safe and timely manner, and companies should strive to make this a reality. One example might be to allow an innovation team to focus on new development for less mission-critical systems using the most advanced cloud native services, while focusing critical system development on more mature services.

Quality assurance and auditing

Once the company's compliance and risk mitigation activities have been solidified, the guardrails are in place to allow for cloud deployments. However, these guardrails and governance methodologies are only as good as when they were developed and implemented. Over time, as workloads are built and deployed to the cloud, a company has to re-evaluate the risk posture they originally implemented and ensure that it keeps up with the current climate. Over time, cloud vendors will release new services, which will need to be evaluated and assigned the right level of data and workloads they are suitable for. Governments and compliance bodies will continue to update or release new frameworks that organizations must follow in order to ensure the safety of customer data. All of these require quality assurance and auditing.

In this context, quality assurance is the process of systems being constantly evaluated and tested to ensure that they meet the standard originally set out in the business problem statement. In the traditional sense, this process makes sure that the code is functionally correct, lacks security and other defects, and meets the other non-functional requirements. This is no different in the cloud. However, the non-functional requirements now include additional cloud native properties. For example, cost optimization in the cloud is critical to prevent cloud sprawl and the quality assurance process should be responsible for verifying that the cloud vendor services being used are appropriate and implemented correctly. Quality assurance extends to not only the code and services, but the deployment pipeline, system availability, and even the blast radius of the distributed architecture. As discussed previously, quality assurance should also be built into the project management processes of the company so that before a workload even reaches production, it is also designed with these philosophies in mind.

Another critical component that systems need is auditability. Regardless of whether the system is within the scope of an external auditor, or only internal, this process assures accountability and traceability to identify defects and security incidents. Over time, even the best implemented systems will drift from their original architecture and security posture. This is natural and expected, as business conditions change and new functionality is implemented. What is important is that the audit process for governance, security, and compliance stays the same or is enhanced along with the system.

Deploying new business functionality doesn't mean that the security posture has to change, so performing continuous auditing of the guardrails will ensure that the drift from the original posture isn't excessive. Cloud vendors often have configuration services that take periodic views of the overall cloud landscape and store them in a digital format, perfect for auditing and comparison testing. These configuration services can usually be extended to not only get a view of the cloud landscape, but also to perform custom system-level verifications and store output alongside the cloud configuration. Through automation, these audit checks can be carried out at short intervals and then programmatically compared to ensure that nothing has been introduced into the environment that will cause drift from the required posture. Automated auditing is how mature cloud native organizations ensure that their systems are always compliant.

While quality assurance and auditing are not specifically part of the **cloud native maturity model** (**CNMM**), it permeates through all three of the axes. Mature CNMM companies are constantly evaluating new and evolved cloud vendor services that will help them to meet their business objectives more quickly and cheaply and stay within accepted risk and compliance requirements. They automate everything, including their compliance checks, auditing activities, and end-to-end deployment and quality assurance processes, so that system drift doesn't cause security problems. They focus their energy on making sure their application designs follow best cloud native practices and automate the code review to check for vulnerabilities, security gaps, cost inefficiencies, and blast radius conditions.

Foundational cloud operating frameworks and landing zones

Not knowing where to start to ensure a secure and operational base environment is a common issue that companies have when beginning the cloud native journey. Even if all of the people, processes, and technology considerations are aligned, this lack of a landing zone can cause slowdowns or even failure during the early stages of cloud native activities. There are many different aspects that go into creating the base landing zone for future cloud workloads, and this section will cover some of these and how to consider the right approach for individual organizations.

Typically, a good starting point is to consider the technology aspect and identify the correct configuration of accounts, virtual networks, security posture, logging, and other base decisions. This will ensure that the base landing zone has the company requirements built in, has ample room for growth, and is capable of being designed by the staff's current cloud skills. For some industries, adding an overlay of one or more specific governance models to ensure proper mapping of external controls to the cloud environment will enable proper auditing ability for regulators. These concepts are explored more in the following sections.

Cloud landing zone

A cloud landing zone is all of the technical and operational aspects that need to be considered and designed before any workloads are actually deployed. There are a range of areas that fall into this category and not all are required for a successful cloud journey. However, as a best practice, it is advisable to take all of them into consideration. At a high level, these aspects are as follows:

- Account structure design, billing, and tagging
- Networking design and interconnectivity requirements
- Central shared services
- Security requirements, logging, and audit ability compliance
- Automation framework and infrastructure as code

Account structure design

The account structure design strategy is the start of it all, and each company will have different requirements for how they will want to set up their accounts. For smaller companies that will have just a few workloads running in the cloud, a single account may be sufficient. As the size and complexity of an organization grows, it is common to have many accounts that allow for desecrate billing, the separation of duties, a reduced blast radius, and the specialization of environment or governance requirements. Using a hierarchical structure, where there is a master account and many sub-accounts, is common. This will give limited visibility across accounts but still keep the ability to federate certain aspects, such as security, networking, and environment workloads.

Often, the top master account is used exclusively for billing and cost aggregation. This will enable a single pane of glass for the billing, but have that broken down into the sub-accounts for charging back, or simply an understanding of which activities are costing the most. It often has the ability to allow for cost optimization across billing constructs as well, supporting volume discount pricing or reserved capacity spreading. The sub or children accounts are usually made up of the individual requirements. Regardless of company requirements, it is important to understand the cloud account strategy early on so as to ensure that it is properly aligned with the needs of stakeholders.

Network design

Once the accounts are designed and ready, network design is the next most critical component. The accounts are mostly administrative constructs, but the ability to deploy workloads and secure data is done by the network design. Most cloud vendors will have a virtual networking concept that allows for a custom design of the network space needed for various requirements. These virtual networks can then be further divided into subnets that allow for network traffic flow requirements, for example, externally routable traffic (in other words, the public subnet) and internal only (in other words, private subnets). Similar to account design, a virtual network design is critical since, once created, it is hard to modify, and so growth and workload needs should be considered.

Typically, a single account may contain many virtual networks and these can interact with each other, or even with virtual networks in other accounts. Therefore, they are an additional way of reducing blast radius issues and isolating workloads or data.

Central shared services

Once the accounts and virtual networks are identified and mapped out, the next major focus area concerns what will run as a central shared service. Some services are going to be standard across the entire cloud estate, and trying to replicate them in different accounts or virtual networks is counterproductive or even risky. In most cases, companies with multiple accounts and virtual networks should consider a shared services account or virtual network to store all of these services. This can be considered a virtual hub and spoke design that has each virtual network connecting back to the hub where a single instantiate of the service is deployed. Good examples of central shared services include logging storage, directory services, authentication services, CMDB or service catalogs, and monitoring.

Security and audit requirements

Finally, security and audit requirements should be pervasive across the cloud estate. The entire account, network, and shared services concepts will be underpinned by a holistic security and audit ability design strategy. As discussed in the central shared services section, directory and authentication services are important for securing access to workloads, data, and accounts. In addition, a critical consideration for security and audit is having a robust logging framework and a configuration audit process.

There are many different logs that can be captured inside a cloud account for workloads, some provided by the cloud vendor, and others built into individual applications. The more logs that are collected, the better decisions can be made for all aspects of the workload. Having a central logging framework enables the instances, container, platform service or other workload component to act as a stateless machine that doesn't need to exist in order for troubleshooting to take place. Combining the workload logs with other logs, such as network flows, API calls, packet latency, and others will give an insight into how the overall cloud environment is behaving, and it can be done in the future to replay events through log aggregation. This is a powerful method for understanding and securing workloads as the cloud estate grows and becomes ever more complex.

Audit ability is another critical component to consider. As discussed previously, there are cloud vendor services that keep snapshots or views of the overall environment configuration at specific intervals that are useful in many ways. First and foremost, this allows for consistent audit checks to be carried out to prove that the cloud environment is following agreed governance requirements. Second, it also allows for cloud administrators to check for environment drift, misconfigurations, malicious configuration changes, and even for cost optimization.

Automation and Infrastructure as Code are the key enablers for this type of logging and audit control deployments and are directly related to the cloud native maturity model that a company wants to increase as they mature in terms of their cloud journey.

External governance guidelines

There are many different governance guidelines developed or evolved to support secure and compliant operating environments in the cloud. Depending on the industry vertical, critical data requirements, or external compliance demands, companies have options on how to enhance their base cloud landing zone. Even for organizations that do not fall into a specific industry or compliance requirement, aligning one or more of these governance guidelines will ensure strict adherence to internationally recognized hardening of cloud computing resources and will help with internal audit processes of control mapping. A few important governance guidelines and models for deploying compliant workloads in the cloud are outlined here.

National Institute of Standards and Technology (NIST)

There are many different NIST-based assurance frameworks that can be implemented. One popular one that Amazon Web Services has done extensive work on in creating reference documents, quickstart guides, and accelerators is for NIST SP 800-53 (Revision 4) (`https://www.wbdg.org/files/pdfs/dod_cloudcomputing.pdf`), NIST SP 800-171 (`http://nvlpubs.nist.gov/nistpubs/SpecialPublications/NIST.SP.800-171.pdf`), the OMB TIC Initiative – FedRAMP Overlay (pilot) (`https://www.fedramp.gov/draft-fedramp-tic-overlay/`), and the DoD Cloud Computing SRG (`https://www.wbdg.org/files/pdfs/dod_cloudcomputing.pdf`) (`https://aws.amazon.com/about-aws/whats-new/2016/01/nist-800-53-standardized-architecture-on-the-aws-cloud-quick-start-reference-deployment/`). Using the guidance and accelerators outlined by AWS, an organization can deploy a standardized environment that helps workloads that fall within the scope of these NIST publications.

Payment Card Industry Data Security Standard (PCI DSS)

For customers who need to process credit card data for their customers, follow the PCI DSS (`https://www.pcisecuritystandards.org/`) compliance standard recommended. Amazon Web Services has a detailed reference architecture and control mapping to help customers set up a PCI DSS-compliant environment available at `https://aws.amazon.com/quickstart/architecture/accelerator-pci/`.

Health Insurance Portability and Accountability Act (HIPAA)

Customers who wish to run sensitive workloads regulated under HIPAA, and who plan to include **protected health information (PHI)**, must understand the implications and have the right authority to operate on behalf of a specific cloud vendor. Not all cloud vendor services come within the scope of the HIPAA Business Associate Addendum and it will fall to the customer to identify the type of data and workload they are designing. Additional information about how to achieve this on AWS can be found at `https://d0.awsstatic.com/whitepapers/compliance/AWS_HIPAA_Compliance_Whitepaper.pdf`.

Center for Internet Security (CIS)

The CIS (`https://www.cisecurity.org/cis-benchmarks/`) has a consensus review process comprising subject matter experts to identify benchmark recommendations of how to deploy and configure services to meet security needs across a wide range of controls. A full explanation of how to achieve this on Amazon Web Services can be found at `https://d0.awsstatic.com/whitepapers/compliance/AWS_CIS_Foundations_Benchmark.pdf`.

Cloud migration versus greenfield development

After the decision to move to the cloud is made and the frameworks and guardrails are in place and some initial success achieved, almost always, the big question will come down to migration of large amounts of workloads. A cloud migration is defined as the movement of applications, data, or other components from their existing location (usually on-premises) to the cloud. A greenfield development project is one in which there are no legacy constraints imposed on the design and, therefore, a completely new implementation is the outcome. Migrations and greenfield development often exist side by side, where legacy workloads are being migrated into the target cloud operating environment and all new projects are designed as cloud native.

This section will break down common migration patterns, tools that are used in migrations, and how greenfield cloud native development fits into the migration story. This book is not designed to go into the details of cloud migrations. However, migrations are an important part of the cloud native architecture process and it is therefore important to know where the intersections are.

Migration patterns

Migrations are often broken down into patterns using The 6Rs (**Rehost**, **Replatform**, **Repurchase**, **Refactor**, **Retire**, and **Retain**). Each of these 6Rs has a place in the cloud native discussion. However, retire, retain, and repurchase are not as applicable for the cloud native discussion. Often, the decision to retire or retain an application workload is specific to the complexity or the expected life remaining until a new replacement can be implemented. Therefore, it is usually cheaper to retain or retire than try to migrate. Repurchase can have implications to the overall enterprise architecture, specifically when the decision is to replace an existing workload with a **Software as a Service** (**SaaS**) offering that is cloud-based, but completely managed by another company. The remainder of the section will focus on rehost, replatform and refactor.

Rehost

Rehost, often referred to as *lift-and-shift*, is the quickest path to the cloud and, in its purest form, literally means moving a workload exactly as is from its existing location (usually on-premises) to the cloud. This migration pattern is often chosen because it allows for relatively small amounts of upfront analysis work and provides a quick return on investment. There are many tools in the market that support this type of migration, doing block-level replication or image packaging to get the instances to the cloud. In addition, there are tools that allow for database servers to have their data migrated, including schemas, in a similar manner. The drawback of this type of migration is that typically, the speed of migration means that the true benefits of the cloud are not being realized. Often, rehost migrations are executed due to a compelling event (for example, a lease on a data center ending) and speed is the most important requirement. There is also a belief that rehosting in the cloud will accelerate the ability to replatform or refactor applications once in the cloud, thereby reducing the risk of making the changes during migration, as seen in the following diagram:

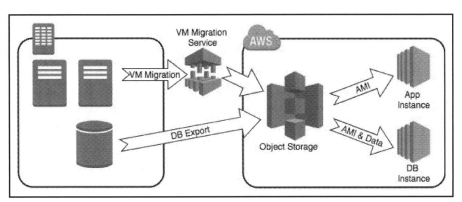

Replatform

Replatform is similar to rehost. However, in the migration process, there are changes to the workload architecture to take advantage of the cloud native vendor services, for example, moving the application exactly as is, but changing the database from self-managed instances to a vendor-managed database platform. While this change seems minor, it introduces a change to the workload architecture and must be managed as a mini-refactor with testing and documentation. Replatforming is also a pattern that can be done at the time of migration from on-premises to the cloud, or once the application is already in the cloud, as seen in the following diagram:

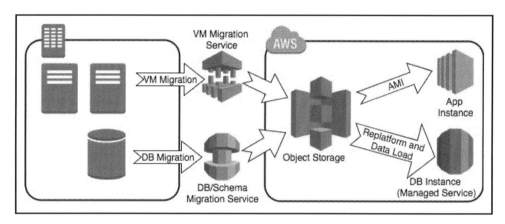

Refactor

Refactor is the process of redesigning the workload to be cloud native. This type of migration pattern is, in essence, a rewrite of the application to align with the CNMM discussion in `Chapter 1`, *Introducing Cloud Native Architecture*, add automation, and architect the application to have a cloud native design. While rehost and replatform are more aligned to what is usually thought of as a migration, refactoring an application during the migration process is becoming increasingly popular as companies realize that lift-and-shift movement to the cloud will not let them realize the benefits from their business case. Refactoring still applies to migrations since, in most cases, the data is being transformed to a newer database engine (in other words, NoSQL), the application is being redesigned to decouple the service components (in other words, microservices) and, most importantly, the business logic stays the same (or is enhanced) during this process, as seen in the following diagram:

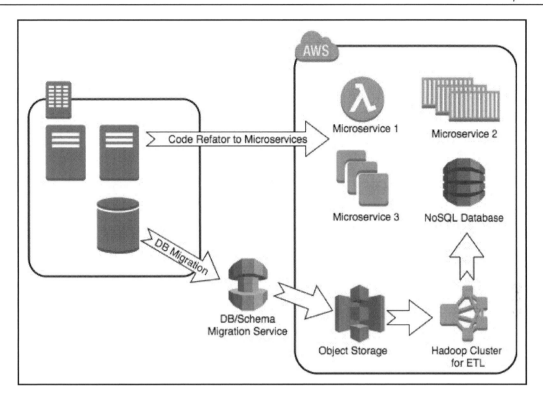

Migrate or greenfield development?

Throughout this chapter, cloud drivers and considerations were discussed, and we dived deeper into how an enterprise would migrate existing workloads into the cloud. While some of these patterns contain development activities to refactor or replatform the application, they are still migration patterns. So, the question is: when does an organization use greenfield development instead of migrations? Typically, when a company decides to be cloud first, they will focus a significant amount of effort migrating their existing workloads to the cloud. At the same time, they will start all new development activities in the cloud, which is greenfield development. Usually, a new project or workload will still require interface points with the legacy applications, whether they are in the cloud or still being migrated, and therefore, a common intersection between these two activities is the integration of interface points.

As the migration activities subside, the focus on new development in the cloud is a top priority. This phase after migration is usually an exciting time at the organization, since the cloud skills are strong and the optimism of how the cloud can change the company are high. Being a cloud native architect during this time will allow for big ideas to be put forward and old barriers to be removed.

Summary

In this chapter, we identified what exactly is reason why companies make the decision to move to the cloud. Understanding these key drivers – agility, cost, security, governance, expansion, talent, and innovation – and their level of maturity within the company, will drive the final decision to make the journey. Once the decision is made, it is critical to define and implement the operating model, which will assure stakeholders, as well as change and project management, that risk and compliance requirements are managed and implemented to ensure success in the cloud. Finally, we reviewed the major migration patterns that will enable workloads to be moved to the cloud. While some organizations will skip the migration and start a fresh in the cloud, most companies will require this step, and it is important that they do it correctly. A cloud-first company will migrate existing workloads, but create all new applications in the cloud in compliance with cloud native architecture patterns.

In the next chapter, we will review the application-level requirements for cloud native architectures, including the system development life cycle, **service-oriented architectures (SOA)**, microservices, and serverless computing. We will dive into different frameworks and methodologies and understand how they fit into cloud native design principles.

3
Cloud Native Application Design

In this chapter, we will dive deep into the development of cloud native architectures, using microservices and serverless computing as a mature CNMM state. Starting with the evolution of computer systems from monolithic and moving through much more mature architectures, this chapter will cover containers, orchestration, and serverless, how they fit together, and why they are considered mature on the application-centric design axis.

From monolithic to microservices and everything in between

Client-server applications have always been popular. However, as networking technology and design patterns have evolved, the need to have less tightly coupled applications intercommunicating has given way to **service-oriented architectures** (**SOAs**). An SOA is the concept of breaking down the components that make up a monolith or server into more discrete business services. SOA components are still self-contained. However, they are significantly smaller in scope than the traditional monolithic application and enable faster maintenance and decoupled interactions. The traditional client could still be considered a component of an SOA application, but, instead of communicating directly with a monolithic server, there would be an intermediation layer, or server bus, that accepts the call and distributes to other services for processing. These other services could offer data persistence or collect additional information to make a business decision. The SOA approach has opened up the ability to distribute systems and allow a massive change in interaction among other systems, even those outside a company's internal systems.

Cloud computing continues to evolve these patterns because of increasingly lower costs for these services, as well as the rising availability of resources to create services. Microservices, which are similar to SOAs, are an evolution that allows for a specific service to be broken down into even more discrete components. A service in an SOA is a black box that performs a full business function. Microservices are made up of that function, which is broken down to perform subsets of the larger business function. This will further increase system maintenance and speed to make functionality updates and also reduce the blast radius of code or hardware faults. A cloud native architecture, as defined in `Chapter 1`, *Introducing Cloud Native Architecture*, of this book, will have various maturity levels on the cloud native maturity model, including using cloud native services, application-centric design and automation, and application design principles. Microservices offer a way to achieve all of those principles so as to enable scale and fault tolerance that is hard to achieve with any of the other traditional ways of system design.

System design patterns

The evolution of systems design is one where various pressures impacted the way systems were built and deployed to solve ever more complex business problems. This section will cover these patterns in more detail and provide additional insights into how they work and the challenges they faced, forcing evolution. To understand how solution architecture has progressed, it is important to define a few key concepts, namely primitives, subsystems, and systems.

Regardless of the design pattern, primitives are the base level of the overall solution, often referred to as functions, tasks, or microservices, depending on the style. By design, a primitive is supposed to be the most basic unit that is capable of performing an action. Primitives are often so specialized that, by themselves, they are not capable of having a direct impact on the subsystem they belong to. Instead, they perform one task quickly and efficiently. Subsystems are logical groupings of primitives that form a discrete business function. Subsystems do not have to be a single component, although they can be depending on the design architecture. They do, however, need to have a logical flow that results in a business function being achieved. The primitives that make up the subsystem could be function calls within the same code block or a completely separate microservice, as long as the results end in a completed outcome for the system. Systems are the top level of the solution, and are often made up of many subsystems that intercommunicate with each other, or other systems, to complete an entire process from beginning to end.

Cloud native architectures are the product of this evolution. It's important to understand the makeup of an architecture and the originations of the patterns so further evolution can continue and the best design for a specific business requirement can be used and evolved over time. There are three main design patterns, namely monolithic, client server, and services. Each uses the concept of systems, subsystems, and primitives. However, the implementation of each is the key differentiators that allow for them to be more robust and cloud native.

Monolithic

From the early days of information technology and the advent of computing power to speed up computational tasks, the preferred design pattern for an application was monolithic. Simply put, a monolithic design pattern is one in which all aspects of the system are self-contained and independent from other systems or processes. This pattern worked great with the large mainframe monoliths that existed and allowed for the code logic, storage devices, and printing to all be done in the same location. Networking, as we know it today, was not possible and what little connectivity was available was significantly slower, preventing additional systems from being interconnected. As new business requirements were identified, they were designed directly in the existing monolith, making them critical and very tightly coupled. Ultimately, monolithic design patterns enabled all tasks to be executed to complete a desirable outcome.

As technology advanced and the needs of computational power were evolving, system designers found that adding new functionality into a monolith was cumbersome and potentially introduced hard-to-identify bugs. They also realized that reusing components and tasks was a great way to save time, money, and reduce code change bugs. This modular approach to systems design, which was still mostly monolithic, enabled reuse and allowed for more targeted maintenance updates to take place without impacting the entire application or system. This philosophy continued to evolve as technology advanced and allowed for the splitting apart of some of the largest monoliths into separate discrete subsystems, which could then be updated independently. This concept of decoupling components is a key driving factor into the evolution of system designs and will continue to get more and more discrete as technology advances.

Client server

Eventually, as technology costs lowered and design patterns continued to advance to more sophisticated levels, a new style of architecture became popular: client server applications. The monolith still existed to provide the backend processing power and data storage required. However, because of advances in networking and database concepts, a frontend application, or client, was used to provide a user experience and transmit data to the server. The client application is still tightly coupled with the server application. However, it allows for potentially many clients connecting into the server and therefore distributing the application to a field workforce or public users on the internet. This evolution of the modular approach also changed the way IT departments deployed and maintained systems, with different groups responsible for the client and server components, and skill sets started to specialize and focus on how to further drive efficiencies.

Services

Client server applications worked very well, but the coupling of components caused slow and risky deployments for mission-critical applications. System designers continued to find ways to separate components from each other to reduce the blast radius of failure, increase the speed of deployments, and reduce risk during the process. A services design pattern is where business functions are broken down into specific objectives to complete in a self-contained manner that doesn't require knowledge of or dependencies on the state of another service. This self-contained independent state of the service is in itself the definition of decoupling and marks a major evolutionary change from monolithic architectures. The change to services design is directly related to the reduction in the price of compute and storage and the increase in network sophistication and security practices for intercommunication. Lowering costs allows for many computing instances of services to be created across wider geographical regions and with a more diverse set of business functional requirements.

Services are not just custom code designed to solve a business problem. In fact, as cloud vendors mature their services, often a managed offering is created to help remove the undifferentiated heavy lifting of some piece of a system. These individual services fit into the services category and often make up specific functions in a large distributed and decoupled solution, for example, using a queueing service or storage service as a function of the design. In a monolithic system architecture, all of these components would need to be developed and would exist in a single application stack with tightly coupled interconnectivity and significant risk of failures, slowdowns, or faulty code. Mature cloud native architectures are specifically designed to take advantage of these vendor services in addition to custom functions, all working as one to react to different events, and ultimately driving business outcomes with as little complexity as possible.

While services-based architectures are very popular with cloud native architectures, the evolution of services design has taken time. From the first iteration of SOAs, to microservices, to functions, each pattern breaks up the functionality even more to decouple their interactions as much as possible.

Service-oriented architectures (SOAs)

A services design pattern that has been around since before the cloud is the SOA. This is the first major evolution of breaking down a monolithic application into separate parts to reduce the blast radius and help make application development and deployment processes faster to support business velocity. SOA design patterns are often still a large application split into subsystems that interact with each other just as they would in a monolithic system. However, they often have an intermediation layer in between (for example, an **Enterprise Service Bus (ESB)**).

The use of an ESB to mediate service requests allows for heterogeneous communication protocols and further service decoupling, often through the exchange of messaging. The ESB allows for message translation, routing, and other forms of mediation to ensure that the consumer service is receiving the messages in the right form at the right time. Because SOA design patterns are often combined to make a large and complex enterprise system, individual services often contain a full set of business logic for a specific subsystem. This design allows for the service to be partially self-contained and send messages, through the EBS, to provide or request data from other subsystems.

This SOA design approach drastically increased the ability for systems to be more distributed, serve business needs faster, and take advantage of cheaper compute resources. However, there are some drawbacks that are associated with SOAs as well. Because services interact with other components through an ESB, it can quickly become a bottleneck or single point of failure. Message flow becomes very complicated and any disruption to the ESB could cause significant slowdowns or queueing of messages, clogging up the entire system. In addition, because each service requires a specific message type formatted with its requirements, testing of the full composite application becomes very complicated and not isolated, slowing down business velocity. For example, when two services have significant business logic updates, each with new and enhanced message formats, the deployment will require an update to both subsystems and the ESB, potentially disrupting the entire composite application.

Microservices

The evolution of SOAs has led to continued breakdown of business functionality into even smaller components, often referred to as microservices. These are still services, as defined earlier. However, the scope of the services and the way they intercommunicate has evolved to take advantage of technology and pricing. Microservices are often used to help reduce some of the challenges faced with SOAs, while continuing to mature the services model. There are two key differentiators for microservices designs when compared to SOA: the scope of service and communication methods.

Microservices are designed the further specialize the scope of the service. With SOAs, a service will act as a full subsystem that has a large block of business functionality where a microservices architecture will break down that subsystem into components closer to primitives that perform a subset of the main service. The microservice might have business logic or it might just perform a workflow task, such as a database transaction, auditing, or logging. If it contains business logic, the scope will be much smaller than an SOA service and will usually not be a standalone component able to complete a full business task. This breakdown of the functionality allows for the service to scale independently from other components and often execute based on an event to reduce the time the cloud resources are being used and paid for.

The other key differentiator of a microservice is the communication method. SOAs will often communicate with heterogeneous protocols through an ESB, where microservices expose an API that can be called from any consumer service. This exposure of an API allows for the service to be developed in any language that will have no impact from other services and their development language or approach. Because of the decoupled nature of the API layer, changes to the service logic often require no coordination between consumer services, and even when the API itself is modified only the consumer services need to be notified, which can often be done via dynamic API endpoint identification and navigation.

Why services matter

A key differentiator of the cloud is the way applications are designed and deployed, with services-based architecture being the most popular. Services matter because they allow for applications to be designed into ever smaller components that have faster deployment velocity allowing business ideas to come to market quicker. In addition, the smaller a service or function, the smaller the blast radius, meaning that a fault or bad code only impacts a relatively small amount of connected services. This reduced blast radius has a significant improvement on the risk profile of code deployments and the time required to roll back if something bad was introduced:

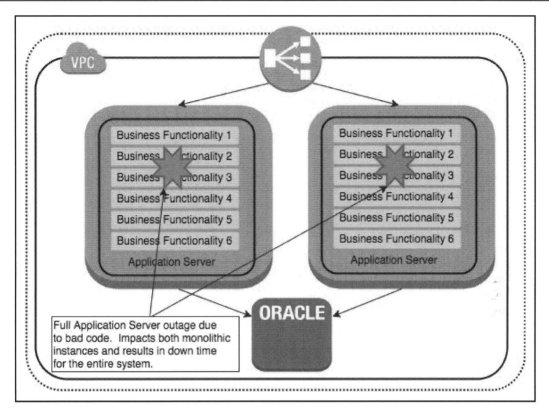

A monolithic system deployed for high availability

The preceding diagram shows a monolithic system, deployed to multiple instances for high availability, but using a design pattern to deploy the full application functionality into an application server on each instance. In this case, the business functionality boxes are an example of a subsystem that would have many different functions, or primitives that are included to complete the required functionally. In this example, the deployment of new code must be done at the system level and will likely require scheduled downtime and a full redeploy of the entire application artifact. If any of the newly deployed code has an unintended bug in a subsystem or primitive, the entire application will be impacted since it's all deployed together. This unscheduled outage will roll back the entire application artifact, even subsystems that were working as intended in other parts of the system. This design is not very flexible and causes long and stressful **big bang** deployments that need to be planned for weeks or months in advance.

By decoupling systems and the business functionality into separate subsystems, the interaction points between these subsystems is significantly lowered and often they will never communicate at all. Using subsystems and primitives in the form of services allows for the changes being made to be vastly less impactful to the wider organization, causing the risk associated with those changes to go down because the blast radius is reduced to only those services directly related to it. Depending on the requirements, a subsystem might still be an isolated coupled component or broken into many primitives:

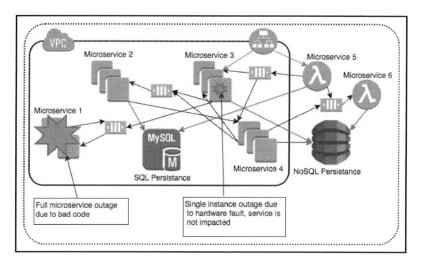

The original monolithic application

In the preceding diagram, the original monolithic application was redesigned and deployed into separate subsystems and primitives, using a mix of instances, containers, functions, and cloud vendor services. Not all services interact with each other or persist data, so if there are problems in the environment most are still usable. Subsystem 1 shows as having an outage due to bad code being deployed, which will be discovered and resolved by the appropriate services team. Meanwhile, all other services are still operating with no impact, unless they were to interact with subsystem 1. The diagram also shows the impact of a single instance outage due to hardware fault, a common occurrence that should not impact the entire system or any individual service. Subsystem 3 would detect that it lost an instance in its fleet and automatically deploy a new instance or container to keep up with incoming requests. Primitive Microservices 5 and 6 are executed as event-based code blocks that interact with other primitives to persist data, interact with message queues, or perform a business function.

Services matter since they allow for separation of functionality, reduce blast radius, increase business velocity and, if done correctly, reduce the cost to run the full system.

Containers and serverless

Cloud native architectures have matured over the years as the patterns evolve to take advantage of the newest advances in cloud technologies. Microservices are currently the hot topic for architecture trends since they allow for massive decoupling of components while utilizing cloud native services in ways that would be impossible with on-premises software. However, microservices are just a pattern. There are multiple ways to construct a microservice with various technologies and approaches, and containers and serverless approaches are the most common. This is not to say that microservice systems cannot be designed with more traditional virtual instances; in the right use case, that is still very applicable. What it means is that containers and serverless technologies allow for systems to be designed and deployed at scale and with agility that typically comes with microservices. They are more aligned with the goals of microservices. This section will explore containers and serverless, explaining what that means, and how they can be used to design cloud native architectures.

Containers and orchestration

Containers are a natural progression of additional isolation and virtualization of hardware. Where a virtual instance allows for a bare metal server to have multiple hosts, hence gaining more efficiencies and usage of that specific server's resources, containers behave similarly but are much more lightweight, portable, and scalable. Typically, containers run a Linux, or, in some cases, Windows operating system. However, a lot of the bloat and unused components are removed, and they handle the traditional startup, shutdown, and task management, and not much else. Developers are then able to include specific libraries or languages and deploy the code and configurations directly to the container file. This is then treated as the deployment artifact and published to a registry to be deployed or updated across the fleet of containers already running in the cluster via the orchestration service.

Because of the lightweight nature of containers, they make for an ideal technology to run in a cloud environment and for extreme decoupling of an application into microservices. The scaling aspect of containers can take place across nodes to maximize the resources on that instance and by using many hosts to form a cluster that are all maintained and scheduled by the orchestration service. For file storage, the service can use local ephemeral filesystem locations, or if the data needs to persist, the files can be stored in a persistent volume which is mounted and accessible by all containers in the node. To make the container placement and scaling easier, some orchestration tools use pods, or containers coupled together to act as a single unit that are instantiated together and scale together.

Registries

A container registry is simply a public or private area for the storage, and serving, of pre-built containers. There are many options for a registry that can be used, and all the major cloud vendors have a hosted version of registries that can be made private for a specific organization. In addition, there are many public hosted registries, such as the Docker Hub registry, that holds publicly available pre-built container files that have lots of common configurations ready to use. Depending on the needs of an organization, any of these would work. However, once the learning phase is completed, it's recommended that hosted private registries are always used. In addition to being much more secure for private container images, if hosted in the cloud environment, this also provides close proximity to the orchestration service for a faster deployment pipeline.

Registries play a critical role in the CI/CD pipelines that will be used for deployment of applications. We have a simple pipeline where the developer checks code into the repository of choice (in this case, a GIT repository). That push triggers a build using Jenkins, which will build the container, test the newly formed container using predefined scripts, and push that container to the registry service. Once in the registry, the orchestration tool will trigger a pull from the registry that will take the new container and perform an update or deploy. There are a few ways to achieve the final deployment: either a rolling update for zero downtime or a new deployment following the configuration requirements.

Orchestration

The orchestration of containers is where the hard part comes in. If an application was designed to use containers as a large monolithic stack that performs all the tasks required for the subsystem to execute, then deploying those containers becomes a pretty easy task. However, this also defeats the purpose of using containers and microservices, which is to decouple the components into small services that interact with each other or other services. As a subsystem is broken down into many separate primitive microservices, the ability to coordinate those services, made up of one or many containers, becomes very difficult. Some services will be relatively small and will only be used sparingly, while others will be very high volume and require strict scaling and high availability configurations In addition, the deployment of new containers to the cluster is critical and usually needs to be done with little or no downtime, making a service that performs those updates very valuable.

There are many types of container orchestration tools on the market, and each cloud vendor will have one or more managed versions, or an organization can choose to set up and maintain their own orchestration tools, depending on their requirements. One of the most popular orchestration services is Kubernetes, which can run on any cloud platform, on-premises, or a hybrid of both. There are reasons to use a cloud vendor's container orchestration service over a third-party tool, most notably the native interaction of the containers and other cloud services provided by the vendor. However, even now cloud vendors are deploying their own managed Kubernetes services as well. Here are some of the key concepts from a Kubernetes deployment:

- **Kubernetes master**: This is responsible for maintaining the desired state for your cluster.
- **Kubernetes node**: Nodes are the machines (VMs, physical servers, and so on) that run your applications and cloud workflows. The Kubernetes Master controls each node; you'll rarely interact with nodes directly.
- **Pod**: This is the basic building block of Kubernetes; the smallest and simplest unit in the Kubernetes object model that you create or deploy. A pod represents a running process on your cluster.
- **Service**: An abstraction that defines a logical set of pods and a policy by which to access them, sometimes called a microservice.
- **Replica controllers and ReplicaSets**: These ensure that a specified number of pod replicas are running at any one time. In other words, they make sure that a pod or a homogeneous set of pods is always up and available.
- **Deployment**: Provides declarative updates for pods and ReplicaSets.
- **DaemonSet**: Ensures that all (or some) nodes run a copy of a pod. As nodes are added to the cluster, pods are added to them. As nodes are removed from the cluster, those pods are garbage collected. Deleting a DaemonSet will clean up the pods it created.

Container usage patterns

Containers are a great tool for designing and implementing cloud native architectures. Containers fit well in the cloud native maturity model that was outlined in `Chapter 1`, *Introducing Cloud Native Architecture*. Specifically, they are a native cloud service from the vendor, they allow for extreme automation through CICD, and they are great for microservices due to their lightweight and scalable attributes. There are a few key patterns used where containers are a central component, namely microservices, hybrid and migration of application deployment, and business innovation through agility.

Microservices with containers

Containers are often synonymous with microservices. This is due to their lightweight properties, containing only a minimal operating system and the exact libraries and components needed to execute a specific piece of business functionality. Therefore, applications, whether designed as new or a broken down monolithically, will be designed to contain exactly what is needed, with no additional overhead to slow down the processing. Microservices are made to be small and perform specific business functionalities, which are often designed by different teams, but deployed at the same time. Therefore, a small team could develop a specific service using containers, with their desired programming language, libraries, API implementation style, and scaling techniques. They are free to deploy their business function, via a container push to the registry and a CICD deployment without impacting any other service in the mesh of interacting services. Alternatively, other small teams could develop their own services, using their own style, and not have to worry about anything about the API of the other services.

The use of containers for microservices works well for keeping small groups agile and moving fast. It also allows for the architecture standards board to implement guidelines that all services must follow without impacting the agility of the design team. For example, a logging framework, security approach for secrets, orchestration layer, and the CICD technology could be mandated but the programming languages would be open to what the team wants to use. This would allow the composite system to be managed centrally and each service to be designed individually.

Hybrid and migration of application deployment

Containers are a great way to run a hybrid architecture or to support the migration of a workload to the cloud faster and easier than with most other methods. Since a container is a discrete unit, whether it's deployed on-premises (such as a private cloud) or in the public cloud (for example, AWS), it will be the same. This pattern then allows for the architecture team to deploy the full composite application (multiple microservices, containerized applications, and so on) to on-premises and use the cloud environment to be the **disaster recovery (DR)** or failover site, or vice versa. It also allows for a low risk migration of a containerized application from on-premises to the cloud, making this a favorite way to perform large-scale migrations after the applications have been containerized. Unfortunately, it's not quite that simple; there are changes that are needed to support the surrounding components that make up the system depending on which cloud and orchestration solution is being used. For example, if using Kubernetes both on-premises and in the cloud, there could be changes needed to the Kubernetes manifest file to support different ingress methods, persistence volumes, load balancers, or other components.

More complex use cases are also possible, including running active workloads across on-premises and the chosen cloud vendor or moving containers from various clouds (often called multi-clouds). The purpose of implementing this architecture would be to take advantage of pricing constructs or moving away from problematic clouds (for example, those with latency issues, downed data centers, and so on) without having to go into a full business continuity scenario. However, the complexity of this type of workload distribution across clouds is very high, and would not be possible for many applications. Only those workloads that were specifically designed to ensure that data persistence and **online transaction processing** (OLTP) was properly handled would be successful. At this stage of the maturity of cloud broker tooling, distributed databases, and networking latency, it is recommended to use only a single cloud platform for cloud native applications.

Container anti patterns

In the world of cloud computing, containers are not only a popular way to achieve cloud native architectures, but they are quickly becoming the standard with which to design microservices. However, there are some use cases where containers are not always suited, specifically using containers for multiple concerns. The concept of concerns, or focus areas of a component, is that each module or class should have responsibility over a single part of the functionality. In the case of containers, multiple concerns would mean having a web server and database running in the same container. Following the services approach, breaking down monoliths into discrete components will ensure the applications have a lower blast radius and are easier to deploy and scale independently. This is not to say that a container should only have a single thread, but that it should have only a single role. There are ways for containers to share persistent disks and intercommunicate, but putting multiple components or concerns on the same container is not the right way. Simply put, containers are not virtual machines.

Treating containers as virtual machines is not limited to deploying multiple concerns into a single container. Allowing SSH daemons (or other types of console access) on a container defeats the purpose of the container in the first place. Since containers are a discrete component, they should be set up, configured, and have their code deployed as part of the initial development phase. That in turn becomes the deployment artifact which is pushed to the repository and deployed via the orchestration tooling used. Allowing direct console access to the container means that modifications can be made, the container is no longer an immutable component, and the consistency of the contents can no longer be trusted. Instead, if the container needs an update due to a bug or enhancement, that should be done to the base container, tested through proper channels, and pushed to the repository for deployment.

If the application requires multiple concerns or SSH access, consider using cloud-instance virtual machines instead of containers. Alternatively, to become more cloud native, work on the application to decouple it or enhance the CICD pipeline to allow for faster and more consistent deployment processes.

Serverless

Serverless does not mean the absence of servers; however, it does mean that resources can be used without having to consider server capacity. Serverless applications do not require the design or operations team to provision, scale, or maintain servers. All of that is handled by the cloud provider. This approach is probably the first time ever where the developers can focus on exactly what they are best at: writing code. In addition to the flexibility and focus this allows, the cost implications to serverless applications is a huge advantage over more traditional approaches, even containers. Serverless pricing is typically done by the runtime of the service, priced at the 100 millisecond duration. Designing services that execute a piece of code at such short intervals meets the definition of a microservice and takes maximum advantage of serverless technology.

In most cases when serverless is discussed, the first thing thought of is Function as a Service. The big three cloud providers each have their version of this: AWS Lambda, Azure Functions, and Google Cloud Functions. Each behaves roughly the same and allows for the deployment of code and execution as an event. For the most part, this type of serverless service is where the place of code execution is considered a core component for all serverless design patterns. However, there are other cloud vendor services that fall into the serverless category, and in most cases these primitives are used together to form subsystems in the cloud environment. According to AWS, there are eight high level areas that have serverless services. These are compute, API proxy, storage, data stores, inter process messaging, orchestration, analytics, and developer tools. With one or more services in each of these categories, complex system designs can be achieved that are cheaper, more scalable, and have significantly less management overhead than traditional services to achieve the same business outcome.

Scaling

Serverless applications are able to scale by design, without the requirement of having to understanding individual server capacity units. Instead, consumption units are the important factor for these services, typically throughput or memory, which can be automatically updated to have more or less capability as the application requires. In addition, for functions (such as AWS Lambda), since they are short lived (less than five minutes), they do not auto scale like an application deployed to a cloud server instance when the CPU is heavily used. Functions are designed to execute as an event so every time that event happens they trigger the function, which executes exactly once and dies off. Hence, the scaling capabilities of functions happen by the nature of the events triggering them, not by adding additional instances via an auto scaling group. Functions are designed to be triggered often by the event source, such as every time a message is put in a queue or a stream, which could be thousands of times a second.

For example, take a typical web server cluster running Apache for serving a web application's front page. Every time a user makes a request to the site, a worker thread is created to serve the page to the user and wait for additional interactions. As the users increase, more threads are created and eventually the instance is working at full capacity and additional instances are required, which are instantiated via an auto scaling group, providing more threads to serve users. This design works fine; however, it doesn't maximize the resources required, instead creating a full instance for use when required, charging the company by the minute as it's running. This same design using an API proxy and function will still be able to dynamically serve the user, but the thread or function will only execute when called and then go away, charging the company per execution at a 100 millisecond amount.

Serverless usage patterns

The ways to utilize serverless technology is limited to only the imagination of the design team involved in the system creation. Every day new techniques are developed that further expand the designs of what can be achieved with serverless, and due to the fast pace of innovation by the cloud providers, the new features and services in this area are increasing all the time. However, with multiple years of maturity at this point, a few core serverless design patterns have emerged, namely web and backend app processing, data and batch processing, and system automation.

Web and backend application processing

The easiest way to describe this design pattern is to compare it with a traditional three-tier application architecture. For many years, the dominant approach to a scalable web app was to set up a load balancer, web servers, app servers, and databases. There are many types of third-party tools and techniques to support this design and, if done properly, a fault tolerant architecture can be achieved that will scale up and down to support the spike in traffic that the application will experience. The challenge with this approach is that it does not fully take advantage of the cloud native services and still relies on capacity planning, people to manage the environment, and lots of configuration to ensure proper cluster setup and failover. This exact same three-tier application can be designed using fully serverless technologies that will enable the administration, execution, fault tolerance, and other administration to be handled by the service, at a fraction of the cost.

We have a fully serverless implementation of a three-tier application. The static frontend page is hosted in an object storage, Amazon S3, where it is served to users who call it from their browsers. Since this service allows for pages to be served, it will handle all of the requirements of load distribution and processing power automatically and not require a web server to be set up to host the web application. Once the user interacts with the page in a way that requires dynamic processing, an API call is made to Amazon API Gateway, which acts as a scalable entry point to execute the code to dynamically execute the user's request via an AWS Lambda function, which is called on an event per API call. The Lambda function has virtually unlimited abilities perform other actions. In this use case, the function will update an Amazon DynamoDB table for data persistence. Other backend functionalities can be performed by forked functions, such as putting messages in queues, updating a topic for further messaging, or executing an entirely new subsystem backend that performed whatever requirement the system has.

Data and batch processing

One of the biggest advantages of using the cloud is the ability to process large amounts of data quickly and efficiently. The two most common high-level approaches are real-time and batch data processing. Similar to the previous example, each of these patterns has been around for a while and there are ways to achieve them using more traditional tools and approaches. However, adding serverless will increase velocity and reduce pricing.

We have the real-time processing and analysis of a social media data stream, and it could just as easily be a click stream analysis of all web properties to support ad analytics. The stream or click stream comes in via a streaming data service, Amazon Kinesis, which executes a Lambda function on each micro batch of data that is processed and analyzed, based on the requirement. The Lambda function then stores the important information in a DynamoDB table, which could be sentiment analysis (if the social media stream is used) or popular ad clicks (if the click stream is used). Once the metadata is stored in the table, additional reporting, analysis, or dashboards can be designed and implemented as another subsystem using additional serverless services.

To show how data processing can be achieved for batch data processing, consider the case where batch files are placed in an object storage, Amazon S3. These files could be anything, images, CSV files, or other blobs that need to be processed or modified in some way before the data processing is completed. Once the file is placed in the object store, an AWS Lambda function executes and modifies the file for the purposes required. This batch process could be to execute other subsystems that use the data, modify the image to change its size, or to update various data stores with parts of the data required. In this example, a DynamoDB table is updated, a message is put in a queue, and a notification is sent to the user.

System automation

Another popular serverless design pattern is to perform common environment maintenance and operations. Following the CNMM requirement to have full automation, functions are a great way to execute the tasks of the system demands. As cloud landscapes grow, automation will ensure that the critical tasks to support that growth stay consistent and do not require the organization to linearly scale up the operations team supporting the environment. The possibilities for how to implement services that perform these administration tasks is limitless, bound only by the requirements and creative thinking of the operations team.

Some common administration use cases are to set up functions that execute on a schedule and check every instance across all accounts for proper tagging, correctly sized instance resources, stopping unused instances, and cleaning up unattached storage devices. In addition to routine administration tasks, serverless application designs can also be used for security administration. Examples include using functions to execute and verify the encryption of objects put in storage or disks, verifying account user policies are correctly applied, and performing checks against custom compliance policies on instances or other system components.

Serverless anti patterns and concerns

Serverless is a growing and critical way to achieve success with cloud native architectures. Innovation is happening all the time in this space, and will continue for many years. However, there are some patterns that do not directly apply to serverless architectures. For example, long-running requests are often not valid given the short-lived time for a function (less than 5 minutes). In cases where a request will take longer than the duration of the function service being used, containers are a possible alternative, since they do not have a time to live duration like functions.

Another example of an area of concern for serverless is when an event source executes in a manner that is not consistent with expectations, hence triggering the function more than expected. In a traditional server instance application, this scenario would saturate the CPU quickly and bog down the instance until it crashed, stopping the scenario. In a serverless environment, since each function is a discrete unit, they will never stop executing, even if that is not the desired intention. At best this will cause an increase in the cost of that function, at worst this could cause data corruption or loss depending on the nature of the function. To prevent this, testing should be done to ensure that triggers are appropriate for that function. In addition, as a failsafe, setting up alerts on total invocations for that function is a good idea, which will notify operations if the function is firing out of control and allow for human intervention to stop the processing.

Finally, knowing the cloud vendor's services and which ones work in conjunction with each other is important. For example, some AWS services are trigger sources for Lambda and others are not. The Amazon Simple Notification Service can trigger a Lambda function every time a message is put on the topic; however, the Amazon Simple Queue Service cannot. Therefore, knowing how the services fit together and when to invoke a function and when a custom solution (for example, listeners on an instance instead of a function) is required will ensure that the subsystems fit together using the best methods.

Development frameworks and approaches

There are many frameworks and approaches taken to design horizontal scalable applications in the cloud. Due to the nature of each of the cloud providers, each has their own specific services and frameworks that work best. In Chapter 9, *Amazon Web Services*, a comprehensive outline of doing this with AWS can be found. In Chapter 10, *Microsoft Azure*, Microsoft Azure's approach is detailed. Chapter 11, *Google Cloud Platform*, breaks down the patterns and frameworks that work best for that cloud. Each of these are similar, yet different, and will be implemented differently by each customer design teams.

Summary

In this chapter, we dived deep into the development of cloud native architectures, using microservices and serverless computing as a design principle. We were able to learn the difference between SOAs and microservices, what serverless computing is and how it fits into a cloud native architecture. We learned that each of the mature cloud vendors has a unique set of frameworks and approaches that can be used to design scalable architectures on those platforms. The next chapter will help you learn the technique of effectively choosing a technology stack.

4
How to Choose Technology Stacks

The world of cloud computing is vast, and while there are a few dominant players in the cloud vendor space, there are other parts of the ecosystem that are critical to success. How to decide which cloud vendor to use? What types of partners should be considered and what do they bring to the table? How will procurement change or stay the same in the cloud? How much do you want to rely on the cloud vendor to manage services? These are all important and valid questions that will be answered in this chapter.

Cloud technology ecosystems

Consideration of the cloud ecosystem and how to leverage it is a critical step in the cloud native journey. There are three main areas to focus on when thinking about partners on this journey: cloud providers, ISV partners, and system integrators. Together, along with the company people going on the journey, they will make up the foundation of the people, processes, and technology used to transform the business with cloud computing.

Public cloud providers

This book is focused on public cloud providers, which, in the fullness of time, will most likely be the dominant way companies consume IT resources. The cloud, as it is today, began in 2006 when **Amazon Web Services** (**AWS**) launched its first public services (Amazon Simple Queueing Service and Amazon Simple Storage Service). From there, they raced to add features at a very fast pace of innovation, with virtual server instances, virtual networking, block storage, and other foundational infrastructure services. In 2010, Microsoft released Azure, similar to AWS, with features designed to mimic what AWS had started and compete for customers in this space. Also during this time, Google began releasing more platform services, which ultimately became Google Cloud Platform, where it stands today.

While there are other clouds out there, with different niche focus areas and approaches to addressing customer requirements, these three comprise the dominant global market share for cloud services. Making the decision on a cloud vendor can appear complex when originally researching the vendors, mainly because less dominant players in the space try to position themselves as better situated than they are by showing cloud revenues or market share on services that are really not cloud at all. Since there is no one definition of a cloud and how to report revenues for it, and each company can say whatever they want about their services, it's important to understand the richness and scale that a cloud vendor has before making decisions. Each of the three major cloud vendors have very compelling foundational services (often referred to as Infrastructure as a Service) and have moved into higher-value managed cloud offerings (sometimes referred to as Platform as a Service), which offer everything from databases, to application services and Devops tools, to artificial intelligence and machine learning services.

There are many criteria that customers consider when choosing a cloud vendor, some of which have to do with the technology they have used in the past and are comfortable with. Some additional areas to consider are as follows:

- Scale: The cloud vendor business is one of scale and ability to deliver anywhere at any time. Even if a customer doesn't currently need cloud resources on a global scale, or to do a massive scale out in a single geography, using a cloud vendor that can do this is critical to ensure they have the experience, funding, and desire to continue to grow and innovate.
- Security/compliance: The priority of all cloud vendors should be security. If a cloud vendor doesn't focus on this and already has the majority of compliance certifications, it is best to stay clear and choose a vendor that makes this a priority.

- Feature richness: The pace of innovation is ever increasing and cloud vendors are moving into areas that were not even considered a few years ago. Whether it be machine learning, blockchain, serverless, or some other new technology, the cloud vendors that are constantly innovating are the ones to focus on.
- Price: While never the sole a reason to choose a vendor, price should always be considered. Contrary to popular belief, the cloud vendor market is not a race to the bottom in terms of pricing. Scale and innovation allow vendors to lower prices by passing along savings to customers (another reason why scale matters). The three major cloud vendors are all cost competitive at this point, but it's important to continuously monitor the price of services.

Gartner has for many years done deep analysis on the cloud vendor market. The most recent version of the Gartner magic quadrant for cloud infrastructure services can be found here: `https://www.gartner.com/doc/3875999/magic-quadrant-cloud-infrastructure-service`.

Independent software vendor (ISV) and technology partners

Cloud vendors are the base of any cloud native strategy, while ISV and technology partners will form a core component in this journey. In a lot of cases, the cloud vendors have tools that are native to their platforms and will fill the exact needs of customers. However, there are many reasons why they cannot meet all the requirements, and that is where ISV and technology partners come in. Even in cases where the cloud vendor has a specific service to solve a problem, customers often prefer to use third-party tools for various reasons. For one, third-party tools are often more mature or feature-rich, since they have often been around a long time and have adopted the cloud for their products. In other cases, a company may have extensive relationships or skill sets using specific ISV products, making it an easy decision to make them a part of their cloud journey. And finally, there are many cases where the cloud vendor doesn't have a comparable service, so using these third-party vendors will allow companies to solve problems without having to develop the capability from scratch.

At this point in the maturity curve of cloud computing, the vast majority of traditional ISVs have made the decision to adopt a cloud strategy. Similar to other companies, these ISVs spent a lot of time and effort evaluating cloud service vendors and standardized on one (or multiple, depending on the type of product). Common usage models for ISV products include customer managed product deployment or Software as a Service. Typically, the ISV or technology partner will have decided on their chosen pricing model, which directly relates to the consumption model offered to the customer.

Customer managed products

In the case of customer managed products, the ISV has chosen to either create or migrate their existing product to a cloud-based model. Often, this means the vendor has taken significant steps to adopt cloud native architectures themselves and then sell their product to the end customer. In its simplest form, the product has been tested with one or more cloud vendors to ensure it works as intended, ensuring that the customer can install and configure it in a similar manner as doing so on-premises. Examples of this approach would be SAP or various Oracle products. In more complex scenarios, the ISV re-architects the product to take advantage of the cloud vendor's native services and microservices to achieve a level of scale, security, or availability that would be difficult to achieve if using the same product on-premises. Regardless of the approach the ISV has taken, choosing the right product requires careful evaluation of the features and pricing models, and comparisons with similar cloud vendor services if applicable, to ensure the product has the scalability and security needed for a cloud native architecture.

Software as a Service

ISVs and technology partners have often chosen to completely redesign their offerings to be service usage-based, making consumption easier for the customer. To achieve this, the vendors will almost always choose a specific cloud vendor and develop their offering on top of the cloud vendor, making their software available to customers but not giving access to the underlying cloud vendor infrastructure or services. In the case of some very large vendors, they actually prefer to run their own private cloud or on-premises environments that integrate with the customer's chosen cloud services, given their core competency in hyper-scale cloud management.

Software as a Service (SaaS), which is very much cloud computing, is not a core component of the large cloud vendors and should not be considered when evaluating a cloud vendor for the majority of workloads being designed. Some large cloud vendors also have SaaS applications that run on their cloud, similar to what ISVs would do, and could be considered for integration purposes, for example, Microsoft and Office 365 or LinkedIn. That said, SaaS vendors absolutely have a critical role in the cloud native journey for many customers, since they offer their services directly to customers regardless of the customer-chosen cloud. The integration of SaaS offerings with customer workloads and data stores is one of the most common ways these services are used in conjunction with custom-designed cloud native workloads. Examples of large SaaS offerings are Salesforce and WorkDay, which offer very sophisticated business logic that integrates well with company systems.

There are also many cases where the ISV or technology partner has offerings where the customer can procure a self-managed version and deploy it in their chosen cloud, or leverage a SaaS version of the same offering. There are many reasons why a vendor might decide to make their offerings available this way. Often, a customer might want to keep the data and control of the product in their environment, or they already have existing licenses they use. Other times, the customer wants to move fast and since they don't already have the software in use, they go directly to the SaaS version so all they need to do is integrate it with their existing systems. Ultimately, ISV and technology partners want to do what their customers ask for, and this should be an important area to consider when choosing a vendor.

Consulting partners

Consulting partners, or **system integrators** (**SIs**), have been around since almost the beginning of IT itself. The concept is that companies don't have the time, resources, or desire to skill up on new technology or scale out their workforce to handle the demands of their business requirements. Therefore, these SI partners are used to fill gaps and help the company move faster with people who can quickly make an impact and deliver projects and business results. These types of partners come in many shapes and sizes, and the relationship they have with the company can be very transactional, or strategic and long term, depending on how the individual company decides to handle their business. Typically, SI partners can be viewed as either niche players, regionally focused, or global/large scale, each having a key place in a company's journey.

Niche SI partners

Niche partners are those companies that offer very specific services on a type of technology, cloud, or area of focus. Often, these partners will be relatively small in size, but have some of the most experienced experts in their respective areas. They are used as subject matter experts on large projects or to own the delivery of a specific project in their area of expertise. At the stage of cloud computing today, there are niche SI partners that have a core competency in specific cloud vendors, and even specific services at one or all of the cloud vendors. The scale of this partner is not the driving force behind being selected for a customer requirement; their technical depth in the chosen area is the area to focus on. When evaluating niche SI partners, customers should consider the certifications of individual resources on the respective technologies, delivery time frames, and customer references where similar work has been done. Niche SI partners are often used to consult on cloud native design and architecture, big data architecture and data structure requirements, or security and compliance for specific industries or requirements.

An anti-pattern for using a niche SI partner is their ability to scale their people beyond their core competency.

Regional SI partners

Regional SI partners are popular with companies that operate in a specific geography or region, since the partner will usually have all the resources located in that area. Often considered strategic partners with senior executive relationships, these partners will help the customer define their strategy and execute specific projects with customer resources. They will usually have a mix of deep technical experts and enough scale to be able to execute large and complex projects for the customer, which would include project management, technical architecture, development, and testing. As with all partners, regional SI partners are often focused on specific verticals, technologies/clouds, or other areas that enable them to differentiate themselves. They are also very responsive to customer needs and can make the difference between success and failure with a cloud native journey. An example of a regional SI partner helping customers on their cloud native journey is Slalom.

An anti-pattern for using a regional SI partner is their ability to support global initiatives that require potentially thousands of people or having a super-long-term strategic view of the company.

Global SI partners

Global SI partners are popular for their scale and ability to support the largest, longest, and most complex projects customers have. As the name implies, they are global in nature, operating in most countries in the world, with a significant presence in all geographies. From the beginning, global SI partners have played a role in helping outsource IT operations, design, strategy, and delivery for big and small companies alike, allowing them to focus on their core business. Global SI partners often have board room-level relationships and will have been involved in the long-term strategic focus of the company for decades, providing resources and technology that align to the customer's requirements. They will execute complex global deployments across multiple cloud providers, geographies, or technologies. An example of a global SI partner helping customers on their cloud native journey is Accenture.

An anti-pattern for using a global SI partner is that quality can sometimes be sacrificed for scale, allowing for a global reach with more junior resources. In addition, given their global nature, the delivery of critical projects is often done in a region where the customer doesn't have operations, making coordination complicated.

Procurement in the cloud

One of the reasons that the cloud is so popular, and that cloud native architectures are becoming the normal method of designing workloads, is due to the procurement and consumption model used. The easy way to think about this is the ability to procure using **operational expenditure (OpEx)** instead of the traditional **capital expenditure (CapEx)**, which can have a large impact on the way a company handles revenues, taxes, and long-term depreciation of assets. However, that is just the surface of the impact that the cloud has on the way organizations procure their IT resources.

The shift to pay per use consumption by cloud vendors has enabled ISVs to also align their business model, making their products easier to consume alongside the chosen cloud vendor services. This change can have a significant impact on the way that organizations negotiate contracts with ISVs, often lowering their overall bill by only paying for what they used instead of long-term contracts based on the number of CPUs the software sits on. In addition to third-party ISVs modifying their procurement model, cloud vendors often offer a cloud marketplace, allowing ISVs to have a digital catalog to list their wares, making it easier for customers to find, test, buy, and deploy software.

All of these changes are designed to allow customers to fundamentally change their purchasing behaviors to be user-friendly, with faster alignment to business requirements and easier identification of offerings that can solve their business problems.

Cloud marketplaces

Using a cloud vendor marketplace as a location to find and procure software required for their business to operate in the cloud is one way companies are able to have the tools needed at any moment. Fundamentally, customers are looking to either develop new workloads or move existing workloads to the cloud, modernize the workload if it was migrated, and then manage their landscape at scale with a streamlined workforce. The bigger the company, the more complex their business requirements can become due to the range of different stakeholders, business units, and customer segments. Procurement of ISV products can take teams of people and months of time to get the right legal terms and conditions, sizing requirements, billing model, and so on. Cloud vendor marketplaces are one way to help companies minimize these blockers to using the software they need, when they need it.

Depending on the maturity of these marketplaces, there could be thousands of different software packages, across just about every category, available for the company to choose from. With the push of a button, or an API call, purchasing and deployment of the ISV product into the customer cloud landing zone, this software can be deployed in minutes, tested, and integrated to the environment when required. Procurement of software using a cloud marketplace has the additional benefit of ensuring that the software is configured and hardened to the specifications of the vendor. There is usually little or no additional configuration required to get the software working. The cloud services being used are still paid for separately (for example, the cost of the instances, storage, network usage, and so on) and in most cases the software is just an additional pay per use line item on the cloud vendor bill.

Marketplace and service catalogs

Cloud vendors often have a service catalog feature that allows for pre-created application stacks or complex solutions to be stored and deployed when required by users with the right permissions. This approach, when combined with the marketplace, offers a powerful way to allow the service design teams to choose the right software, stage it in the catalog location, and either deploy it or have the operations team deploy it following company guidelines. The following diagram shows where the marketplace and a service catalog offering might fit into an organization's procurement strategy:

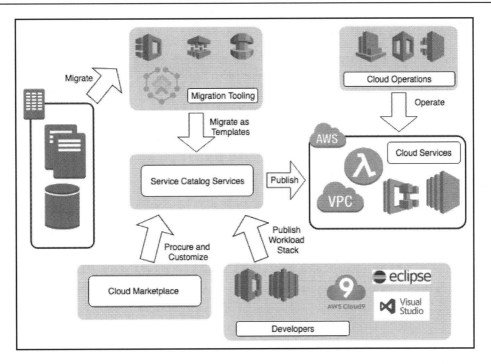

Marketplace and service catalog offering

In this example, the service catalog is acting as an intermediary location for the company to publish customer development patterns, procure cloud marketplace software, or migrate on-premises workloads before being pushed to the target cloud landing zone.

Cloud marketplace anti-patterns

The cloud marketplace can be a powerful tool to allow companies to acquire software with little or no long-term negotiating. It also allows companies to test new software to determine whether it will solve a business problem with ease and little in the way of upfront costs. However, there are cases where using the marketplace is not a fit. For example, if a company already has a long-term strategic relationship with an ISV vendor, with custom patches, or other specific product offerings, then deploying the software themselves is usually preferred. Alternatively, if a company feels they have an especially complicated use case (large scale, additional security, and so on) and the core competency to manage the deployment themselves, it would usually chose to forgo the marketplace and design and deploy the software solution themselves.

Licensing considerations

The previous section identified some areas of consideration with regards to procurement and discussed the common pay-as-you-go model of consumption. Typically, the cost of cloud vendor services would not be considered licenses, but consumption; however, there are often additional license costs associated with it, depending on what software is being used. Traditionally, licenses for software followed a model of paying based how many CPUs or cores the software would be installed on, giving a way for the vendor to understand how much of the software was being used. That worked fine while customers were making large upfront CapEx investments in hardware and knew exactly which servers would run which software. The cloud breaks that model due to its elastic nature. So, how then should customers pay for the licenses of the software being used? ISVs still want to get paid for the amount of use, so they need to identify other ways, typically their key metric of usage. Some common cloud-based approaches are:

- Network throughput, storage amount, or other physical component. They meter and bill by how much network traffic is used, how many Gigabytes (GB) of storage are used, or other hardware metrics that are not CPU-based.
- Per host. Server instances are still very popular in the cloud, and will be for a long time. Depending on the software, charging a per host fee will be enough to get an accurate accounting of how much of the software is used. This would usually be charged on a unit of time basis (for example, hours) to account for elasticity and would not be tied to the CPUs.
- Percentage of cloud vendor spend. For software that is used across the entire cloud landscape, such as monitoring or endpoint security, vendors might charge a small percentage of the overall customer cloud spend. This would allow for elastic growth and shrinkage to be accounted for in the payment to the ISV.
- By transaction. Some ISVs have very high transactional rates, but very low sizes of transaction. By metering the amount of transactions and charging a small amount per transaction, the ISV can account for elasticity and still give a pay-per-use model to the customer.

Cloud vendor pricing models

It's important for customers to fully understand the pricing metric for each piece of technology being purchased. This is true especially with cloud vendors, who can have complex pricing models for services that are very new and otherwise hard to price. Since a lot of the technology services offered by cloud vendors are new or offered in a way that is new, the pricing mechanisms can be very different and require a thorough understanding of how much of the service will be used, so there are no surprises in the cost of usage. For base infrastructure services, such as virtual instances or blob storage, the metric for pricing is usually per hour or per month, with the rate going up as the size goes up. However, for managed cloud services, the price can be more complicated. The following are some examples from popular AWS services used in cloud native microservice architectures: AWS Lambda and Amazon DynamoDB.

Given the complexity and options for pricing, it's critical for the design team to understand how these services will be used in the architecture. Even small changes to the size of transactions, runtime of functions, or other aspects can cause a significant increase in the bill if the system scales high enough.

Example - AWS Lambda pricing

This example of AWS Lambda pricing is taken directly from the AWS service pricing page, and additional details can be found on that page.

Lambda counts, as a request, each time it starts executing in response to an event notification or invocations call, including test invocations from the console. You are charged for the total number of requests across all your functions.

Duration is calculated from the time your code begins executing until it returns or otherwise terminates, rounded up to the nearest 100 ms. The price depends on the amount of memory you allocate to your function.

The following table shows the free tier seconds and the approximate price per 100 ms associated for different memory sizes:

Memory (MB)	Free tier seconds per month	Price per 100 ms ($)
128	3,200,000	0.000000208
192	2,133,333	0.000000313
256	1,600,000	0.000000417
320	1,280,000	0.000000521
2,816	145,455	0.000004584
2,880	142,222	0.000004688

2,944	139,130	0.000004793
3,008	136,170	0.000004897

Pricing example 1:

If you allocated 512 MB of memory to your function, executed it 3 million times in one month, and it ran for 1 second each time, your charges would be calculated as follows:

- Monthly compute charges
- The monthly compute price is $0.00001667 per GB and the free tier provides 400,000 GB
- Total compute (seconds) = 3 million * (1s) = 3,000,000 seconds
- Total compute (GB) = 3,000,000 * 512 MB/1024 = 1,500,000 GB
- Total compute - free tier compute = Monthly billable compute GB
- 1,500,000 GB - 400,000 free tier GB = 1,100,000 GB
- Monthly compute charges = 1,100,000 * $0.00001667 = $18.34
- Monthly request charges
- The monthly request price is $0.20 per 1 million requests and the free tier provides 1M requests per month
- Total requests - free tier requests = monthly billable requests
- 3M requests - 1 million free tier requests = 2 million monthly billable requests
- Monthly request charges = 2 million * $0.2/M = $0.40
- Total monthly charges
- Total charges = compute charges + request charges = $18.34 + $0.40 = $18.74 per month

Example - Amazon DynamoDB pricing

This example of Amazon DynamoDB pricing is taken directly from the AWS pricing page, and additional details can be found on that page.

Unlike traditional NoSQL deployments that ask you to think about memory, CPU, and other system resources that could affect your throughput, DynamoDB simply asks you to specify the target utilization rate and minimum to maximum capacity that you want for your table. DynamoDB handles the provisioning of resources to achieve your target utilization of read and write capacity, and then auto-scales your capacity based on usage. Optionally, you can directly specify read and write capacity if you prefer to manually manage table throughput.

The following table summarizes key DynamoDB pricing concepts:

Resource type	Details	Monthly price
Provisioned throughput (write)	One **write capacity unit** (**WCU**) provides up to one write per second, enough for 2.5 million writes per month	As low as $0.47 per WCU
Provisioned throughput (read)	One **read capacity unit** (**RCU**) provides up to two reads per second, enough for 5.2 million reads per month	As low as $0.09 per RCU
Indexed data storage	DynamoDB charges an hourly rate per GB of disk space that your table consumes	As low as $0.25 per GB

Manual provisioning example: Assume that your application running in the US East (N. Virginia) region needs to perform 5 million writes and 5 million eventually consistent reads per day on a DynamoDB table, while storing 8 GB of data. For simplicity, assume that your workload is relatively constant throughout the day and your table items are no larger than 1 KB in size.

- **Write capacity units** (**WCUs**): 5 million writes per day equals 57.9 writes per second. One WCU can handle one write per second, so you need 58 WCUs. At $0.47 per WCU per month, 58 WCUs costs $27.26 per month.
- **Read capacity units** (**RCUs**): 5 million reads per day equals 57.9 reads per second. One RCU can handle two eventually consistent reads per second, so you need 29 RCUs. At $0.09 per RCU per month, 29 RCUs costs $2.61 per month.
- Data storage: Your table occupies 8 GB of storage. At $0.25 per GB per month, your table costs $2.00.

The total cost is $31.86 per month ($27.14 of write provisioned throughput, $2.71 of read provisioned throughput, and $2.00 of indexed data storage).

Open source

Similar to traditional on-premises environments, customers will have a large range of software options to choose from when starting on their cloud native journey. As pointed out already, licensing considerations are critical to understand before making any decision. Open source software can be very effective in the cloud, and often the preferred method for companies to fill important gaps in their technology landscape. Whether it's using some of the fantastic projects found at the Apache Foundation or from other locations, customers should consider these options when making decisions.

For example, a very popular security information and event management (SIEM) solution is the ISV Splunk, which will do large-sale log aggregations and event management. While often considered best of breed for these types of solutions, there are some alternative open source projects that are similar, specifically the **ELK** stack (short for **ElasticSearch, Logstash, Kibaba**). Both achieve similar results, each with different pricing models that can be attractive to different types of customers. Often the open source alternative will come with strong community support but a less polished configuration model, causing the customer to need skills in the technology to set it up and make it run effectively.

It's also important to remember that with open source software, the physical resources (for example, virtual instances, storage, networking, and so on) are still going to have costs associated while in use; only the software will be free.

Cloud services

Cloud providers have a lot of services, and innovation is accelerating; therefore, understanding how to choose the right service to solve business problems can be a tough prospect. The large cloud providers have designed their services to be like building blocks that can be used together to solve problems that may never have been considered for that specific service. This approach allows customer design teams to be creative and think outside the box with experimentation and fail fast projects. The key is to have a good understanding of what services are actually available. Foundational infrastructure services, once the growth drivers of the cloud, have matured to a state where they are often decided on by default. Setting up landing zones with specific networking addresses, subnets, security groups, and routes is done with Infrastructure as Code, using a consistent and approved model. However, there are still some important foundational considerations, specifically regarding operating systems.

Moving up the service stack is where the large public cloud vendors start to differentiate from their peers. The offerings vary by provider and can include anything from managed database platforms to fully trained machine learning facial recognition. Understanding how these services fit into a cloud native strategy, how to price them for at-scale usage, and if there are alternatives that have a more niche feature to meet architecture needs is critical along the journey.

Cloud services – vendor versus self-managed

In the early days of the cloud, the foundational infrastructure services were reason enough to develop new workloads there. However, as those services matured and the cloud vendors quickened their pace of innovation, they began to develop other services that were managed versions of existing software customers had been using. The reason for this is simple: the goal of the large cloud providers is to innovate on behalf of the customer so that the undifferentiated heavy lifting of managing environments is reduced, freeing up time and resources for business requirements. One of the early areas where this approach was used successfully was with databases. The large cloud vendors will have managed versions of popular database platforms for customers to use. But should a customer use the cloud managed version or deploy and manage them on their own? The answer to that question really comes down to whether an organization has the core competency in that technology and believes they can do it cheaper and faster than the cloud vendor can. Even then, companies that decide to manage their own software should be prepared to have a fast rate of iteration so that they keep up with the latest software for that service; otherwise, they will be passed as the cloud vendor innovates on the service.

Self-managed approach

Setting up databases, sometimes with clusters or other high availability approaches, and including the correct disk type and networking requirements, can be challenging. For years, this skill set, often referred to as a database administrator (DBA), was one that required very skilled and experienced professionals to do correctly. The cloud does not change this, and those same DBAs are needed to install, configure, and manage database platforms. In the early days of the cloud, this was the approach taken as companies moved or developed workloads in the cloud, self-managing their software. Using virtual instances, ISV vendor software, and experienced professionals, most workloads can be run just the same in the cloud as they did on-premises.

Using open source packages and having access to the latest technology is one reason that companies can still manage their own software. While cloud vendors innovate fast, they still take some time to get a production-ready version of a hot new technology, so to shorten the time to market with that technology, companies will choose to do this themselves. Other reasons for companies to do this is that they feel they have a strong competency in a specific package or pattern, and prefer to own the setup and management of that software. The more complex or mission critical a software package, the more difficult and expensive the resources will be to manage it.

Managed cloud services

Vendor-managed cloud services are a way for customers to use the technology they need without having to deal with the undifferentiated lifting of managing the operations of the technology. Cloud vendors spend a lot of time and resources to design services that mimic or exceed the way that companies manage similar technology on-premises. For example, cloud vendors have database services that offer the same popular database platforms, but are automatically configured to span data centers, take incremental backups, tune themselves, and even failover or self-heal when there is a fault. This type of service typically uses automation to allow for huge numbers of these to be running at any time for their customers, and they are responsible for all aspects of the operations (operating system, software patching, backups, and so on).

As cloud vendors grow in maturity, more and more services are being offered that are managed by the vendor, and customers should consider these as they become available. Mature cloud native organizations will attempt to leverage as many of these vendor managed or serverless offerings as possible, to allow the focus of their resources to be on developing business value.

Vender lock-in

Throughout the history of IT, there has been a common theme of vendors making their products sticky and hard to migrate away from. While this trend is seemingly done to support customer requirements, if often makes it difficult, if not impossible, to switch to a newer technology, leaving customers locked into the vendor they originally chose. The best example of this behavior is the old guard database vendors that use proprietary code and stored procedures, which for large databases can represent a significant amount of investment and be critical to the application. This type of innovation is great while it's still going strong, allowing for customers to use new features as soon as they are released by that vendor. But what happens if that vendor slows down or pivots from that platform, and the innovation isn't keeping pace with customer needs? All that investment in stored procedures and code written to the database specification will prevent that customer from switching to a faster moving, more innovative platform.

The cloud is different in this regard. The old way, of IT being the cost center, and setting up and managing software packages using company servers and hardware, is over. Cloud native companies have learned that using the old model will only commoditize their offerings and allow for no way to differentiate them in the market. The only way to prevent this is to offload that undifferentiated heavy lifting of IT service management and focus resources on the business requirements. Cloud vendors innovate across a number of areas, constantly, and show no signs of slowing down. They devote significant effort and resources to security and cutting-edge services, which have proven to be impossible for individual companies to keep up with. Cloud native organizations embrace these managed cloud services and while some people might consider that cloud lock-in, mature companies understand this is the new way of doing business.

Even with this new way of thinking, there are some considerations that organizations should take into account to be able to leverage other cloud vendors if the event should arise:

- Have an exit plan. Every decision that is mission-critical requires a plan of how to exit or migrate if the need arises. Know which applications are capable of moving quickly, what data goes with them, and how it's done.
- Design loosely coupled and containerized applications. Following the 12-factor app and other cloud native design principles, designing loosely coupled applications will enable easier movement with less risk of blast radius issues.
- Organize and manage critical data closely. Know exactly what data you have, where it resides, and its classification and encryption requirements. This will ensure that if the decision is made to move to a different cloud, the order of operations for the data is already known.
- Automate everything. Using Infrastructure as Code and other DevOps philosophies will allow for minimal changes to the automation to support another cloud. Automation is key to a cloud native company.

Operating systems

Foundational infrastructure services typically include cloud virtual instances. These instances require an operating system to run, and for the cloud, that often comes down to choosing between a flavor of Linux or a version of Windows. In addition to virtual instances, containers also require a flavor of operating system to run, albeit a slimmed down version, to deploy code and the frameworks that make them execute. Even with mature cloud native architectures, there will most likely be some instances still being used to handle various tasks and edge cases that cannot use serverless or a similar technology. Therefore, operating systems in the cloud are going to be around for a while and are an important choice to make.

Windows versus Linux

The old question of Windows versus Linux is one that most customers have to agree on at some point. However, for any cloud deployment of size, most likely there will be a mixture of both Windows and Linux, with different versions and flavors of each. Therefore, it's important to know which versions are needed and which are offered by the cloud vendor. Typically, the cloud vendor will have many different flavors of each operating system; some will have an associated licensing cost, others will be free to use. The price of the operating system can add up to be a significant portion of the bill, so trying to minimize their use, or using those that are free to use, is recommended for customers who are going fully cloud native.

Do operating systems really matter any longer?

The real question is do operating systems really matter any longer? The answer is yes and no. Yes, because containers are still a common technology for developing microservices and therefore an operating system is required. No, because as the architecture matures, more and more managed cloud services will be leveraged with serverless as a core component of cloud native architecture. Because managing the operations and licensing of operating systems can add up fast, mature cloud native companies limit their use to only legacy workloads and areas that still require specific libraries to be installed.

Since the cloud is an API-driven environment, the definition of operating systems is changing somewhat. Of course, virtual instances and containers still require operating systems. However, the full-scale cloud environment itself is turning into an operating system of sorts. Microservices, events, containers, and vendor managed services are now intercommunicating via API service calls, object storage, and other decoupled methods. This trend to think of the cloud, and the cloud native workloads that are deployed there, as a large scale operating system is going to continue to grow in popularity.

Summary

In this chapter, we learned the answers to the questions you may ask while deciding on which technology stack to choose. The next chapter talks about scalability and availability in cloud architectures.

Scalable and Available

5

In the previous chapters of this book, we defined what a cloud-native architecture is and the impact these architectures have on people, processes, and technology. The journey to building cloud-native systems is neither straightforward nor short. It can take years to fully realize the potential of going cloud-native as your organization and culture matures. Skill sets and problem solving approaches need to change over time. Mistakes are made, lessons are learned, and systems evolve. We introduced a framework for defining the journey to cloud-native. The journey impacts your business, people, governance, platform security, and operations. Each application and each company can have varying levels of maturity depending on where they are in their journey. In order to better understand this journey, we established a Cloud Native Maturity Model. This is a useful model to understand where your organization, application stack, or system currently is on the journey, and what features it may need to become more cloud-native. Furthermore, we introduced the **software development life cycle (SDLC)** of cloud-native applications and learned how to choose the best technology stack that works for our use case.

In the next four chapters of this book, we seek to define the core pillars of cloud native design. These design pillars are core features that make a system cloud-native. These features on their own are not exclusive to cloud applications or systems. However, when taken together, they are a set of features that no other platform but cloud can bring to the table. We will introduce these pillars one by one in the following chapters. For each pillar, we will state core design tenets to guide your architecture and deployment. We will examine particular use cases on how these tenets can be applied to different layers of an application stack. We will discuss tools, open source projects, cloud-native services, and third-party software solutions that can help support these objectives.

In this chapter, the reader will first gain an understanding of the scale at which modern cloud providers operate. There has been a clear departure from ordinary scale (the scale of data centers with which most seasoned IT practitioners are familiar with) to *hyper-scale*. This hyper-scale cloud infrastructure inherently forms many of the constructs and approaches discussed in this chapter. We will also introduce the core tenets of a scalable and available cloud system, which will help the reader make informed architecture decisions. Finally, we will discuss the current tools available to users to help build self-healing infrastructures which form the basis of resilient, cloud-native architectures.

The following topics will be covered in this chapter:

- Global Cloud infrastructure and common terminology
- Cloud infrastructure concepts (regions and AZs)
- Autoscaling groups and load balancers
- VM sizing strategies
- Always-on architectures
- Designing network redundancy and core services
- Monitoring
- Infrastructure as Code
- Immutable deployments
- Self-healing infrastructure
- Core tenets of scalable and available architectures
- Service oriented architectures
- Cloud Native Toolkit for scalable and available architectures

Introduction to the hyper-scale cloud infrastructure

When deploying systems or stacks to the cloud, it is important to understand the scale at which leading cloud providers operate. The three largest cloud providers have created a footprint of data centers, spanning almost every geography. They have circled the globe with large bandwidth fiber network trunks to provide low latency, high throughput connectivity to systems running across their global data center deployment. The scale at which these three top-tier cloud providers operate are so much larger than the other players that it's necessitated the industry to adopt a new designation, hypercloud. The following diagram depicts the global footprint of AWS, the largest cloud provider by total compute power (estimated by Gartner):

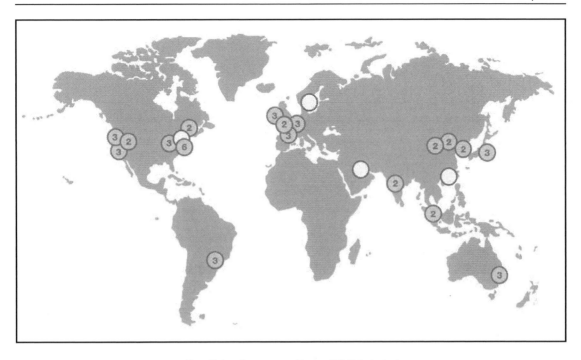

Figure 5.1: https://aws.amazon.com/about-aws/global-infrastructure/

In this image, each orange dot represents an autonomous *region*. The number within each orange dot represents the number of AZs. Green circles represent regions that have been announced but are not yet generally available.

In addition to the fleet of data centers that have been built and are managed, hypercloud providers have deployed high bandwidth trans-oceanic/continental fiber networks to effectively manage traffic between each of their data center clusters. This allows customers of the respective platforms to create distributed applications across multiple geographies with very low latency and cost.

Now let's have a look at the image that captures AWS global data center and network trunk infrastructure (AWS shared their global schematics publicly for the first time at their annual developer conference re:Invent in November 2016, which was presented by AWS VP and the distinguished engineer James Hamilton). The image is as follows:

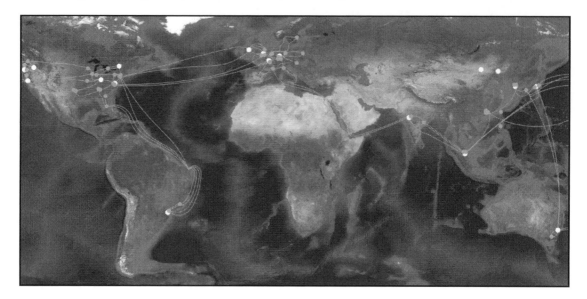

Figure 5.2

Google Cloud Platform (**GCP**) and Microsoft Azure provide similar geographic coverage. All three hypercloud platforms provide core cloud services from an infrastructure abstraction called a **region**. A region is a collection of data centers that operate together under strict latency and performance requirements. This in turn allows consumers of the cloud platform to disperse their workloads across the multiple data centers comprising the region. AWS calls this **availability zones** (**AZs**) and GCP calls it **zones**.

 Cloud Native Architecture Best Practice: Disperse workloads across multiple zones within a region to make the stack highly available and more durable against hardware or application component failure. This often costs nothing extra to implement, but gives stacks a distinct operational advantage by dispersing compute nodes across multiple isolated data centers.

The following diagram shows three different AZs within one region:

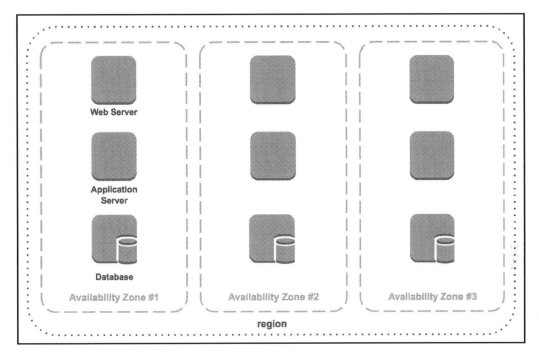

Figure 5.3

As shown in the previous diagram, dispersing compute workloads across multiple AZs within a region reduces the *blast radius* in the event of a service interruption (whether it's an application or machine failure). This usually costs nothing extra from a cost perspective, as the AZs are purposefully built to be highly performant and extensible with each other within a region.

A key concept to understand and minimize when designing cloud-native systems is the *blast radius*. We define the blast radius as *the applications or ancillary systems that can be affected by the failure of a core design component*. This concept can be applied to a data center or a single microservice. The purpose is to understand the dependencies within your own architecture, evaluate your appetite for risk, quantify the cost implications of minimizing your blast radius, and design your stack within these parameters.

Central to minimizing your blast radius in the cloud is effectively utilizing the distributed quality of the regions and zones. There is a series of services that are offered by major providers that help architects do this effectively: load balancers and auto-scaling groups.

Load balancers are not a unique development to cloud, but the major platforms all have native services that provide this functionality. These native services provide much higher levels of availability, as they are running on many machines instead of a virtual load balancer running on a VM operated by the cloud consumer.

Cloud Native Architecture Best Practice: Use the native, cloud-offered load balancers whenever possible. These relinquish operational maintenance from the cloud consumer to the cloud provider. The cloud user no longer has to worry about maintaining the uptime and health of the load balancer, as that will be managed by the CSP. The load balancer runs across a series of containers or fleet of VMs, meaning that hardware or machine failures are dealt with seamlessly in the background without impact to the user.

The concept of load balancers should be familiar to all who work in the IT industry. Flowing from and adding to the concept of LBs are cloud services, which allow users to provide DNS services coupled with load balancing. This combination allows users to build globally available applications that extend seamlessly to geographies of your choosing. Services such as Amazon Route53 on the AWS platform allow users to engineer latency-based routing rules and geo-restriction to connect end consumers to the most performant stack (or to preclude availability of these services based on the end users' location). An example of this would be restricting access to your application to users based in Iran, Russia, or North Korea for the purposes of following the current sanctions laws.

Cloud Native Architecture Best Practice: Use cloud-native **Domain Name System** (**DNS**) services (AWS Route53, Azure DNS, or GCP Cloud DNS). These services integrate natively with load balancing services on each platform. Use routing policies such as **latency-based routing** (**LTR**) to build globally available performant applications that run across multiple regions. Use features such as Geo DNS to route requests from specific geographies (or countries) to specific endpoints.

Another important tool in the cloud-native toolbox is the deployment of **auto scaling groups** (**ASG**) – a novel service abstraction that allows users to replicate and expand application VMs dynamically based on various alarms or flags. In order to deploy an ASG, a standardized image of the application must first be pre-configured and stored. ASGs must almost always be coupled with load balancers in order to be used effectively, since traffic from the application consumer must be intelligently routed to an available and performant compute node in the ASG fleet. This can be done in several different ways, including round robin balancing or deploying a queueing system. A basic auto-scaling configuration across two AZs is shown in the following diagram:

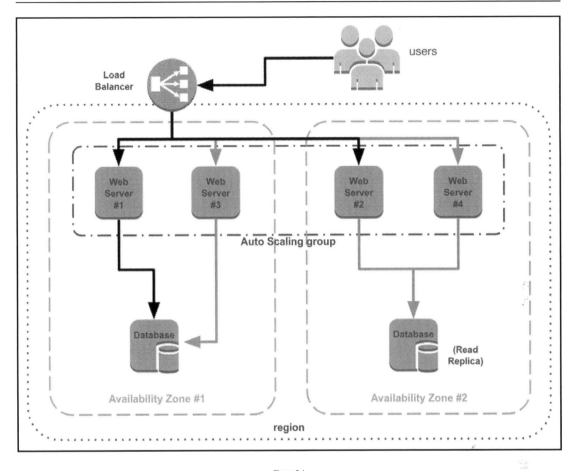

Figure 5.4

The ASG in the previous diagram is set to a minimum of two VMs, one in each availability zone (**Web Servers #1** and **Web Servers #2**). Traffic to these nodes is depicted in black. As more users access the application, the ASG reacts by deploying more servers to the ASG across the multiple AZs (**Web Servers #3** and **Web Servers #4**), with the additional traffic depicted in gray.

Now we have introduced the critical elements in a resilient cloud system: load balancing, auto-scaling, multi-AZ/ region deployments, and global DNS. The auto-scaling feature of this stack can be replicated using elastically expanding/contracting fleets of containers as well.

 Cloud Native Architecture Best Practice: When architecting a stack, it is more cost-effective to use smaller, more numerous VMs behind a load balancer. This gives you greater cost granularity and increases redundancy in the overall system. Creating a stateless architecture is also recommended, as it removes dependencies on a single application VM, making session recovery in the event of a failure far simpler.

Let's have a look at the comparison between auto-scaling groups with different VM sizes:

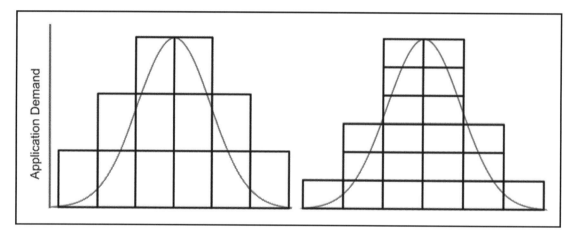

Figure 5.5

There is an advantage to creating auto-scaling groups with smaller VMs. The blue line in the preceding graph represents the demand or traffic for a given application. The blocks each represent one virtual machine. The VMs in the auto-scaling group deployment on the left contain more memory, computing power, and a higher hourly cost; the VMs in the right deployment have less memory, computing power, and hourly cost.

In the preceding graph, we have demonstrated the advantage of using smaller compute nodes in an ASG fleet. Any spaces within a block that appear above the blue line are wasted resources that are paid for. This means that the performance of the system is not ideally tuned to the application's demand, leading to *idle* resources. By minimizing the VM specs, significant cost savings can be achieved. Furthermore, by reducing the size of the VMs, the application stack becomes more distributed in nature. The failure of one VM or container will not jeopardize the entire health of the stack since there are more VMs in the group to fail over to.

Utilizing load balancers services with auto scaling groups; dynamic routing; stateless architectures utilizing highly available and performant DB services, dispersed among multiple zones (or groups of data centers); represents a mature, cloud-native architecture.

Always-on architectures

For many years, architects have always had two primary concerns: the *availability* of a given system and the *recoverability* of the system (often referred to as **disaster recovery**). These two concepts exist to address inherent qualities of a system deployed on a limited, on-premise infrastructure. In this on-premise infrastructure, there are a finite number of physical or virtual resources performing very specific functions or supporting a specific application. These applications are built in such a way that it negates the ability to run in a distributed manner across multiple machines. This paradigm means that the overall system has many single points of failure, whether it be a single network interface, a virtual machine or physical server, a virtual disk or volume, and so on.

Given these inherent fault points, architects developed two principle assessments to gauge the efficacy of a system. The systems' ability to remain running and perform its function is known as availability. If a system does fail, the recoverability of a system is gauged by two measurements:

- **Recovery time objective (RTO)**: The time needed to bring the system into an acceptable functional state after a failure
- **Recovery point objective (RPO)**: The acceptable length of time the system can lose data during an outage

When considering a completely cloud-native architecture, several important factors affect these old paradigms and allow us to evolve them:

- **The cloud provides architects (for all practical purposes) an infinite amount of compute and storage.** The *hyper-scale* nature of the leading cloud providers that we discussed earlier in this chapter demonstrates the size and scope of modern systems.

- **Services provided by cloud platforms are inherently fault tolerant and resilient in nature.** Consumption or integration of these services into a stack provides a level of availability that can rarely be matched when trying to construct a highly available stack utilizing home grown tools. For example, AWS **Simple Storage Service (S3)** is a fault tolerant and highly available object storage service that maintains 99.999999999% durability (meaning the chance of an object becoming permanently lost is miniscule). **Service Level Agreement (SLA)** availability for the S3 standard is 99.99%. Objects you upload to S3 are automatically replicated across two other AZs in the region for redundancy at no additional cost to the user. The user simply creates a logical storage vehicle called a **bucket** and uploads their objects there for later retrieval. The physical and virtual machine maintenance and oversight is handled by AWS. To try and approach the level of availability and durability provided by AWS with your own system would require an immense amount of engineering, time, and investment.

- **Native services and features are available that aid architects and developers in monitoring, flagging, and performing actions to maintain the health of a system.** For example, the Cloudwatch monitoring service from AWS gives metrics on performance and health of virtual machines in a stack. You can combine Cloudwatch metrics with auto-scaling groups or instance recovery, which automate system responses to certain performance levels. Combining these monitoring services with serverless function execution, architects can create an environment where the system can respond to metrics in an automated fashion.

Given these cloud features, we believe the new paradigm for cloud architectures allows us to achieve an **always-on** paradigm. This paradigm helps us plan for outages and architect in such a manner that the system can self-heal and course-correct without any user intervention. This level of automation represents a high level of maturity for a given system, and is the furthest along the Cloud Native Maturity Model.

It is important to note that every human endeavor will eventually fail, stumble, or become interrupted, and the cloud is no exception. Since we lack precognition and are constantly evolving our capabilities in IT, it is *inevitable* that something will break at some given point. Understanding and accepting this fact is at the heart of the always-on paradigm—planning for these failures is the only guaranteed way to mitigate or avoid them.

Always-on – key architectural elements

There are defining features of cloud-native architectures that allow for an always-on, technically resilient architecture. This is not an all or nothing proposition, and many deployments will feature a mix of the features we are going to be talking about. Do not overwhelm yourself or your architects by believing all these features can be incorporated into a deployment overnight. An iterative, evolutionary approach is needed to adopt the key design elements we will be discussing. As Werner Vogels (CTO Amazon) says, "Everything always fails." If we plan for inevitable failure, we can design systems to avoid it.

Network redundancy

Connectivity into the cloud and across all your environments should be provided in a highly available, redundant manner. There are two main implications for this in a cloud-native world. The first implication is the physical connectivity from an on-premise environment or customer into the cloud. All hypercloud providers provide a private express network connection alongside ISP partners (for example, AWS Direct Connect, Azure ExpressRoute, and GCP Cloud Interconnect). It is a best practice to back up the primary, high bandwidth connection with a failover option (another private connection or a VPN tunnel over the internet) by utilizing separate physical links.

Cloud Native Architecture Best Practice: Utilize redundant network connections into your cloud environment by using two physically different and isolated network fibers. This is especially important for enterprises that are relying on their cloud environments for business critical applications. In the case of smaller or less critical deployments, either a combination of private fiber and VPN, or two VPN links may be considered for lightweight environments.

The second implication is the redundancy of physical and virtual endpoints (both in the cloud and on-premise environment). This is largely a moot point for cloud endpoints since each of them are provided in an *as-a-service* gateway configuration. These virtual gateways are running on the cloud providers' hypervisor across multiple physical machines across multiple data centers. What is often overlooked is that the cloud-native mentality must extend down from the cloud to the customer endpoint as well. This is necessary in order to ensure no single point of failure exists to hobble a system's performance or availability to end customers. Thus, a cloud-native approach extends to a consumer's on-premise network connectivity. This means utilizing multiple, redundant appliances with parallel network links, mirroring the way cloud providers build out their physical data centers' connectivity.

Cloud Native Architecture Best Practice: For enterprises and business critical environments, utilize two separate physical devices on the customer side (on-premises) as the termination point of your cloud connection. Architecting for always-on in the cloud is a null point if your connection to the environment is hobbled by a hardware-based, single point of failure on the customer side.

Let's have a look at the following diagram showing connection between cloud provider and corporate data center:

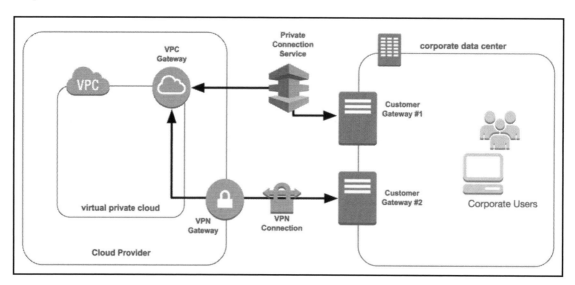

Figure 5.6

When connecting from a corporate data center, office location, or customer site into a cloud environment, use redundant connectivity pathways to maintain cloud environment availability. In the event of an appliance failure, physical fiber outage, or service interruption, a redundant pathway should always be available. This can be a combination of a high cost, high performance primary line and a low cost, low performance secondary line (that is, VPN over the internet).

Redundant core services

Making key services and applications that are consumed by the rest of the IT stack redundant is another important design facet of cloud-native architectures. The enterprise has a lot of legacy services that are only just beginning to adapt to the cloud native model. When migrating to the cloud, it is critical to re-architect or refactor these applications to dependably run in the new environment.

An example of this is the **Active Directory** (**AD**), a critical component for enabling productivity for almost every enterprise. AD maintains and grants access to people, machines, and services by authenticating and authorizing their actions.

There are varying levels of cloud native maturity for standing up AD services. At one end of the spectrum, companies simply extend their network to the cloud and utilize the same AD infrastructure that exists on-premise. This represents the least performant pattern and minimizes the benefits of what the cloud has to offer. In a more advanced pattern, architects extend the forest to the cloud by deploying **domain controllers** (**DC**) or **read-only domain controllers** (**RODCs**) in the cloud network environment. This provides higher levels of redundancy and performance. For a truly cloud-native AD deployment, leading cloud platforms now provide native services that stand up fully managed AD deployments that run at scale and cost fractions of maintaining your own physical or virtual infrastructure. AWS provides several variants (AWS Directory Service, Managed Microsoft AD, and AD Connector), while Microsoft provides Azure AD and Google Cloud has Directory Sync. The following diagram shows three different active identity options, ranging from least (Option #1) to most performant (Option #3), based on where the domain controllers are hosted.

A range of AD deployments are demonstrated in the following diagram:

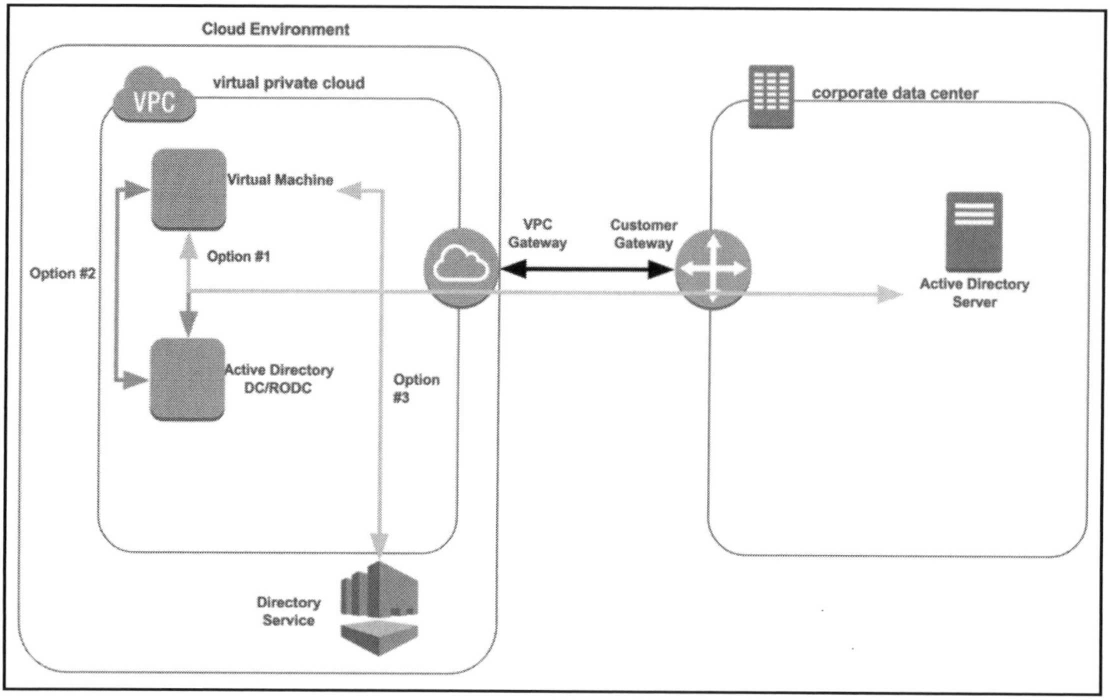

Figure 5.7

The first option is to rely on connectivity to the on-premise AD server for AD authentication and authorization. The second option is to deploy a DC or RODC in the cloud environment. The most cloud-native method is to offload this *undifferentiated heavy lifting* to a native cloud service. The cloud service deploys and manages the AD infrastructure, relinquishing the cloud consumer of these menial tasks. This option results in substantially better performance and availability. It is deployed across multiple AZs automatically, provides scale-out options with a few clicks to increase the number of Domain Controllers, and supports the advanced features needed from an on-premise AD deployment (such as single sign-on, group-based policies, and backups).

In addition to this, the cloud AD services natively integrate with other cloud services, easing the burden during the VM deployment process. VMs can be very easily added to domains, and access to the cloud platform itself can be federated based on identities and users in the AD. It should also be mentioned that these cloud services are generally (if not fully) supportive of **Lightweight Directory Access Protocol (LDAP)**, meaning alternatives to Microsoft AD such as OpenLDAP, Samba, and Apache Directory can be used.

Domain Name System (DNS) follows a similar pattern to AD, with varying levels of cloud nativity based on the deployment model. For the highest level of availability and scalability, utilize leading cloud services such as AWS Route53, Azure DNS, and Google Cloud DNS (which are discussed later on in this book). Hosted zones (public and private) supported by these internal services give the best performance per unit cost. Aside from AD and DNS, other centralized services include AV, IPS, IDS, and logging. These topics will be covered more in-depth in `Chapter 6`, *Security and Reliability*.

Apart from the core services an enterprise may consume, most large-scale application stacks require middleware or queues to help manage the large and complex traffic flows through the stack. As you might suspect, there are two major patterns an architect can use for a deployment. The first is to manage their own queueing system that's deployed on the cloud's virtual machines. The cloud users will have to manage the operational aspect of the queue deployment (examples such as products from Dell Boomi or Mulesoft), including configuring multi-AZ deployments to ensure high availability.

The second option is to use a queue or message bus service offered by the cloud platforms. The undifferentiated heavy lifting is managed by the CSP—all that remains to the architect or user is to configure and consume the service. The leading services one may consider are AWS **Simple Queue Service (SQS)**, AmazonMQ, Amazon **Simple Notification Service (SNS)**, Azure Storage Queues and Service Bus Queues, and GCP Task Queue.

Cloud-based queue services reside on redundant infrastructures, guaranteeing at-least-once delivery, while some support **First In First Out (FIFO)**. The ability of the service to scale allows the message queue to provide highly concurrent access to many producers and consumers. This makes it an ideal candidate to sit at the center of a decoupled Services Oriented Architecture (SOA).

Monitoring

To cloud-native applications, monitoring is the equivalent of the body's nervous system. Without it, signals to expand and contract auto-scaling groups, optimize infrastructure performance, and the end user experience would be impossible. Monitoring needs to be applied at all levels of the stack to maximize feedback, help guide intelligent automation, and inform IT owners on where to focus efforts and dollars. An adage that should serve as a mantra for all architects and engineers is: *If you can't measure it, you can't manage it.*

Monitoring in a cloud-native environment must principally cover four areas:

- **Infrastructure Monitoring**: Collects and reports on the performance of hosts, network, databases, and any other core cloud services that are consumed within your stack (remember, even cloud services can fail or be interrupted, thus they must be monitored for health and performance).
- **Application Monitoring**: Collects and reports on the use of local resources supporting application runtime, as well as application performance that's unique to your cloud-native app (for example, Query return time).
- **Real Time User Monitoring**: Collects and reports all user interactions with your website or client. This will often be the "canary in the coalmine" when the system begins to show faults or experience service degradation.
- **Log Monitoring**: Collects and reports logs that are generated from all hosts, applications, and security devices into a centrally managed and extensible repository.

 Cloud Native Architecture Best Practice: Across all monitoring use cases, it is advised to keep a historical trail of data whenever possible. Interesting and novel usage patterns emerge from these historical datasets that can help inform when to pre-emptively scale or identify problematic or underperforming service components.

Across all four of the previously stated use cases, cloud natively supports the creation, ingestion, and storage of logs. AWS Cloudwatch and CloudTrail, Azure Monitor, Google Cloud Stackdriver Monitoring, and IBM Monitoring and Analytics are all examples of the native services provided on these platforms.

The following diagram depicts the different sources of logs encountered in a hybrid environment (cloud and on-premise):

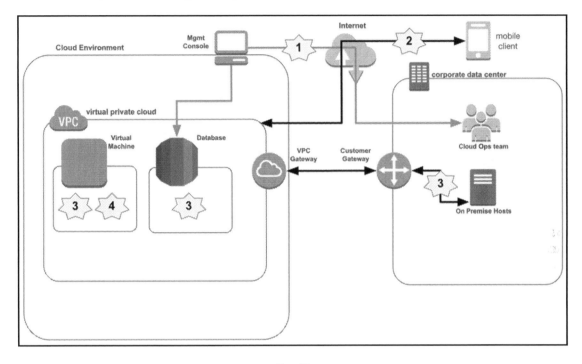

Figure 5.8

The sources can be:

- **Source 1:** Logging of API calls made to change settings and configurations of the environment by IT teams and machines
- **Source 2:** End user logs generated by the mobile and desktop of web clients
- **Source 3:** Infrastructure performance logs generated by resources in the cloud and on-premise
- **Source 4:** Custom logs generated by your application that are specific and deemed pertinent to the overall health of the stack

In most cases, there are several solution variants to choose from, ranging from native cloud services, third-party products deployed and managed on the cloud compute resources, and a combination of both. For the enterprise, popular (albeit sometimes expensive) options include Splunk, Sumo Logic, Loggly, and Dynatrace. These third-party solutions provide extensive capabilities that collect, store, and analyze high volumes of data that's generated across all four use cases. Standard APIs are available to build and feed data sources natively into the products.

Encroaching on this space and constantly providing more features and capabilities, CSPs have launched their own logging and monitoring services which integrate natively with other services on the platform. An example of this is AWS CloudTrail and Cloudwatch. These services help provide a mature, turnkey service that provides logging capabilities natively on the platform. They both integrate easily with other services offered by AWS, thus increasing their value to the user.

AWS CloudTrail helps enable governance, compliance, operational, and risk auditing of the AWS environment by logging each unique account interaction. CloudTrail leverages the fact that underlying every account event (a user or machine initiated configuration change) is done through APIs. These API requests are captured, stored, and monitored through CloudTrail. This provides operations and security teams a full 360° view into **who** changed **what** and **when**. AWS CloudWatch is a complementary service that allows users to collect and track metrics from the platform or from custom generated sources at the application level. CloudWatch also allows users to build custom dashboards, thus making aggregation of relevant metrics for operations teams and reporting much more simple. Finally, CloudWatch allows users to set alarms that can automatically trigger events (such as sending an SMS or email notification) when certain resource conditions are met (such as having a large CPU utilization or under-provisioned DB read capacity).

The following screenshot is an example of a custom dashboard built with AWS CloudWatch:

Figure 5.9: A custom dashboard built with AWS CloudWatch

Each graph in the preceding screen is a customizable widget that can represent myriad metrics collected from other services on the platform. Custom metrics can also be ingested into and monitored by the service.

CSPs other than AWS offer similar services with a constantly expanding set of features and rich capabilities. It is worth noting that this is a noticeable theme within the industry — third-party partners' (3PP) offerings are constantly encroached upon by the CSPs as they expand their services and features. This push and pull is a boon to cloud consumers as the whole industry is propelled forward more quickly in this highly competitive environment:

Cloud Native Architecture Best Practice: Build several dashboards, each giving you insight into one application stack or relevant operational group. This one-to-one relationship will allow you to quickly and easily view all relevant data for one autonomous stack, making troubleshooting and performance tuning much simpler. This can also be used to simplify reporting.

Building upon *Figure 5.8*, we can now flesh out services to specific use cases, which is shown in the following diagram:

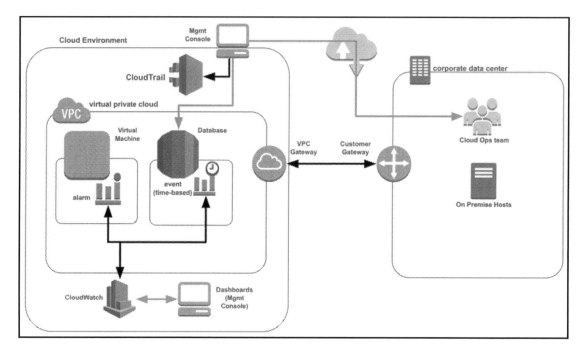

Figure 5.10

AWS CloudTrail serves as an audit trail for every API call made to the cloud environment. This allows owners to maintain complete visibility into who is performing what actions with which resources. Amazon CloudWatch provides native metric gathering and reporting capabilities. These custom dashboards can even collect and report logs from on-premise hosts and systems.

Instantiating services such as CloudWatch and CloudTrail, then creating a customized dashboard based on the usage environment and application you are supporting, are critical first steps to setting up a cloud-native environment and application.

Infrastructure as Code

The very nature of the cloud materially separates the cloud user and the resources they are provisioning and consuming. This eliminates the possibility of being able to physically troubleshoot non-performant or failed devices. This necessitates the digitization of all functionality that was done by walking to resources and interacting with them. This is certainly not the sole reason, but it was a leading design imperative in the nascent days of the cloud. CSPs have built their platforms from the ground up with APIs. Each service and feature can be utilized, configured, consumed, or otherwise interacted with programmatically through a set of defined APIs. The syntax, descriptions, **command-line interfaces** (**CLIs**), and usage examples are published and maintained by each CSP and are available for free for all to scrutinize and utilize.

Once software defined configuration had taken root, it became possible to express the whole IT environment or stack through code. The concept of **Infrastructure as Code** (**IaC**) was born. Many of the same concepts, approaches, and tools that developers used to collaborate, test, and deploy their applications could now be applied to infrastructure (compute resources, databases, networks, and so on). Suffice to say this development has been one of the largest contributions to the rapid advancement of IT systems in general, as it allowed infrastructure architects to iteratively evolve their systems as quickly as developers.

In order to set up a highly available, scalable, and resilient application, it is important for cloud architects to adopt many of the principles at the heart of software development today. We will cover this in more detail in `Chapter 8`, *Cloud Native Operations*, but the evolutionary approach afforded by treating your IaC is the enabling factor to reach a high stack maturity (that exhibits high levels of availability, scalability, and resiliency). Do not assume that your cloud-native application will be mature and resilient from day one. With each day, new efficiencies and failovers must be built into it. This evolutionary approach is core to achieving success (often called the "cloud journey" in industry parlance).

Cloud Native Architecture Best Practice: Manage a series of IaC stacks instead of building one large monolith IaC stack. Common approaches are to separate core network configurations and resources into one stack (this is typically a one time configuration that sees very little change over time and is a common resource used across all applications, thus necessitating its own dedicated stack). Segregate applications into their own stacks or multiple stacks. Shared resources between applications should rarely be included in the stack of a single application — manage it in a separate stack to avoid missteps between two teams.

Building upon *Figure 5.6*, we can now define our entire cloud network infrastructure as a code template (we will call this the network stack), as shown in the following diagram:

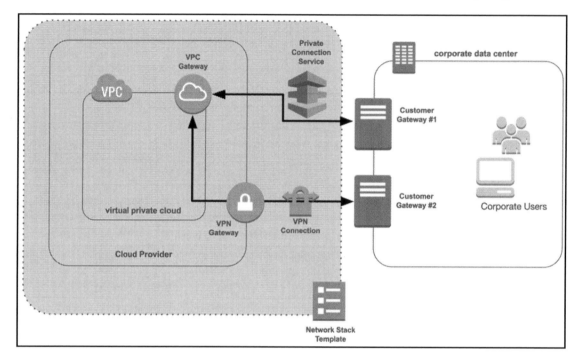

Figure 5.11

Everything within the gray dotted line is defined as code within the network stack template. Any changes that need to be made to the network stack can be managed by making changes to the code contained therein.

Building upon *Figure 5.4*, we can see one approach to managing an application with IaC. The web server configuration, auto-scaling group, and elastic load balancer are defined and managed in the Web Stack Template. The database configuration and resources are managed in the Database Stack Template, as shown in the following diagram:

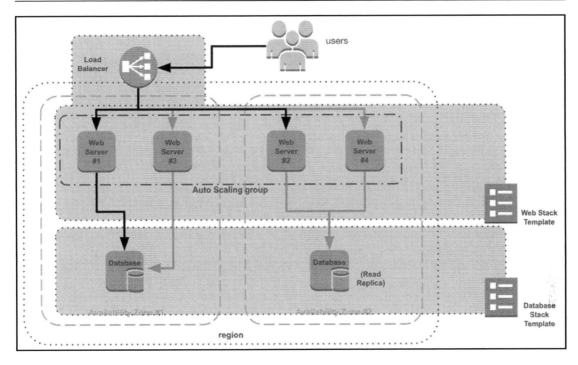

Figure 5.12

There are native cloud services and third-party options to use here. AWS CloudFormation, **Azure Resource Manager** (**ARM**), and GCP Deployment Manager are examples of native CSP services. Code can often be written in **JavaScript Object Notation** (**JSON**) or **Yaml Ain't Markup Language** (**YAML**), previously known as **Yet Another Markup Language**.

A popular third-party tool is Terraform by HashiCorp. Terraform works across all major clouds and on-premise, allowing users to create a unified IaC landscape across a hybrid infrastructure environment. Terraform supports its own format for configurations (otherwise known as templates), creatively named terraform format, but JSON is also supported. While not strictly IaC, there are many tools that perform configuration management, such as Vagrant, Ansible, Chef, and Puppet.

A mature deployment in AWS, for example, would utilize both CloudFormation with a configuration management tool such as Chef to automate and reduce deployment errors.

Immutable deployments

Immutable means something does not change over time or is unable to be changed. An immutable deployment is the approach that once an application stack is deployed and configured, its state is fixed. If there are any necessary modifications, the entire application stack or stack element is redeployed.

Cloud VMs are inherently no more reliable or durable than on-premise machines. Their primary advantage is that they are *standardized* and *easy to replace*. Imagine you are building a complex Lego building set. If you break one yellow 4 x 2 brick, you wouldn't wait to repair that brick, so you can continue building your structure. You would reach into the bucket and find the next identical brick and continue building. Treating cloud resources in a similar fashion is appropriate. More succinctly and ruthlessly put, a common adage is "Treat your resources like cattle, not pets." Be ready to cull the underperforming cattle in order to free your pastures for healthy ones.

If we continue with the Lego analogy, we can gain several advantages by treating the whole completed structure (a castle, for example) as immutable. Any changes that we want to make to the castle (adding a drawbridge, for example) would be built and tested in a second castle that we would build. The first functions normally until we have completed testing and are ready to promote the new castle with its updated drawbridge.

Treating application stacks in this manner, by replacing the entire system at the lowest level possible each time, triggers several benefits:

- Replacing a system at the lowest level encourages you to automate every deployment step.
- Failing back to a previous version is easy and straightforward since the healthy, old stack remains running until the new stack is tested and ready, as opposed to rolling updates, where the live stack is updated with the changes you want to make. If something goes wrong, one has to roll back the updates, hoping that they can reverse all changes made. Each phase of a rolling update and rollback bring the system down. This is unnecessary with immutable deployments.
- By encouraging automation, every change will need to exist as a script. There will be tough lessons for teams who continue to make manual changes, as no server is special and may be de/re-commissioned at any time.
- Scripting everything means you can build production-like systems for development and testing very easily by changing a few lines of code.
- Most importantly, new infrastructures can be tested in isolation, without risking the production stack. For business critical applications, this is paramount to ensure revenue generating systems are unaffected.

Treating your deployments as immutable isn't a configuration change, but a mindset and cultural shift that needs to occur in the organization. It's become an option because of the new capabilities that cloud offers, specifically IaC (whether it be AWS CloudFormation, Azure ARM, or Terraform).

There are other cloud tools available as well that help provide yet more automation and ease the deployment burden. Cloud services such as AWS Elastic Beanstalk manage the operational burden of a deployment, leaving the user to focus on building and owning the code development of the application. The user simply uploads their code to the service and Elastic Beanstalk handles the rest (with a few configuration parameters given by the user). Services such as Elastic Beanstalk have immutability at the heart of the deployments, allowing you to provision a new 2.0 stack alongside your original 1.0 stack. You can perform testing and slowly accept more user traffic in the 2.0 version. When you are sure the 2.0 stack is ready for production, you can complete the cutover. If the new stack is faulting, you can fail back quickly to the original environment. This is done simply by changing the load balancing settings to direct traffic from the old to the new stack (or vice versa).

Furthermore, there are now cloud services that enforce configuration rigidity and help you maintain immutability. Services such as AWS Config and Config Rules help track configuration changes over time, allowing users to monitor changes of resources and view states. These metrics can be consumed through the API to feed your own notification/remediation system, or you can use Config Rules to automatically enforce certain actions based on how the resources have changed.

Immutability is a key design paradigm to adopt in the journey to cloud native maturity. By managing deployment changes at the lowest resource level, you are encouraging automation and increasing the availability of the application.

Self-healing infrastructures

Another important paradigm to adopt for cloud-native applications as it relates to scalability and availability are self-healing infrastructures. A self-healing infrastructure is an inherently smart deployment that is automated to respond to known and common failures. Depending on the failure, the architecture is inherently resilient and takes appropriate measures to remediate the error.

The self-healing aspect can apply at the application, system, and hardware levels. The cloud has completely taken responsibility for "hardware self-healing". No such thing *technically* exists, as we have yet to figure out a way to repair broken hard disks, torched CPUs, or to replace burned-out RAM without human interaction. As cloud consumers, however, the current state of affairs mimics an idealistic future. CSPs deploy people behind the scenes to repair and replace failing hardware resources quickly and furtively. By our strict definition, we have yet to approach self-healing physical infrastructures since human intervention is still needed. However, as cloud consumers, we do not need worry about this, as we are completely divorced from the physical layer.

At the system and application level, we have many methods at our disposal to help build self-healing infrastructures and cloud-native applications. A few examples are given as follows, and we will cover tools to use later in this chapter:

- **Auto-scaling groups** are a perfect example of self healing systems. While we typically associate ASGs with scalability, ASGs can be tuned to discard and reprovision unhealthy VMs with new ones. Sending custom health metrics or heartbeats to your monitoring system is key to utilizing this capability. It's important to architect apps as stateless, since this will allow sessions to be handed across one VM to another within an ASG.
- **DNS Health Checks** available on the cloud platforms allow users to monitor and act upon the health of a specific resource, the status of native monitoring services, and the states of other health checks. You can then intelligently and automatically reroute traffic based on the health of the stack.
- **Instance (VM) Autorecovery** is a feature that CSPs such as AWS provide to automatically recover an unhealthy instance when there is an underlying hardware failure. If there is a loss of network connectivity, loss of system power, software issues on the physical host, or hardware issues on the physical host that impact network reachability, AWS will replicate the instance and notify the user.
- **Database failover or cluster** features are available through managed DB services on the major CSPs. Services such as AWS RDS (Relational Database Service) give users the ability to provision multi-AZ deployments. By using SQL Server Mirroring for SQL; Multi-AZ deployments for Oracle, PostgreSQL, MySQL and MariaDB; and clustering for Amazon's proprietary DB engine called Aurora, these services support highly available DB stack components. In the event of a failure, the DB service automatically fails over to a synchronized standby replica.

Core tenets

Cloud-native applications must be scalable and available. In order to achieve this bar, resilient systems in the cloud must make use of the concepts introduced in this chapter. We've summarized the core tenets that one should abide by to build cloud-native applications as follows:

- Compute is distributed and the application is stateless:
    - Distribute across multiple zones and geographies. Take full advantage of the scale of hyper-cloud providers and build your own systems to be multi-zonal or multi-regional.
    - A stateful application keeps data about each session on the machine and uses that data while the session is active. A stateless application, however, does not keep any session state data on the server/host. Instead, the session data is stored on the client and passed to the server as needed. This allows compute resources to be used interchangeably as needed (for example, when an ASG expands or contracts the number of compute resources in a group).

- Storage is non-local and distributed:
    - Utilize cloud storage services which provide redundancy to your data by design. Services from AWS such as **Simple Storage Service (S3)** and **Elastic Block Store (EBS)** automatically replicate your data across multiple AZs and multiple hard disks.
    - Utilizing distributed caching solutions such as Redis and Memcache helps support stateless application architectures. This offloads common data and objects from the elastic web and app layers into a common data store.
    - Use database solutions that distribute data and tolerate hardware or node failures. Multi-AZ database deployments or fully managed NoSQL DB services like AWS DynamoDB provide inherent redundancy and resiliency.

- Create physically redundant network connections:
    - Even the most advanced applications can fail if network connections are severed and there is no failover plan. Architect redundant network connectivity to the cloud from your existing data center or network exchange. This is a foundational architecture decision that will pay dividends in an extreme failure event. This mentality also applies to network hardware on-premise. Do not terminate a private link and its redundant VPN connection on the same network gear. Have at least two physically separate resources to rely on.

- Monitor extensively and exhaustively:
    - Without intelligent, thorough, and continuous monitoring, you cannot build a scalable and highly available system. By monitoring at all levels of the stack, you can build automation to enable self-healing infrastructures and find common failure modes. Furthermore, as you build a historical record of how the system behaves over time, patterns emerge for you to intelligently scale ahead of anticipated traffic increases and address system performance bottlenecks.

- Use IaC:
    - By expressing stacks as code, you can apply all the benefits of agile software development methodologies to the deployment and management of IT systems. This is a crucial point in order to build cloud-native applications, since without it, several of the concepts introduced in this chapter would not be possible.

- Every deployment is immutable:
    - Enforce a policy of adopting changes to a system at the lowest level possible. If you need to apply an update or patch an application, deploy a new updated VM based on a new image or launch a new container with your updated application. This is as much a cultural shift for the organization as it is a technological one.

- Design and implement the self-healing infrastructure whenever possible:
    - Reduce your operational overhead by deploying resources and building systems that repair themselves. Expect and anticipate failures, even in the cloud. CSPs services and virtual machines are not immune to hardware or network failures, nor should you expect 100% uptime. Take this into account and deploy across multiple geographic zones and distribute.

- Deployment anti-patterns are automatically reported and prevented:
  - By treating IaC and adopting immutable deployments, every change to a stack can be monitored and inspected. Build in configuration checks and rules into the environment to prevent changes. Build code checks into your pipeline to flag non-compliant systems before they are deployed. This will be covered in more detail in `Chapter 8`, *Cloud Native Operations*.
- Create and maintain an Operational Control Pane:
  - Create custom dashboards tailored to your application and system. Use a combination of built-in cloud logging services and custom metrics to aggregate critical data into one view. Furthermore, create rules to flag or notify admins when metrics exceed normal behavior.
- Scalability versus Elasticity—know the difference and architect appropriately:
  - The scalability afforded by cloud gives users almost infinite capacity to grow their application. Scalability requirements for your application will depend on where your users are based, your global ambitions, and which specific resource type is needed. Elasticity is an architectural feature which you must design and build into your system. This means that your system can expand and contract to match a user's demand. This leads to performance and cost optimization.

Service-oriented architectures and microservices

The origin of cloud development for the leading CSPs stems from the pain of managing monolithic systems. As each company (Amazon.com retail site, Google.com's indexing of the web) was experiencing tremendous growth, the traditional IT systems were incapable of keeping up with the rate of expansion and evolving at a necessary pace to enable the innovation that was needed. This story is true and well-documented in the public sphere for both AWS and GCP. As their internal systems matured around these services (provided initially as internal only to product development teams), Amazon took the step to provide these services to external customers on a utility-based billing system.

Many businesses and architects now see the virtue in this decoupling process, calling the fully decoupled environment a **service-oriented architecture (SOA)**. We define SOAs as *digital environments where each constituent system providing the lowest level of application functionality is run independently and interacts with other systems solely through APIs*. In practice, this means each service is deployed and managed independently (ideally as a stack managed by IaC). Services can be dependent upon other services; however, this exchange of data is accomplished through APIs.

SOAs and microservices are at the mature end of the CNMM for scalability and availability. Decoupling your application or IT environment requires years of work and technical discipline.

Cloud-native toolkit

Now that we have a firm understanding of the and strategies around architecting scalable and available systems, in this section, we will introduce tools, products, and open source projects to help implement these strategies. These tools will help you design more mature systems along the Automation and Application Centric Design axes of the CNMM.

Simian Army

The Simian Army is a suite of tools made available by Netflix on GitHub as an open source project. The *army* consists of monkeys (different tools) ranging from Chaos Monkey and Janitor Monkey to Conformity Monkey. Each monkey specializes in a certain objective, such as bringing down a subsystem, removing underutilized resources, or resources that do not conform to predefined rules (such as tagging). Using the Simian Army tool is a great way to test your systems in a *gameday-like* situation, where your engineers and admins are on the alert and are ready to remedy the system if it fails to deal with the outcome of the Simian Army's attack. Netflix has these tools running consistently during the work day, allowing engineers to constantly test the effectiveness of their design. As subsystems are taken down by the army, the self-healing aspects of the applications are subjected to punishing tests.

The Simian Army is on GitHub at `https://github.com/Netflix/SimianArmy`.

Docker

Docker is a software container platform that allows you to package up an application with all its dependencies and requisite libraries into a self-reliant module. It moves the architecture design center of gravity from host/VM to containerized applications. Containers help eliminate the risk of incompatibilities or version conflicts between the application and the underlying OS. Furthermore, they can easily be migrated across any machine running Docker.

As it relates to cloud-native applications, containers are an effective way to package applications for runtime, great for version management, and efficient in operating deployments. Docker is a leading solution in this space, and its **Community Edition** (**CE**) is free to use.

In addition to Docker, there are several noteworthy open source projects that can help maximize the use of Docker and help create cloud-native systems:

- **Infrakit** is a toolkit for infrastructure orchestration. It emphasizes the immutable architecture approach, and breaks down automation and management processes into small components. Infrakit provides infrastructure support for higher-level container orchestration systems and makes your infrastructure self-healing. It has many plugins to other popular tools and projects, such as Swarm, Kubernetes, Terraform, and Vagrant, and supports AWS, Google, and VMWare environments (https://github.com/docker/infrakit).
- **Docker Swarm(kit)** is a cluster management and orchestration tool for Docker Engine 1.12 and later. It allows your Docker container deployment to support service reconciliation, load balancing, service discovery, and built-in certification rotation. **Docker Swarm** standalone is also available, but has seen its active development cease as Swarmkit has surged in popularity (https://github.com/docker/swarmkit).
- **Portainer** is a lightweight management UI for Docker environments. It's simple to use and runs on a single container that can run on any Docker engine. When building an operational control pane, UIs such as Portainer are indispensable in pulling together a master view of the environment and systems. (Go to https://github.com/portainer/portainer and https://portainer.io/ to learn more).

Kubernetes

With the popularity and success of Docker expanding in the mid 2010s, Google recognized the trend of containerization and contributed significantly to its adoption. Google designed Kubernetes from scratch to orchestrate Docker containers, basing it off of their internal system infrastructure orchestration system called Borg. Kubernetes is a powerful, open-source tool that helps mount storage systems, check application health, replicate application instances, autoscale, roll out updates, load balance, monitor resources, and debug applications, among many other capabilities. In 2016, Kubernetes was donated to the Cloud Native Compute Foundation, ensuring it would remain free to use and supported by an active community (`https://kubernetes.io/`).

Terraform

Terraform by Hashicorp is a popular tool for building, changing, and versioning **IaC** (**IaC**). As opposed to native cloud platform services such as AWS CloudFormation or Azure ARM, Terraform works across CSPs and on-premise data centers. This gives a distinct advantage when handling infrastructure resources across a hybrid environment (`https://github.com/hashicorp/terraform`).

OpenFaaS (Function as a Service)

Combining a few of the tools mentioned previously (Docker, Docker Swarm, and Kubernetes), OpenFaaS is an open source project that allows you to easily build serverless functions. The framework helps automate the deployment of an API gateway to support your function and collected metrics. The gateway scales according to demand, and a UI is made available for monitoring purposes (`https://github.com/openfaas/faas`).

Envoy

Originally developed at Lyft, Envoy is an open source edge and service proxy designed for cloud-native applications. Proxy services are key to adopting service oriented architectures—of which mature designs provide the best scalability and availability (`https://www.envoyproxy.io/`).

Linkerd

Another open source project supported by the Cloud Native Compute Foundation, Linkerd is a popular service mesh project. It's designed to make SOA architectures scalable by transparently adding service discovery, load balancing, failure handling, and smart routing to all inter-service communication (`https://linkerd.io/`).

Zipkin

Based on the Google Research paper titled *Dapper, a large-scale distributed systems tracing infrastructure*, Zipkin is an open source project that operationalizes what was conceived in the paper. Zipkin helps architects troubleshoot and optimize latency within their microservice architectures by asynchronously collecting span data, and rationalizing this data through a UI (`https://zipkin.io/`).

Ansible

A popular open source configuration management and orchestration platform, Ansible is part of RedHat's software offering. It relies on agentless communication between nodes and control nodes. It supports playbooks to automate and deploy application infrastructure stacks (`https://www.ansible.com/`).

Apache Mesos

Mesos is, in essence, a cluster manager that provides your applications the ability to scale beyond a single VM or physical machine. Mesos allows you to easily build a distributed system across a pool of shared resources. By providing common functionality that any distributed system needs (for example, failure detection, task distribution, task starting, task monitoring, task killing, and task cleanup), Mesos has become a popular choice the supporting big data Hadoop deployments. Mesos was created at the University of California at Berkeley's AMPLab and became an Apache Foundation top-level project in 2013 (`http://mesos.apache.org/`).

Saltstack

Another open source configuration management and orchestration project, the Saltstack project is an option for managing cloud-native deployments at scale. Consider using salt if your deployment is heavily skewed towards the use of Linux-based OS distributions. Salt was written by Thomas S Hatch and was first released in 2011 (`https://github.com/saltstack/salt`).

Vagrant

An open source project owned by Hashicorp, Vagrant gives users a consistent method of configuring virtual environments. When used in conjunction with automation software, Vagrant ensures scalability and portability across all virtual environments. The first release of Vagrant was written in 2010 by Mitchell Hashimoto and John Bender (`https://www.vagrantup.com/`).

OpenStack projects

OpenStack is an open source project umbrella for building smaller, open source projects, mimicking all the services found in today's leading CSPs. OpenStack projects range from compute, storage, and networking to data and analytics, security, and application services.

Compute:

- Nova – Compute Service: `https://wiki.openstack.org/wiki/Nova`
- Glance – Image Service: `https://wiki.openstack.org/wiki/Glance`
- Ironic – Bare Metal Provisioning Service: `https://wiki.openstack.org/wiki/Ironic`
- Magnum – Container Orchestration Engine Provisioning: `https://wiki.openstack.org/wiki/Magnum`
- Storlets – Computable Object Store: `https://wiki.openstack.org/wiki/Storlets`
- Zun – Containers Service: `https://wiki.openstack.org/wiki/Zun`

Storage, backup, and recovery:

- Swift – Object Store: `https://wiki.openstack.org/wiki/Swift`
- Cinder – Block Storage: `https://wiki.openstack.org/wiki/Cinder`
- Manila – Shared Filesystems: `https://wiki.openstack.org/wiki/Manila`
- Karbor – Application Data Projection as a Service: `https://wiki.openstack.org/wiki/Karbor`
- Freezer Backup, Restore and Disaster Recovery: `https://wiki.openstack.org/wiki/Freezer`

Networking and content delivery:

- Neutron – Networking: `https://docs.openstack.org/neutron/latest/`
- Designate – DNS Service: `https://wiki.openstack.org/wiki/Designate`
- DragonFlow – Neutron Plugin: `https://wiki.openstack.org/wiki/Dragonflow`
- Kuryr – Container Plugin: `https://wiki.openstack.org/wiki/Kuryr`
- Octavia – Load Balancer: `https://wiki.openstack.org/wiki/Octavia`
- Tacker – NFV Orchestration: `https://wiki.openstack.org/wiki/Tacker`
- Tricircle – Networking Automation for Multi-Region Deployments: `https://wiki.openstack.org/wiki/Tricircle`

Data and analytics:

- Trove – Database as a Service: `https://wiki.openstack.org/wiki/Trove`
- Sahara – Big Data Processing Framework Provisioning: `https://wiki.openstack.org/wiki/Sahara`
- Searchlight – Indexing and Search: `https://wiki.openstack.org/wiki/Searchlight`

Security, identity, and compliance:

- Keystone – Identity Service: `https://wiki.openstack.org/wiki/Keystone`
- Barbican – Key Management: `https://wiki.openstack.org/wiki/Barbican`
- Congress – Governance: `https://wiki.openstack.org/wiki/Congress`
- Mistral – Workflow Service: `https://wiki.openstack.org/wiki/Mistral`

Management tools:

- Horizon – Dashboard: `https://wiki.openstack.org/wiki/Horizon`
- Openstack Client – Command-line Client: `https://www.openstack.org/software/releases/ocata/components/openstack-client-(cli)`
- Rally – Benchmark Service: `https://rally.readthedocs.io/en/latest/`
- Senlin – Clustering Service: `https://wiki.openstack.org/wiki/Senlin`
- Vitrage – Root Cause Analysis Service: `https://wiki.openstack.org/wiki/Vitrage`
- Watcher – Optimization Service: `https://wiki.openstack.org/wiki/Watcher`

Deployment tools:

- Chef Openstack – Chef Cookbooks for OpenStack: `https://wiki.openstack.org/wiki/Chef`
- Kolla – Container Deployment: `https://wiki.openstack.org/wiki/Kolla`
- OpenStack Charms – Juju Charms for OpenStack: `https://docs.openstack.org/charm-guide/latest/`
- OpenStack-Ansible – Ansible Playbooks for OpenStack: `https://wiki.openstack.org/wiki/OpenStackAnsible`
- Puppet OpenStack – Puppet Modules for OpenStack: `https://docs.openstack.org/puppet-openstack-guide/latest/`
- Tripleo – Deployment Service: `https://wiki.openstack.org/wiki/TripleO`

Application services:

- Heat – Orchestration: `https://wiki.openstack.org/wiki/Heat`
- Zaqar – Messaging service: `https://wiki.openstack.org/wiki/Zaqar`
- Murano – Application catalog: `https://wiki.openstack.org/wiki/Murano`
- Solum – Software development life cycle automation: `https://wiki.openstack.org/wiki/Solum`

Monitoring and metering:

- Ceilometer – Metering and data collection service: `https://wiki.openstack.org/wiki/Telemetry`
- Cloudkitty – Billing and chargebacks: `https://wiki.openstack.org/wiki/CloudKitty`

- Monasca – Monitoring: `https://wiki.openstack.org/wiki/Monasca`
- AODH – Alarming service: `https://docs.openstack.org/aodh/latest/`
- Panko – Event, metadata indexing service: `https://docs.openstack.org/panko/latest/`

There are many more tools (open source and not) that are available, with many up and coming projects that are under incubation now. This list should not be seen as the be-all and end-all list of definitive tools, but simply a shortlist of some of the most popular tools being used at the time of writing this book. The important takeaway here is that automation and freedom is key. We will dive deeper into tool selection and management for your cloud-native operations in `Chapter 8`, *Cloud Native Operations*.

Summary

In this chapter, we introduced you to hyper-cloud scale and all the implications this aggregation of organized compute means to IT consumers. The global scale, consistency, and reach of these cloud platforms has changed the way we need to think about scalable and available systems.

We introduced the concept of always-on architectures, and the key architectural elements that comprise these systems. Network redundancy, redundant core services, extensive monitoring, IaC, and immutable deployments are all important elements to architect into any cloud-native system.

Building on this always-on approach, we introduced the concept of self-healing infrastructures. For large-scale, cloud-native deployments, automating the recovery and healing of a system is a key feature. This allows systems to recover on their own, but more importantly frees up critically important human resource time to work on improving the system, allowing evolutionary architectures.

We wrapped up this chapter by introducing some of the most popular tools available to architects and IT professionals today. These tools cover all matter of use cases, from configuration managements, automation, monitoring, testing, and microservice mesh management.

In the next chapter, we will talk about the security in the cloud architectures.

6
Secure and Reliable

Security is often the first criterion considered by most decision makers in enterprises when they decide to adopt any new technology. The ability to deploy securely, then protect and react to security threats, is paramount to success. This has been true since the dawn of computer systems and will remain no different for the foreseeable future. Overall IT system security is compounded by the risk of losing business due to exposed, leaked, or mismanaged customer data. There are dozens of examples *just in the past decade* of businesses going under due to security events.

The once-dominant internet search giant Yahoo, while in acquisition discussions with Verizon, announced it had been the victim of an attack. The hack exposed the real names, email addresses, dates of birth, and telephone numbers of 500 million users in 2014. This was surpassed months later by another announcement from Yahoo of a security event that compromised 1 billion accounts and passwords. These events knocked an estimated $350 million off the acquisition price of Yahoo by Verizon.

There are dozens of examples similar to Yahoo, where improper management, inadequate response, and poor architecture decisions have led to equally bad outcomes for companies. In 2014, eBay had 145 million user accounts compromised, Heartland Payment Systems in 2008 had 134 million users' credit cards stolen, Target in 2013 had up to 110 million customers' credit/debit card and contact info stolen—and the list goes on. Each security breach costs these companies millions in fines, broken consumer trust, and an untold amount of lost business revenue.

We know security is an important element of any IT system, so why and how did these companies fail? They certainly did not lack the resources, manpower, or willpower to get it done. The answer to this question leads us to cloud native security methodology.

In the pre-cloud world, IT assets were housed in a centrally managed, on-premises location. In the best of circumstances, physical access to these data centers was controlled and monitored (often lax enforcement would set in). In the worst of cases, the compute resources were dispersed across multiple locations, with poor tracking and monitoring of physical assets. Inconsistent hardware, poor access control, and deficient overhead management would lead to a weak security posture.

The general approach to security is to insulate these resources with a hard outer shell. Maintaining the security boundary was tantamount to having secured the entire IT landscape. It disregards threats that could arise from the inside, or what to do with a threat once it has penetrated this shell. This shell is oftentimes a firewall placed at a critical network junction, where all traffic could be monitored. IDS/IPS (Intrusion Detection Systems and Intrusion Protection Systems respectively) are deployed in similar fashion. Once a threat can bypass the secured network exchange point, the entire stack running behind the firewall becomes an attack surface. There is very little to stop an attacker from exploiting vulnerabilities once inside the protected edge. Furthermore, there is very little protection from threats emerging from within the protect shell:

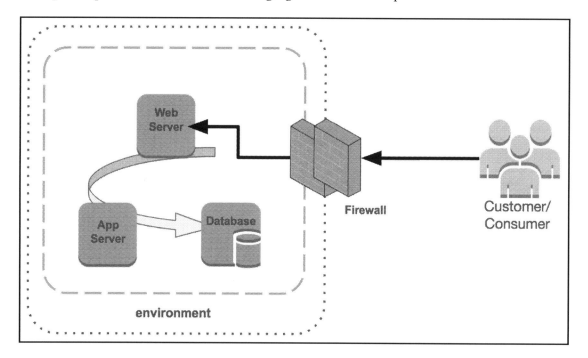

Figure 6.1

This outdated security posture often comes hand-in-hand with an outdated security operations and organization model. Security teams report to different managers and are aligned to separate goals than the development or infrastructure teams. The security team is usually not aligned to the end business goals (capturing more market share, increasing revenue, decreasing infra costs, and so on)—they're perceived and operate as inhibitors to development and innovation.

Oftentimes this perception is not far from reality, but at no fault of the security engineers. The organizational model for how security engineers work with developers and infrastructure architects creates this friction. Instead of being viewed as partners working towards the same goal, adversarial zero-sum relationships become the norm. It's become *du jour* for architects and developers to gripe about the lack of agility injected into the sprint process by security engineers. The *fail fast and innovate* mentality of the developers runs headlong into the *control change and review* mentality of the security organization.

Security in a cloud native world

What if we could reorganize and reorient our teams to make security an **enabler** to development, and not a blocker? Public cloud platforms allow this evolution in a number of ways:

- Providing and extending security products/services into the platform natively
- Exposing the native security features as APIs
- Integrating security features into the core IT services (network, identity and access management, encryption, DLP, and more)
- In addition, there are some innate benefits:
    - A shared responsibility model where security responsibilities are shouldered by the cloud provider and the customer security team
    - At-scale and deep security experience offered by cloud provider
    - Updates and features incorporated into services on a continual basis

Each of the hypercloud providers has world-class teams of security professionals who number in the thousands. Their job each day is to battle against the myriad threats in existence and enable cloud consumers to circumvent these challenges successfully. As time has progressed, cloud providers have steadily moved up the stack in terms of the services they provide. Starting first with **identity and access management** (**IAM**), firewalls and the **web application firewall** (**WAF**), then on to agent-based OS security, such as Amazon Inspector or Azure Security Center, and **data loss prevention** (**DLP**), such as Amazon Macie.

Security at every layer

There is no shortage of options when it comes to what firewall and VPN appliances are available for data centers or cloud environments. The important factor when it comes to choosing them isn't necessarily the security product, but the given deployment and the features available (including access controls, authentication, and authorization ability). Ensuring these are built into the application layer rather than relying solely on network security is critical. An application-level security implementation makes access control scalable, portable, and immutable. Access can then be governed based on the real identity of an application or (micro)service rather than on human provisioning.

By our definition, a cloud native application is a secured application. A secured system by logical extension must be a reliable system. Application code is packaged and deployed across multiple cloud regions; executed in various containers; and is accessed by many clients or other applications (for more details, please refer to `Chapter 5`, *Scalable and Available*). This makes it even more critical to bake security into each microservice. The simple fact that applications are now dispersed across multiple geographic areas (scaling up and down constantly) necessitates a more automated and nuanced security approach.

For the majority of enterprise history, writing security code has been less interesting and less important than business logic. Often security-related tasks are left until the last minute in a development cycle, leading to major trade-offs in a product's security features. If you are trying to build a cloud native solution that can scale to support large volumes, run across different regions, and can self-provision, then it is imperative the chief architect considers security as one of the core building blocks of the architecture.

If security is to be part of the design from the ground up, as opposed to bolted on to the solution at the last minute, then let's examine a few essential features of a secure cloud native stack:

- **Compliant**: Maintain system compliance and audit trails through automation. Generate and build change logs that can be used for compliance reports (for example, GxP, FFIEC, and so on). Deploy rules to prevent unauthorized deployment patterns.
- **Encrypted**: Sensitive data should be encrypted while traveling through the network or when residing on storage targets. Protocols such as IPSec and SSL/TLS are essential to securing data flows through multiple networks.

- **Scalable and available encryption resources**: Do not rely on a single encryption resource to perform encryption functions. These resources, as with all cloud native patterns, must be dispersed and decentralized. This is not only more performant but eliminates any single point of failure.
- **DLP**: Do not allow any PII or sensitive data to be written to logs or other non-authorized targets. Logs are relatively insecure and often contain information in plaintext. Log streams are often the softest targets for intruders.
- **Secure credentials and endpoints**: Keep service credentials and source/target endpoints outside of the memory. Utilize native tokenization services, with minimized privileges, to keep blast radius to a minimum. When creating credentials for human operators, create identity and access management (IAM) rules with segregated and specific policies. Review and monitor usage continuously.
- **Caching**: Cloud native applications scale in and out across multiple instances. Applications should leverage an external cache (for example, Memcache and Redis) to support a stateless design. Apps should never store information in memory longer than needed for the request-execution time. Consequently, in the event of a single machine failure, the request can be easily rolled over to another machine in the application server fleet.

Cloud security services

As discussed in earlier chapters, one of the benefits of building in a cloud environment is the access the cloud native developers receive to dozens of services that easily integrate into the environment. This is especially important when it comes to security, as there are many features *baked in* to the platform that a user can and should leverage. The current list of services and features are outlined next.

Network firewalls

Security groups (SGs) and NACLs act as firewalls for virtual machines in your cloud network plane. SGs act at the machine **network interface (NI)** and are generally more flexible and useful in day-to-day deployments. SGs can be modified on the fly and rules cascade down to all NIs within the group. SGs by default restrict all incoming traffic (except from other machines in the same SG) and allow all outbound traffic. NACLs are similar, but are applied across a whole subnet and by default allow all traffic.

A detailed comparison between SGs and NACLs is made in the following table:

SGs	NACLs
Operates at the instance level (first layer of defense)	Operates at the subnet level (second layer of defense)
Supports allow rules only	Supports allow rules and deny rules
Stateful: Return traffic is automatically allowed regardless of any rules	Stateless: Return traffic must be explicitly allowed by rules
We evaluate all rules before deciding whether to allow traffic	We process rules in number order when deciding whether to allow traffic
Applies to instance only if someone specifies the security group when launching the instances, or associates the SG with the instance later	Automatically applies to all instances in the subnets it's associated with (backup layer of defense, so you don't have to rely on someone specifying the correct SG)

As shown in the following diagram, security groups should be applied to groups of instances utilizing similar ports for their transport layer communication (layer 4), whereas NACLs should be used when precluding connectivity between two large subnet masks:

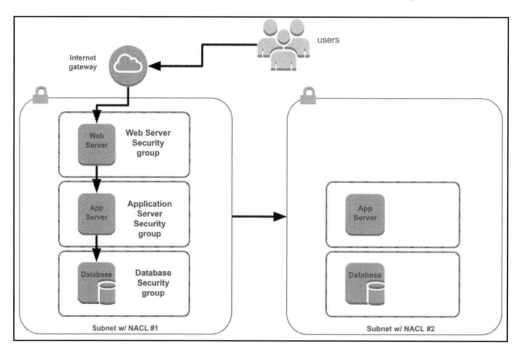

Figure 6.2

In this example, we want the users (over the internet) to connect to Subnet #1, but not to Subnet #2. NACLs would be best to enforce that rule at the subnet level, whereas specific application ports would be set at the security group layer.

When determining how to utilize SGs and NACLs in your deployment, consider these factors while in the design phase:

- What does my subnet pattern look like across the network plane?
    - Example: I need private and public subnets to quarantine my non-web applications from the internet.
- Are common servers grouped together in certain subnets?
    - Example: A web-tier, an app-tier, and DB-tier subnet.
- Which VM clusters or subnets will not connect outside the private network plane and which will?
    - Even in a completely flat network plane, certain VMs' traffic patterns will be similar and can be grouped accordingly.
- Which ports and protocols are used by my applications?
    - Understanding applications' common traffic patterns will help create appropriate firewall rules.
- Are any targets in the public network space?
    - Understand which applications must reach out in the public domain to get patches/updates and where they must connect to.

With these questions answered, a security and network engineer can better lay the groundwork for enabling a scalable and secure firewall posture for the cloud environment.

Logs and monitoring

Several types of native logs exist on cloud platforms, allowing users to create a wide and deep log stream for auditing and monitoring. Despite the large and growing offering, there are still gaps that exist, primarily in the application logging territory. We will cover methods to address these gaps with open source or third-party solutions.

Network logs

Network logs allow the cloud user to view network traffic within their private cloud network plane. AWS VPC flow logs, Azure flow logging, and GCP Stackdriver logging are all native services that run on each respective cloud platform and provide network logging and analysis tools.

These flow logs contain a wealth of information, including (but not limited to):

- Source and destination IPv4 or IPv6 address
- Source and destination port
- IANA protocol number
- Number of packets
- Size in bytes
- Start and end time of capture window
- Action/Status (whether traffic was permitted by firewall rules or not)
- Account IDs
- Interface ID (logical identifier for virtual network interface of traffic)

These logs are maintained in the native cloud service, but can be exported into other storage targets that allow cloud users to assimilate and compile a myriad of different log sources into one central repository.

Audit logs

Audit trail logs allow all management/logical events administered within the cloud environment to be captured and stored. AWS CloudTrail, Azure control management logs, and GCP Cloud Audit Logging are all native services that provide administrative audit trails to understand how users are interacting with the cloud environment.

In order to build validated environments (GxP, HIPAA), or just to maintain a scalable and sustainable enterprise cloud environment, it is paramount to be able to track the actions of the hundreds of users who may be interacting with the cloud environment. The native audit logs enable this capability.

Since all cloud providers' services are built on top of scalable APIs, all interactions with the cloud environment can be boiled down to API calls (even changes made using the GUI). The logs these API calls generate contain a wealth of information, including (but not limited to):

- Event type, name, time, and source
- Access key ID
- Account ID
- Username
- Region

- Source IP address
- Request parameters
- Response elements

These logs are stored within cloud storage targets or within the cloud services themselves, but can be exported and assimilated with other logs for centralization, giving users a 360-degree view of multiple accounts.

Monitoring tools

Monitoring tools give the cloud user a dashboard to view the metrics and behavior of the cloud environment over time. Think of these services as native cloud infrastructure monitoring tools that integrate seamlessly with other cloud services. AWS CloudWatch, Azure Monitor, and GCP Stackdriver monitoring are all native services that run on each respective cloud platform and provide similar levels of functionality.

Early in the development cycle of these services, they first integrated with other cloud services out the box. As time has progressed and more functionality has been added, these services now support the ingestion of custom metrics, allowing cloud users to feed application metrics that they configure into the monitoring services. *Utilizing one pane of glass* to have a complete stack monitoring solution has and should always be a goal of security-ops and administrative-ops teams.

Some important features to call out with these services are:

- Detailed monitoring every minute
- Set and trigger alarms when monitoring metrics reach certain thresholds
- Automate actions based on alarms
- Build custom dashboards with graphs and statistics

Unlike other monitoring solutions, the cloud monitoring services are *always on*, providing a distinct advantage in performance and availability (since they run in a distributed fashion and are managed by the cloud provider). These services integrate with other cloud services, increasing interoperability. Log files can be encrypted, mitigating one of the most common attack patterns.

Configuration management

Since all administrative operations within the cloud environment (whether through GUI or CLI) are API calls, tracking configuration states and changes becomes an attainable goal. Services such as AWS Config allow users to monitor deployment patterns, retain configuration states, and monitor changes to the cloud resources over time.

The security benefit of such a capability cannot be overstated. The ability to create an inventory of cloud resources as well as software configurations on the VMs gives users peace of mind in maintaining security posture and tracking any configuration drift. Any changes that are made can trigger notification mechanisms to alert administrators. A secondary benefit is the ability to audit and assess the compliance of the cloud environment.

Identity and access management

Probably the most fundamental and important service when it comes to the security of a cloud environment, **identity and access management (IAM)** allows cloud users to provision access to users, machines, and other services to manage, change, operate, and consume cloud services in a scalable and secure manner. All major cloud providers have a robust IAM service that integrates with AD and other LDAP identity solutions.

The fundamentals components of the IAM service can be broken down into these core concepts:

- **Users**: An entity that is created to represent a person or service that uses it to interact with the cloud environment. A user is defined by a name and carries a set of cloud access credentials (secret and access keys).
- **Roles**: An entity that represents a type of access pattern that might be needed by an individual, machine, or service. A role is similar to a user, but is meant to be assumed by anyone or anything that requires the privileges contained in the role.
- **Policies**: A policy is a code statement that explicitly or implicitly grants/rejects access to cloud services, resources, or objects. Policies are attached to roles or users to grant or restrict what they can do in the environment.
- **Temporary security credentials**: A service that grants temporary, limited privilege credentials for IAM users that are authenticated/federated by the IAM service.

In a similar vein, cloud providers have developed robust services to authenticate and authorize users on mobile applications (known as authN and authZ). AWS's Cognito, Azure Mobile App Service, and GCP Firebase are examples of these services. This allows developers to integrate a scalable and highly available authN/authZ service into their mobile apps which can integrate seamlessly into their cloud environment on the backend.

Encryption services and modules

Hyperclouds offer fully managed services that generate and manage cryptographic encryption keys. These keys can be used to encrypt data ingested and stored on other cloud services, or be called upon to encrypt data stored at the application level. The physical security, hardware maintenance, and availability of the keys are managed as a service, leaving the users to focus on how the keys are consumed and ensuring their data is properly protected. AWS offers **Key Management Service (KMS)**, Azure Key Vault, and GCP Key Management Service.

The keys are generated following the Advanced Encryption Standards 256 bit (AES-256) specification established by the United States National Institute of Standards and Technology (US NIST). They meet advanced standards such as the Federal Information Processing Standards Publication 140-2 (FIPS 140-2), allowing sensitive information that requires high levels of encryption security to be encrypted by these cloud native services. The use of these services is key to achieving scalable, compliant architectures in the cloud, which we will cover later in the chapter.

Web application firewalls

There exist cloud native services that provide **web application firewall (WAF)** capabilities in a turnkey fashion. These services allow you to create rules that can filter web traffic based on conditions that include IP addresses, HTTP headers and body, or custom URIs. These services make it effortless to deploy a scalable, highly available level of protection from attacks that seek to exploit vulnerabilities in custom or third-party web applications you may deploy. These services make it simple to create rules that can mitigate common exploits like SQL injection and cross-site scripting. Rules can also be configured to block based on GeoIP to restrict access from known trouble spots in the world (for example, China, or Russia).

In addition to custom rule sets that users can configure, managed rule sets are available through native WAF services. These managed rule sets are updated daily to adjust to new CVEs and threats discovered by the cloud security teams. This extends your security team to the global, focused security teams at the cloud provider.

Both AWS WAF and Azure WAF provide these capabilities natively on their platforms. AWS WAF is also fully supported through APIs, opening new possibilities to integrate into a full DevSecOps process.

Compliance

Compliance is a derivative of overall security. A compliant environment is generally a secure one, because it adheres to best practices governing the use, maintenance, and operation of a given dataset or environment. In order to achieve compliance, administrators need to provide documentation, audit trails, and demonstrate operational controls to third-party auditing parties that certify compliance. In a cloud environment, the segregation of duties between the cloud provider and the cloud consumer for security mean that the two organizations need to work together to achieve compliance. Cloud providers do this by providing automated tools to access and generate compliance reports for the cloud providers' portion of the security model. AWS's Artifact tool, Microsoft Trust Center, and Google's Cloud Compliance page provide easy-to-access portals for viewing and downloading copies of different compliance attestations. These include a large and growing list of compliance reports, such as ISO 27001 Security Management Standard, ISO 27017 Cloud Specific Controls, PCI DSS Payment Card Industry Data Security Standard, SOC 1 Audit Controls Report, SOC 2 Compliance Controls Report, SOC 3 General Controls Report, ITAR International Traffic in Arms Regulation, various country-specific Personal Privacy Acts, FFIEC Federal Financial Institutions Examinations Council, CSA Cloud Security Alliance controls, CJIS Criminal Justice Information Services, and many others.

Automated security assessments and DLP

Cloud services are moving further up the stack (from traditional Infrastructure-as-a-Service) and providing more tools to help build and assess the security of code deployed by customers. These services help identify deviations from security best practices in applications, before and during deployments. They can be integrated into your DevOps process to automate assessment reporting as you are moving through the deployment pipeline. AWS Inspector, Azure Security Center Qualys cloud agents, and Cloud Security Scanner provide some or all of the features noted previously.

Moving further up the stack, cloud services are also providing users with the ability to natively discover, classify, and protect sensitive data stored in cloud environments. These services utilize machine learning to perform these classifications on a large scale, without the need for human supervision. By continuously monitoring the cloud environment, administrators can be confident that business critical data (such as PII, PHI, API keys, and secret keys) are automatically detected and proper action is taken based on notifications. AWS's Macie, Azure Information Protection, and the Google Cloud Data Loss Prevention API allow users to discover and redact sensitive data within the environment.

Cloud native security patterns

Now that we have a broad understanding of the native security tools available to us in the cloud, we can dive into some examples of how to design and build common deployments. It is important to realize that each use case will not leverage all security tools and will not exactly match other security patterns. We aim to demonstrate a palette of different approaches to varying problems and give the reader the ability to select and combine different solutions.

As our **first example**, let's consider a three-tier web application:

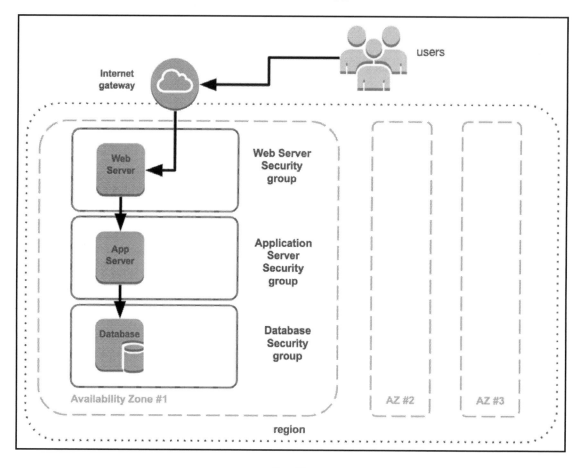

Figure 6.3

Security groups should be used to separate tiers within a stack, as shown in the previous diagram of a three-tier web application. Each tier has its own security group, which has unique rules that expose minimal attack vectors.

For our first security pattern example, let's use a basic three-tier web application. The 3 tiers comprising this pattern are the web, application, and database. A user routing from the internet will not directly connect/interface with the application or DB tiers. The DB tier will not interface with the web tier. Given these network patterns, we should build our security group rules accordingly:

Security Group	Direction	Protocol	Port	Destination	Notes
Web Tier SG	Inbound	TCP	22, 80, 443	0.0.0.0/0	SSH, HTTP, and HTTPS
App Tier SG	Inbound	TCP	22, 389	\<Corporate network\>	SSH, LDAP
	Outbound	TCP	2049	10.0.0.0/8	NFS
DB Tier SG	Inbound	TCP	1433, 1521, 3306, 5432, 5439	App Tier SG	Default ports for: Microsoft SQL, Oracle DB, MySQL/Aurora, Redshift, PostgreSQL

We've exemplified configurations for three different security groups corresponding to each tier of a three-tier web application

By using three separate security groups for each tier, we are able to create the smallest attack surface for each group of instances while enabling functionality. After configuring each security group and ensuring the stack can operate, we need to apply the security methods and approaches discussed earlier in the chapter. Ensuring the configuration doesn't drift from the original structure is essential to maintaining a secured environment.

This is where service configuration management comes into play. Either through custom scripting (utilizing the APIs available from each CSP) or utilizing services such as AWS Config, changes can be detected and acted upon when configurations change outside of set bounds. This is critical when dozens of individuals are operating in a production-like environment. Expect changes to happen that are against policy and have the tools in place to detect and mitigate them.

If we further build on the three-tier web app example, we can layer on a simple WAF loop that captures some advanced functionality. A URL honeypot can be built to detect botnets, capture their IPs, and add those IPs to rules on the WAF in an automatic fashion:

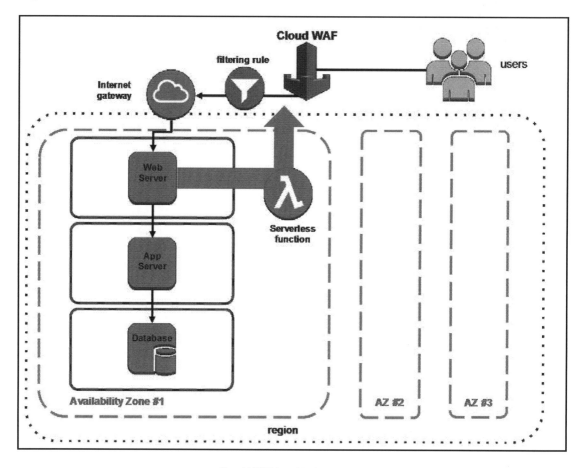

Figure 6.4: WAF along with other components

As shown in this diagram, Web Application Firewalls are a cloud native method of increasing security. WAF services from cloud providers are API driven, allowing programmatic loops to be built, such as the automated honeypot scenario.

This is done by adding hidden URLs to the public site that are invisible to ordinary users, but will be caught during the scraping process that bots use. Once the hidden URLs (the honeypot) are navigated to by the bot, a function can pick up the IPs from the weblogs and add them to the WAF rules to blacklist that specific IP. A serverless function service is available on AWS, called Lambda, and can support this pattern easily.

As our **second example**, let's look at another example of an enterprise environment:

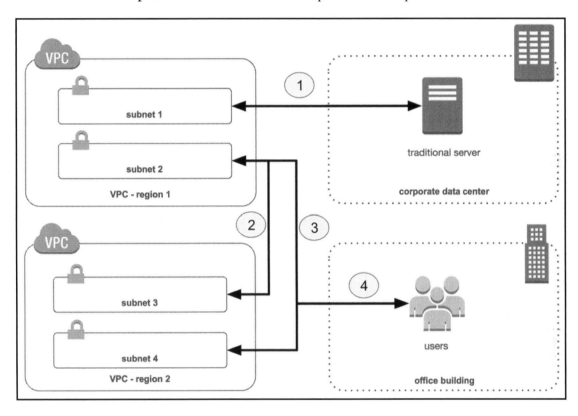

Figure 6.5

An enterprise IT environment typically looks like the network topology as shown—spread across multiple office locations and regional cloud environments. The cloud native security approach requires us to utilize nuanced approaches at several layers to mitigate vulnerabilities.

Enterprise environments are typically spread across multiple sites and cloud providers. This is done to minimize business risk, reduce blast radius, support workloads that are required to stay on-premises (such as nuclear reactor power control applications), and to support satellite office locations. This creates a large attack surface and requires security controls at several network interchange locations.

The first tools we can reach for are familiar to all IT veterans: site-to-site VPNs and private fiber connections provided by ISPs and CSPs (for example, AWS Direct Connect). The second is to utilize **network access control lists** (**NACLs**) to prevent all non-standard network pathways. For example, in the previous diagram we have several different subnets across two cloud regions plus two corporate locations. If we have office productivity apps running in subnet 2, we can enable NACLs to restrictively only allow packets from the CIDR range of the office users. Let's say DBs are also in subnet 2; we can add rules to allow connectivity to subnet 3 and 4 to work with the application servers running in region 2.

Furthermore, we can restrict our **high performance compute** (**HPC**) cluster utilizing **personal identifiable information** (**PII**) data running in subnet 1 to only communicate with our on-premises servers in using network pathway 1. The use of NACLs allows us to provide a high level of control to connectivity across disparate enterprise sites.

Looking at each VPC individually, we should understand the type of traffic ingress and egress. This gives us a baseline of good traffic, the ability to catch improper packets from non-approved pathways, and a tool to debug applications as they misbehave. CSPs have services such as AWS VPC Flow Logs, which captures and generates logs containing the source/destination IP, packet size, time, and other metrics for packets entering and leaving the VPC. These logs can be ingested into SIEM tools to monitor non-approved or abnormal behavior:

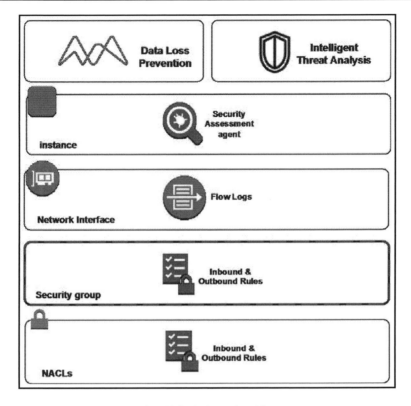

Figure 6.6: Cloud native security workflow

A cloud native security approach involves layering security services at every layer of the stack. From the bottom network layer, up to network interfaces, within an instance's OS, running against data stored across the environment and finally against user behavior within the overall environment.

In addition to the wide spread of the network we need to protect, we must also consider how to deal with the hundreds or thousands of users that will interact with the environment. How can we safely and responsibly enable them to work and be productive while mitigating risks of accidental keystrokes?

Identities

A cloud native identity management system contains three principle aims:

- **Enable the productivity of individuals within the organization** to perform their day-to-day responsibilities. These include DB administrators, security officers, and developers.
- **Enable machines that perform automated actions within the environment**. These functions, applications, or machines are increasingly important as environments become larger.
- **Enable users/consumers to securely connect to your public-facing services**. This entails securing and authenticating your consumers' identities.

CSPs have well-developed IAM services (such as AWS IAM) that allow the creation of custom **policies** dictating what can be done within the cloud environment. These policies can be attached to **groups**, which aggregate the most restrictive interpretation of several policies into one administrative body. For each individual working within the environment, a **user** can be created with unique logins for console access and a unique key/secret for making API calls to the environment. Each interaction the user makes with the environment will be restricted to what is allowed in the policies attached to the group the user is placed in:

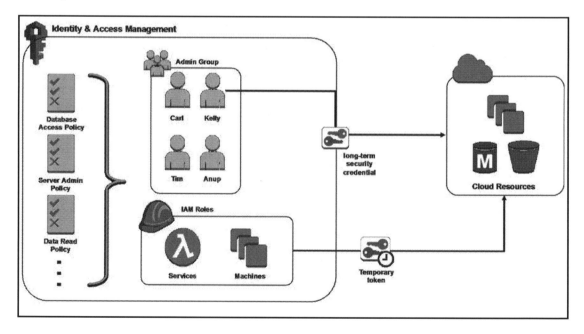

Figure 6.7: Identity and access management

Policies can be used for both roles and groups. They can even be attached to specific users, though this is not best practice. Roles assigned to services and machines are able to implicitly gain access to other parts of the cloud landscape, enabling automation patterns.

When dealing with multiple cloud accounts and other SaaS platforms, it is best practice to provide your staff with a **Single Sign On** (**SSO**) solution. This makes the switching of user profiles across multiple cloud environments (for example Azure, AWS, GCP, Salesforce, and so on) easier and more secure. One of the principal human errors introduced as the IT estate sprawls over multiple vendors is the user managing multiple logins (usually for the same CSP environment), which can prove disastrous (or equally frustrating when logging in with the wrong profile).

Emphasis in a cloud native environment is always on automation engineering. Every IT shop should be focused on enabling machines to do their jobs, freeing up more time for the users to build more machines. In order to safely power this virtuous cycle, we need mechanisms to enable machines while restricting them from being exploited by bad actors. It should be noted that applications that utilize cloud services will use similar mechanisms, so this discussion is not just limited to IT environment management tools, but all applications programmatically interacting with the cloud.

The first option is the use of **roles**. Roles are given to services and machines with certain policies (these are the same policies we built for our groups/users). These roles broker abilities to the attached entities that are handled by the CSP. Keys are programmatically given to the machine and services when making the API calls.

For applications, the embedding of secrets in code is a dangerous vulnerability. Instead, we can utilize the second option, the use of token services that generate and share time-limited credentials to make API calls. This key expires at the end of a set time, upon which the application will need to make a new request to the token service. The AWS **Security Token Service** (**STS**) is a highly useful tool to accomplish the use of secrets in applications.

Mobile security

The web is increasingly mobile driven—most web traffic is now from mobile devices and mobile apps dominate the development landscape. A cloud native security approach must take into account the security of data generated on these apps and the secure flow of data between cloud systems and end users.

In the past, mobile developers have managed these keys through custom code implementations or through third-party tools purchased with per-license or per-user pricing models. This not only introduces increased overhead to the development teams, but also means they must maintain and update this code to deal with new vulnerabilities. Instead of managing backend infrastructure for these capabilities within applications, CSPs have native services we can leverage to do this in an efficient scalable manner.

Services such as AWS Cognito help developers and architects tackle several of these challenges. This starts with defining users and groups that will interact with your app. You can customize and define the attributes that you need to identify unique users. Password complexity, length, and the use of special characters and case conditions can be easily set to ensure a base level of security. The service supports MFA through email and SMS, in which the service also takes care of the SMS messaging infrastructure.

Furthermore, these cloud native services make application client integration straightforward. Supporting OAuth 2.0 standards, services such as AWS Cognito can issue access tokens to end users, allowing access to the protected resources supporting your application front end:

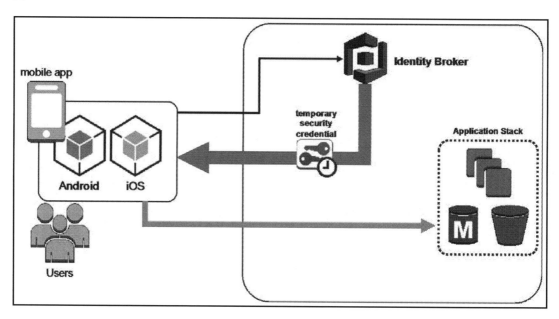

Figure 6.8: Client integration

A cloud native mobile application identity management system built using cloud services helps mitigate the heavy lifting of standing up scalable and secure services. These services use common standards such as OAuth 2.0 to delegate access to resources your application uses.

DevSecOps

A term that has increasingly gained traction in the industry is DevSecOps—the convergence of development, security, and operations. As DevOps practices have become more common and accepted throughout technology practices, security was left behind in the agile-driven practices espoused by DevOps.

DevSecOps applies the same agile *build it and own it* mentality to security, pulling it into the fold of continuous integration deployment. It is ultimately the belief that a specific set of resources or a small team owns security. It is the culmination of tools, platform, and mindset and the idea that everyone is responsible for security and needs to implement good security practices at every stage of the develop/deploy/operate life cycle.

There are principal guidelines for DevSecOps that constitute a cloud native approach, and these are demonstrated perfectly by the DevSecOps manifesto:

> **Leaning in** over Always Saying "No"
> **Data & Security Science** over Fear, Uncertainty, and Doubt
> **Open Contribution & Collaboration** over Security-Only Requirements
> **Consumable Security Services with APIs** over Mandated Security Controls & Paperwork
> **Business Driven Security Scores** over Rubber Stamp Security
> **Red & Blue Team Exploit Testing** over Relying on Scans & Theoretical Vulnerabilities
> **24x7 Proactive Security Monitoring** over Reacting after being Informed of an Incident
> **Shared Threat Intelligence** over Keeping Info to Ourselves
> **Compliance Operations** over Clipboards & Checklists

Similar to topics covered in `Chapter 5`, *Scalable and Available*, security stands to benefit from defining everything as code, termed here **Security as Code (SaC)**. This means taking the same IaC approach and applying it to security enforcement and operations. Access controls, firewalls, and security groups can be defined within templates and recipes. These templates should be the shared across the organization as the starting point for creating an environment. They can also be used as points of reference to track drift from approved patterns.

Cloud native security toolkit

Now that we have a firm understanding of the approaches and strategies around building secure and reliable cloud native solutions, in this section we will introduce supportive tools, products, and open source projects. It should be noted that these tools help make the end goals discussed in this chapter easier to attain, but come at a price. Naturally, in-house development of these features tuned to your cloud consumption is best, but can prove difficult and timely to do.

Okta

Okta has a growing number of identity-related services, but is best known for it's single-sign on service that allows users to manage login names and passwords for a large number of disparate accounts (across IaaS, PaaS, and Saas). This provides for a much more efficient login experience and helps users (especially admins) to manage multiple user/roles within one cloud account (`https://www.okta.com/`):

Centrify

Centrify is another popular identity and access management tool that integrates with cloud environments. It supports integration with AD and allows for automated account provisioning. This greatly aids in operating securely at scale for large enterprises managing dozens or hundreds of cloud accounts. (`https://www.centrify.com/`):

Dome9

When deploying what we've discussed in this chapter at scale, it can become challenging to visualize and understand true configuration states when troubleshooting. Dome9 helps solves this issue by creating detailed maps of security groups, NACLs, and machines. In addition, Dome9 can integrate into DevOps workflows to scan and flag IaC templates (like `cloudformation`) for anti-patterns (`https://dome9.com/`):

Evident

Evident provides a range of products for different cloud providers; the Evident Security Platform (ESP) allows users to take a consolidated view of the entire cloud landscape (across multiple accounts) and helps them find threats with guided incident response. ESP also integrates with native cloud services such as AWS Config to help detect state drift over time (`https://evident.io/`):

Summary

In this chapter, we discussed how security needs to adapt to a cloud native world. The old processes around applying security are largely obsolete, and a new approach is needed. We discussed the mindset of applying security at every layer and what essential features make up a secure cloud native stack. They are compliant, encrypted with scalable/available encryption resources, utilize DLP technology to automatically prevent exposure of data, employ caching to prevent user data from being written in application memory, and finally have secure credentials and endpoints to enable people to interact with the stack safely.

We introduced a number of cloud security services that exist on CSPs today. These include security groups, NACLs, data loss prevention, identity and access management, log generation and collection, monitoring, configuration management, encryption services and modules, web application firewalls, and automated security assessment tools.

All these services must come together to build a secure cloud native stack. We covered a few novel examples of how these services can be applied in different situations, ranging from IAM management and firewall configuration to mobile security management.

Finally, we introduced some of the third-party tools available in the marketplace that one can use to help close the gap between current security approaches and the more cloud native ones discussed in this chapter.

Optimizing Cost

7

In this chapter, we are going to learn how to frame and communicate the inherent cost advantages of cloud platforms. You will finish this chapter with a firm understanding of the cloud pricing models available today and how to optimize them. These models are viewed differently by businesses, so we will cover which aspects of the model are appealing to certain business leaders.

Once we have a firm understanding of the pricing model, we'll dive into building economic business cases for adopting cloud. We'll demonstrate this through several examples to show you the inherent cost benefits and flexibility that cloud can afford. Finally, we'll cover common toolsets and services available to ensure that we are monitoring, controlling, and optimizing costs in a cloud native way.

Before we begin, let's define **cost** as *the expense that a business incurs in bringing a product or service to the market.* **Price** is defined as *the amount an entity (consumer or business) pays for a product or service.* Finally, **opportunity cost** is defined as *the benefit that an entity (consumer or business) could have received, but gave up, to take another course of action.* Stated differently, an opportunity cost represents an alternative that's given when a decision is made.

Before the cloud

Before we can discuss the cost of building cloud native applications, we need to turn back the clock to examine infrastructure before the cloud, namely on-premises systems. When an enterprise deems it necessary to establish or expand its IT infrastructure, a number of actions have to be taken regarding:

- **Physical space**: Finding space in the existing data center or buying/renting new space for the data center buildout.
- **Electric power**: This can be easily overlooked. Deploying a large scale array of servers requires large power conduits that may not exist in a new location or be available in the current space. In addition, redundancy and backup power generators are often required to continue critical operations in case of a power outage or disaster.
- **Physical Security**: Paramount in enterprise deployments, establishing physical security to the hardware supporting a data center requires key/badged access points, security personnel, cameras, and security equipment.
- **Network connectivity**: Depending on the site chosen, broadband connectivity may not exist or be of insufficient bandwidth to support steady state data center functionality. In most cases, data centers require a physically redundant network connection to support network failover scenarios. This may require digging, burying, and trenching another line on the part of the **internet service provider (ISP)**, which may take months (in the worst case scenario, permits are required from the local and regional governing authorities to bury a single network strand).
- **Cooling**: Computing equipment generates lots of heat, and they need to operate within certain temperature ranges to maintain optimal performance. The newest data centers have passive cooling systems (if built in cold climates), but the vast majority require large air conduits that are built-in to move the waste heat from the computers and pull in cool air.

- **Physical hardware**: After all of the preceding points have been addressed, the actual compute, storage, and network equipment that gives the data center its business value needs to be ordered, shipped, received, racked, stacked, connected, tested, and brought online. This takes teems of data center operations resources to accomplish and dozens of man hours per rack.
- **Staff**: While all of the preceding points are being dealt with, the company in question needs to hire, train, and compensate a large number of staff to design, order, install, test, and operate all the items noted previously.

It's no surprise that data center buildouts are planned out months and years in advance. Large capital investments are needed to bring together the necessary teams and resources so that they can complete the build and become production ready.

Cloud cost view

The advent of cloud has all but eliminated the limitations provided by each of the preceding points. Cloud providers now completely manage the *undifferentiated heavy lifting* for their customers. They've bought the physical space to house the data centers; deployed network, electric, and cooling systems to support millions of machines; managed security of the physical infrastructure, performed background checks, and segregated duties to ensure that no staff has both physical and logical access to systems; designed and deployed state-of-the-art cooling systems; and have a staff of focused operations engineers to maintain their massive fleets of data centers. For a further discussion on the cloud providers' scale, please refer to `Chapter 5`, *Scalable and Available*.

In every one of these points, the CSPs aggregate and reduce costs through economies of scale. A company such as AWS or Azure can spend more time designing more secure systems than other enterprises because they have more resources, money, and commitment for ensuring security. In the case of cooling, CSPs can apply greater engineering know-how to developing greener, more efficient cooling systems than any other enterprise in the market. For example, Google is using seawater to cool its data centers in Finland, which reduces stress on local freshwater sources and local electric generation, and increases efficiency. You can refer to `https://www.wired.com/2012/01/google-finland/` to read more about this.

Apart from the tangible benefits of adopting cloud, there are several intangible cost benefits (opportunity costs), which are enumerated as follows:

- **Reduced complexity**: Adopting the cloud eliminates the *undifferentiated heavy lifting* to manage your business's IT infrastructure. Lengthy license pricing negotiations are eliminated because the cloud provider has pre-negotiated bulk licensing agreements with vendors. In other cases, the CSP provides a marketplace of third-party software that's available on the platform with rates baked into the cost of the compute resource. Finally, the cloud gives your business the ability to devote the human capital previously concerned with managing that complexity to more business critical tasks. This reduction in complexity saves the business dollars, directly and indirectly.

- **Elastic capacity**: Adopting the cloud gives the enterprise the unprecedented ability to expand or contract their IT infrastructure on the fly. This elasticity allows businesses to expand on successes and contract quickly after a failed experiment, or to follow seasonal business needs or daily user fluctuations. Enterprises no longer need to forecast demand years in advance and plan accordingly—they can manage and expand their business today, with cloud consumption mirroring their own business trends.

- **Increased speed to the market**: Enterprises competing for market dominance need *agility* to be successful. The ability to design, develop, test, and launch products supported by IT projects more quickly is a dominant factor in whether a company succeeds or fails. Adopting cloud native architectures is a key factor in increasing the speed with which a company can iterate product development.

- **Global reach**: The hyperscale cloud providers have a global network of data centers that are available to all customers. Any size of customer can leverage the global network to expand its products or services globally within minutes. This greatly reduces time to the market and allows companies to reach new markets with ease.

- **Increased operational efficiency**: Each of the major CSPs provides tools to decrease time spent on basic operational controls and checks, which helps automate many of these functions. Resources (people, capital, and time) are freed up so that they can be spent on building the company's differentiating product. In a similar vein, people within the organization can now spend time solving valuable and difficult problems, leading to higher job satisfaction.

- **Enhanced security**: The CSPs manage their portion of the shared security model (covered in `Chapter 6`, *Secure and Reliable*), which frees up customer resources to focus on their portion of the security model. By providing native security tools on the platform, CSPs amplify and automate security functions on the customer side of the shared responsibility model. These have large effects on how an organization is modeled and operated, enhancing security and freeing up resources to focus on greater *application* security.

These tangible and intangible cost benefits are enormously beneficial to every single organization with an IT department. This is explained well by the upswing in cloud adoption that started in 2013 by large enterprises. The collective realization dawned on these entities that the cloud has many upsides and almost no downsides to adoption—the sole valid exception being the unrealized return on capital investments made recently in the IT infrastructure (for example, Company X just invested $50 million in a new data center that came online last month). Unless Company X can find a way to relinquish their new data center and recuperate commensurate sunk costs, the math is likely not in favor of cloud adoption until the next refresh cycle (this term is used to describe the time in-between the replacement of computers and associated computer hardware).

Cloud economics

In many companies, a central IT organization manages infrastructure and charges back the price of IT services vended to the **lines of business** (**LOB**) plus their own administrative costs (known as a *chargeback model*). It is important to realize that the chargeback price rarely equals the price of cloud (for an equivalent stack). In these pricing exercises, rarely do central IT organizations take into account facility costs, security, cooling, water, and electric in their prices.

The price of a cloud stack must be compared to the chargeback price **plus** capital expenditures (building and equipment), operational expenditures (electricity, cooling, water), staffing, licensing (costs for virtualization software, ISV/third-party tools, and so on), facilities, overhead, and opportunity costs. This is referred to as **Total Cost of Ownership**, or **TCO**. Azure (`https://www.tco.microsoft.com/`) and AWS (`https://awstcocalculator.com/`) have TCO calculators that allow users to make reasonable numerical assertions for TCO based on a few assumptions (labor, electric, storage, facility, and so on).

These TCO analysis tools help you compare tangible costs between the current on-premises deployment and their equivalent environment on the CSP platform. These do not account for intangibles (read: opportunity costs) that are to be gained by adopting a cloud platform.

To find out the pure price of cloud services, we need to shift the discussion to another set of tools. There are pricing calculators available with the major CSPs that allow you to price out a given architecture on the CSP's platform with great accuracy (given your assumptions around data usage, code execution, GB storage, and so on are accurate). The AWS Simple Monthly Calculator (`https://calculator.s3.amazonaws.com/index.html`), Microsoft Azure Pricing Calculator (`https://azure.microsoft.com/en-us/pricing/calculator/`), and the Google Cloud Pricing Calculator (`https://cloud.google.com/products/calculator/`) are all available online and are free to use.

CapEx versus OpEx

When building the business case for cloud, one of the most compelling arguments to senior leadership (read: C-suite) is the ability to shift IT spending from **Capital Expenditures (CapEx)** to **Operational Expenditures (OpEx)**. A capital expense is defined as money spent by a business on acquiring or maintaining fixed assets, such as land, buildings, and equipment. An operating expense is defined as the ongoing cost for running a business/system or providing a service/product.

There are several advantages that make up a compelling business case for leaders to transition to an OpEx model, which are enumerated as follows:

- **Lower, recurring costs versus large, upfront investments**: As mentioned earlier in this chapter, building out a data center requires large amounts of time and resources to bring the compute power online. The cost associated with the time and resource allocation to building a data center is large. In an OpEx model, the business can achieve the same end result without a large, upfront investment.

- **Tax benefits**: Operating expenses are treated differently than capital expenses. In general, business are allowed to write off operating expenses the year they are incurred—or said another way, these outlays can be deducted in their entirety from a business's taxable revenue. However, in general, capital expenses must be deducted more slowly over a schedule defined by the government tax office (for example, IRS in the US). These schedules typically range from 3-5 years, over which the cost of the capital expense can be deducted from a business's tax outlay.

- **Greater transparency**: The cloud enables a great degree of cost transparency, which allows business leaders to justify and draw conclusions from investment decisions. With a native cloud environment, conclusive market tests can be conducted to increase or decrease IT spending (for example, we paid X dollars for Y amount of storage and compute time, leading to a Z% increase in online revenue).

- **Capital depreciation**: Similar to the tax benefits noted previously, businesses can avoid capital depreciation on their upfront expenses by adopting a cloud-based OpEx model. Capital depreciation is the gradual decrease in value of an asset owned by a company. In the IT industry, this is unavoidable as there are always better performing servers, storage devices, and network components coming to market, driving down the value of older equipment.
- **Easier growth**: Tied to the natural elasticity of cloud resources, OpEx models allow for spending that matches natural business growth and contractions, whereas fixed capital investments can lie idle or provide a ceiling to business capacity.
- **No commitment or lock-in**: A concern that business leaders have when purchasing any technology service or product is lock-in—an arrangement according to which a company is obliged to deal only with a specific product or service. This lock-in can be in the form of an exclusive service contract or technology portability limitations (where the barrier to changing systems to work with another product is too costly). This is largely eliminated by cloud as there is no upfront payment or term-based contract necessary to consume cloud services (that being said, term-based discount contracts are available from CSPs. If you are willing to commit to a minimum amount of spend on the platform, CSPs will give incremental discounts over the life of the contract (typically 3-5 years). However, this is in no way mandatory). Companies can choose to increase or decrease their consumption on the platform (or eliminate it altogether) without any limitations.

Cost monitoring

CSP platforms are inherently built to be cost transparent. There are no hidden fees or service charges that a customer can't see until they begin building on the platform. All pricing is posted and kept updated on the sites of the big three and is readily available to anyone interested in pricing out an architecture. As mentioned earlier, pricing calculators are available from the CSPs to help prospective customers price out an environment before building. This trend was first established by AWS when they released their initial cloud services and have remained true to this day.

In a similar vein, once systems have been built on the cloud, each CSP has native services to help monitor, drill down, and explore service consumption and their related costs. AWS's **Billing & Cost Management Dashboard** is a perfect example of these cloud native capabilities. Features such as AWS Cost Explorer allow users to drill down into monthly bills, look at historical spends, and anticipate future spending. Budgets allow users to set custom budgets that can trigger alerts or alarms when the cost or usage of something has exceeded the set limits. These tools allow cloud admins to confidently set guardrails around the usage and costs incurred through cloud services:

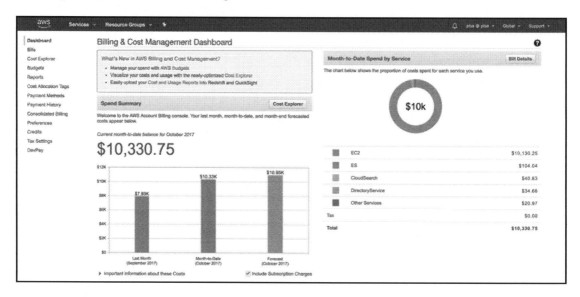

The **Billing & Cost Management Dashboard** of the author's AWS account.

We can very easily ascertain the last, current, and next month's costs in one simple view. On the right, we can see which services we are incurring costs for.

 Cloud Native Architecture Best Practice: Every cloud administrators' second task (after establishing MFA and securing root credentials) should be to familiarize themselves with the cost explorer dashboard and services for their chosen cloud platform.

Central to being able to navigate the thousands or millions of resources that an enterprise will provision in a cloud environment is tagging. Tagging is the fundamental method with which resources can be assigned to cost centers, programs, users, lines of businesses, and purposes. Without tagging, a cloud environment would be almost impossible to properly maintain across a large organization. We will cover best practices for tagging as it relates to cost management in the next section.

Historically, IT budgets have been exposed to capital investment models that are expended upfront. With the cloud, this was shifted to OpEx models where consumers had more control over operational costs. The next step in this evolution is the ability to set hard or soft limits for spending within portions or across the entire IT landscape of an enterprise. These budgets are enforced natively in the platform through APIs or notification services that alert admins when consumption is exceeding these thresholds.

AWS Budgets (`https://aws.amazon.com/aws-cost-management/aws-budgets/`), Azure Spending Budgets (`https://docs.microsoft.com/en-us/partner-center/set-an-azure-spending-budget-for-your-customers`), and GCP Budgets (`https://cloud.google.com/billing/docs/how-to/budgets`) are examples of cloud native methods to control and limit spending. This is a critical feature for large organizations where the activities and spending of certain groups may not immediately be visible to leadership or budget owners.

Cloud Native Architecture Best Practice: Set budgets for each cloud account tied to different groups across your organization. These budgets can be revisited and modified in the future. Perhaps more importantly, the budgets set a soft limit in order to enforce certain behaviors. Giving carte blanche to teams, allowing them to rack up a limitless bill, is not a best practice. Giving teams a budget limit will instill better operational practices and force them to think outside the box, leading to more inventive thinking when it comes to designing systems.

Budget thresholds can be set to alert administrators when costs exceed limits, when the use of certain services/features exceed set limits, or when consumption of pre-paid resources (such as Reserved Instances on AWS EC2) exceed set limits. These budgets can be aligned on different periods (monthly, quarterly, or annually), giving admins flexibility in how they choose to enforce constraints across the organization. Optionally, notifications can be set to alert you when you're approaching certain percentages of the budget:

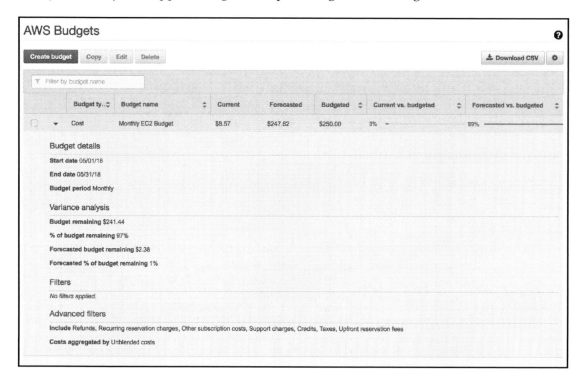

Setting budgets is an effective way of monitoring cloud costs. Systems will automatically notify you when you are approaching or exceed set spend amounts. The following shows you this setting:

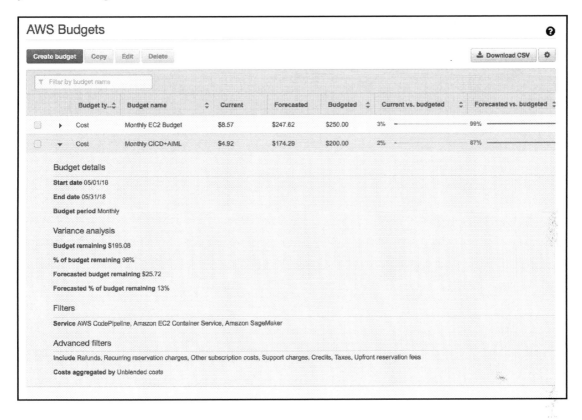

Billing alarms can be configured to trigger email notifications. This allows you to minimize overspending and keep your cloud environment cost optimized. The following screenshot shows the notification setup:

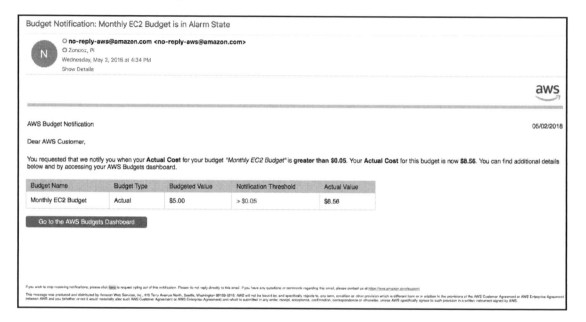

The notification setup information

There are also third-party tools that work across different cloud platforms to aggregate, display, and predict costs—these will be introduced in the Cloud Native Toolkit at the end of the chapter.

When taking into account best practices for deployment and management discussed in the previous chapters, immutable architectures require a unique approach. Since each deployment replicates the entire stack or a modular component of it, we can price it out before deployment. Using AWS Cloudformation, on the final confirmation page before deployment, you can confirm the stack's monthly cost using the **Cost** link beside **Estimate Cost**. This navigates the user to a prepopulated Simple Monthly Calculator:

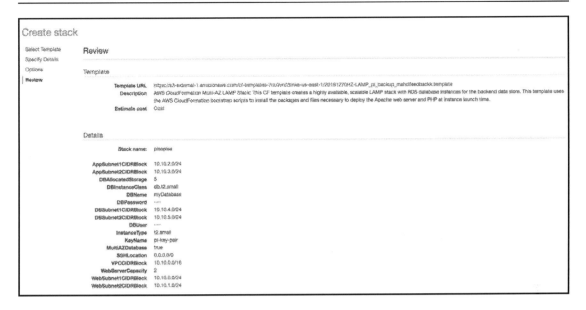

When managing deployments as stacks expressed as code, each stack can be priced out before deployment (as in the preceding case of the CloudFormation stack being deployed on AWS).

The following screenshot shows an example simple monthly calculator estimate, which was generated from a sample CloudFormation template deployment (shown in the previous screenshot):

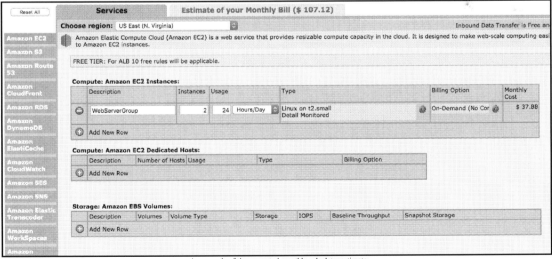

An example of the generated monthly calculator estimate

Tagging best practices

For large enterprises or small startups alike, tagging is the most critical daily activity to be performed in order to enable cost transparency. CSPs can report and display billing transparently, but those charges will mean little to the business or end users if they can't allocate or track costs to key business functions.

Tagging is a native function supported by all leading CSPs and supports customization. Since each business, organization, and consumer has unique internal processes and terminology, it is important to develop a tagging strategy that works for you.

Cloud Native Architecture Best Practice: Tagging will very quickly become burdensome and impossible to maintain if tags are not designated at launch time. Within a couple of weeks, the entire environment can be untagged (and thus impossible to manage) if development life cycles are short enough. A cloud native cost optimized environment automatically detects (and even deletes) resources that aren't tagged. This very quickly forces teams to treat tagging as a critical activity.

Automatic enforcement of tags can be done in a number of ways. Using the command-line interface, a list of untagged resources can be generated for each service (for example, AWS EC2, EBS, and so on). Native CSP tools such as AWS Tag Editor can be used to manually find untagged resources. The optimal cloud native route would be to build a rule requiring tags on native cloud services that do this automatically, such as AWS Config Rules. Config Rules checks the environment constantly for tags that you specify as required. If they are not, manually or automatic intervention can be performed once detected:

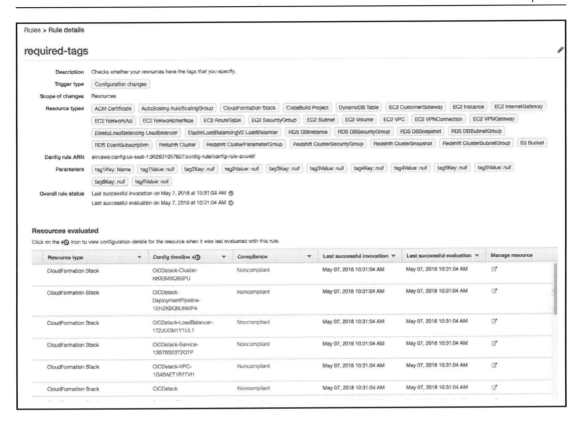

The previous screenshot shows how AWS Config Rules allow automatic detection and reporting of resources that are not tagged.

The following screenshot shows how AWS Tag Editor can be used to manually search for resources without tags, though this is more cumbersome than automatic detection (especially in large enterprise environments where thousands of resources are being used and consumed):

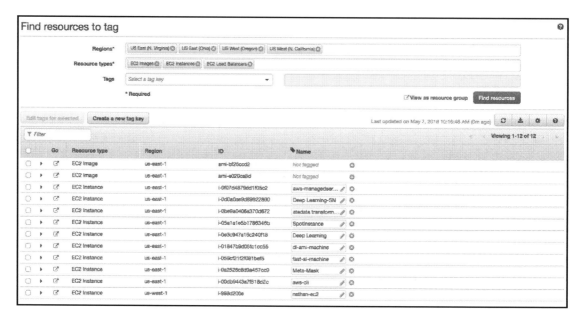

AWS Tag Editor

In a fully mature environment, every deployment is managed as code using deployment pipelines. In this pipeline, a gate should be used to enforce proper tagging of the template. Upon deployment, the tags should flow down to all resources in the template, if written properly. The key to tagging is automation, and by designating tags at the top-level construct (a stack template), we are minimizing the manual intervention needed and increasing the accuracy of our tags.

Cost optimization

Now that we have an approach for collecting, tracking, and viewing costs in a cloud environment, how do we optimize these costs? There are two distinct camps on what is meant by *optimizing costs*. One camp hears *minimize* (to reduce to the smallest possible amount) while the other hears *maximize* (to make the best use of). Both camps are technically correct, since no IT organization has a bottomless budget (hence you minimize to constrain costs within your budget). However, today's leading organizations have changed the way they look at IT outlays. They seek to maximize business benefits and link technology investments to business outcomes. This is what is meant by *maximizing/optimizing* our technology costs. The first question requires technology decisions. The second requires technical experimentation, patience, and business acumen.

Compute optimization

Typically, the largest savings in a cloud environment are realized during a *right sizing* exercise for the compute resources. Since compute typically dominates costs, it is reasonable to expect that the biggest cost savings can be found here. **Right sizing** refers to the act of selecting the most adequately sized virtual machine for the given application (size here refers to the amount of CPU and memory allocated to the machine).

This problem is acutely present in environments that were just migrated from on-premises to a cloud environment. The resource sizing process for on-premises typically goes through many approvals and requisite teams, each layer adding extra cushion to CYA. This results in overpowered machines that are then migrated to comparable VMs in the cloud.

 Cloud Native Architecture Best Practice: After a successful migration, or after the successful deployment of a cloud native application, collect baseline resource utilization for each of your compute resources. Use this data to properly size your VMs to the necessary performance levels.

If your application can run in clusters and is stateless, it is advantageous to use more numerous, smaller instances. This optimizes for better cost (and performance), since you will be able to scale the cluster to better match demand. AWS and Azure have a rich set of VM sizes to choose from that can match any use case. GCP offers Custom Machine types where the user can set the sizing that's available. This offers even more control over matching machine resources to application demand.

Storage optimization

After compute, storage costs typically dominate cloud bills. Some of these costs include the virtual disks/volumes attached to each VM; the object storage services hosting application artifacts, pictures/videos, and documents; archival data service usage; and the backup of this data to backup services.

For all forms of data storage, it is important to establish a life cycle that is as automated as possible. Data and backups should naturally flow down this life cycle until they are put into archives for compliance purposes or deleted. Tags should be used to designate which data stores or objects are needed long-term for compliance purposes. Scripts should be used to manage these, though cloud native services exist to aid users in this effort.

The AWS **Simple Storage Service (S3)** is a highly durable service for storing objects. S3 supports life cycle policies, which allow users to designate a transition from S3-standard to cheaper and lower performant services that Standard-IA (infrequent access), One Zone-IA, and Glacier (long-term archival cold storage). All three of these target transition services are cheaper than the standard S3 service. Objects can also be set to permanently delete after X days of being created. This can be set at the bucket level, which cascades down to all folders and objects.

The data life cycle manager for AWS EBS also provides a native solution to managing hundreds or thousands of volume level backups. For large enterprises, this task would prove cumbersome as automated tools would have to be built to query, collect information, and delete old or expired snapshots. This service from AWS allows users to natively build these life cycles.

Serverless implications

Serverless architectures are a unique costing challenge. Most of the effective cost optimization efforts fall in writing effective code in order to reduce the code's execution time or the number of executions required. This is evident from the pricing model of serverless code execution services such as AWS Lambda, which charges based on the number of executions, execution time, and allocated memory to the container that runs the code (`https://s3.amazonaws.com/lambda-tools/pricing-calculator.html`). Memory size can be optimized by tracking the amount of memory used per execution (this can be tracked in AWS CloudWatch).

Other *serverless* cloud services, such as AWS Kinesis and Athena, follow a similar data-based pricing model (per shard hour and payload units for Kinesis, per TB of data scanned for Athena). These services are almost always cheaper than their comparable services (such as Apache Kafka and Presto), which are hosted on self-managed compute nodes.

Cloud native toolkit

Many of the cloud native tools for cost optimization are natively available on their respective platforms. However, two drivers may (rightly so) drive businesses to use non-native services to optimize costs:

- The independence of a third party to deduce cost optimization areas
- The ability to work across two or more cloud environments (multi-cloud architectures)

This space is getting squeezed as CSPs replicate many of the features provided by these companies natively on the platforms. Many of the tools that provided cost optimization have been forced to pivot to management and operational automation.

Cloudability

One of the last remaining independent tools focused on cost transparency is Cloudability, which gives users a detailed budget and daily reports based on detailed metrics it collects from your cloud environments. It is currently available and integrates with the major CSPs.

AWS Trusted Advisor

This service from AWS could make an appearance in several chapters of this book due to the amount of value it gives cloud users of AWS. Trusted Advisor provides automated cost optimization, security risk, performance optimization, and fault tolerance recommendations. Trusted Advisor will notify users if instances are not properly sized, if resources are idle or unused, among many other checks to minimize cost.

Azure Cost Management

Powered by their acquisition of Cloudyn, Azure Cost Management is an effective way to track use and expenditures for your Azure landscape. It provides recommendations on instance right sizing and identifies idle resources.

Summary

In this chapter, we learned and defined the cost structure of current enterprises managing their own data centers. We established a common set of terminology to help us understand and measure the cost benefit of cloud adoption.

We learned how cloud economics drives huge advantages and savings for customers, as well as how the model for pricing has shifted from capital expenditures to operational expenditures, a key difference between legacy systems and cloud native.

Finally, we established strategies for tagging which helped enable detailed cost analysis and traceback. These strategies help optimize architectures.

In the next chapter, we will talk about operational excellence.

8
Cloud Native Operations

In the preceding chapters, we learned about what makes a cloud native architecture unique and different from previous patterns of building IT systems. In our view, cloud native is not strictly limited to architectural decisions made relating to core technology components of a given system. In order to receive the biggest benefits, operations must evolve alongside our cloud technology adoption. Without a cloud native organization, most of the benefits of the cloud will go waste.

In this chapter, we will learn about how to build an effective organization that can design, build, and maintain a cloud native environment. It is a combination of processes, people, and tools that come together to realize the full potential of **cloud native development (CND)**.

By the end of this chapter, you will understand the following:

- How the cloud has driven changes in what an average technology professional is supposed to do
- What a successful cloud native organization looks like
- How to build mechanisms that enforce cloud native best practices
- What common tools and processes look like
- How to build an organization that empowers builders
- What Cloud Culture is and why it is important

Before the cloud

As always, it's best to start with a bit of perspective. Whether you've begun reshaping your IT environment and organization to be cloud native, or are yet to embark on the journey, you need to understand how the majority of organizations are organized to design, build, and run current IT systems.

As an example, let's consider an insurance company that offers several products to its customer base (home, life, and auto insurance). Internally, it has several teams, which help support its products: policy developers, field sales teams, statisticians, HR, programmers, marketing, actuaries, and so on. Each of these teams consumes the services of the IT team (whether it's servers for emails, clusters to run statistical models, databases to store client information, or websites to be a storefront for the public).

The IT team is in turn separated into several groups based on domain competencies. Network, security, database, and ops are typical teams found in these outdated organization models. These teams sit parallel and separate from the development teams, which are totally focused on writing code:

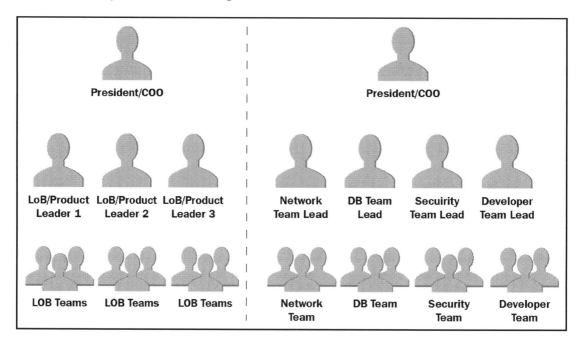

Figure 8.1

The preceding diagram exhibits the organizational structure of a typical company developing a product. There is strict separation between the technology domain experts and the product/service owners.

The problem here is that fundamentally these organizations are at odds with each other. The view of a CEO is that the left-hand side of the diagram is trying to maximize revenue and capture more business/customers. The right-hand side of the diagram is viewed by the typical CEO as a cost center—a group to be minimized and streamlined ad infinitum.

This mentality has ingrained itself in the behavior of individuals, the corporate culture, the psyches of leaders, and the cross-border collaboration efforts between these two groups. IT teams view LOB teams as foreign entities making unrealistic demands to build systems in too short a time, with unrealistic features for very little cost. On the other side, LOB teams find the IT teams disconnected from the core organizational purpose and the customer problem they're trying to address. IT doesn't seek to understand business goals and seems to react with intransigence at every request.

This is further compounded on the IT side since each domain works within teams comprising like-minded individuals. Security professionals work primarily with and sit alongside other security professionals. Likewise for network, DB, operations, and architecture. While this may make sense in a top-down view, this model facilitates echo chambers where the same ideas reverberate from person to person without being challenged or tested in a meaningful way by someone who is a *foreigner* to their area of expertise. Under this model, domain approaches became inflexible and brittle. Any challenge to *this is how we handle X* is met with stern no or long exception processes involving senior leadership and review boards. This siloing of resources also does the individuals a disservice. As they are cut off from the rest of the enterprise and technical teams, the chance to learn and expand their knowledge is more limited in general.

Each of these team leads (security, network, and so on) became protective of their resources and cut out *turfs* to entrench their role within the organization. They sought to put limits, guardrails, and processes around how their team members engage with other teams. They put rules around when and how other teams could leverage their people, and dictated what areas required their approval. Not only do they try to control the rate at which the team members can work, but they limit the ability of other teams to develop quickly without roadblocks.

For endeavors that required a mix of resources across multiple technology teams, a strict review process existed where leaders must review, give input, make a commitment, and provide oversight before a mixed joint team could be assembled. Oftentimes, these joint teams still run into many of the obstacles discussed earlier. These efforts typically devolved into a reporting structure where team leaders still had to be consulted before any real decisions could be made. These structures are the antithesis of an independent, autonomous team that can make decisions and evolve a product iteratively.

The apotheosis of these organizational structures and mentalities is the **Change Approval Board (CAB)**. CABs developed out of a necessity to control any changes to a monolithic system, where a change can have many downstream effects. A minor configuration adjustment could create a cascade of issues downstream, crashing revenue-generating systems and causing dozens of severity 1 events.

The CAB was created out of necessity during a time where systems ran on shared hardware resources, services within the system were tightly coupled, and there was little visibility into the performance of the system overall (other than the output rate of the system). As technology evolved and system architectures progressed, the CAB remained as a holdover institution. CABs are still prevalent across many enterprise IT organizations, despite the technology limitation that necessitated the CAB in the first place no longer existing.

Alongside the CAB arose the **Change Management Database** (**CMDB**) and the Configuration Management Database. The purpose of these systems was as follows:

- Control and track the planned changes made to a monolithic system
- Track the current state of a sprawling system

Both of these systems arose out of necessity, but are obsolete in a cloud native world. This is because of the manual processes needed to keep the information stored within the CMDBs relevant. The practicality of maintaining these systems is lacking when they often store very little higher-order information that makes a data store like this useful to a user. The data stored has to be refreshed and maintained regularly, otherwise it goes stale and loses all relevance. In order to maintain its relevance, a significant amount of upkeep is required from the organization. This requires expending time and effort, which can drag on the productive time of resources to develop and build products. We will introduce the successors of CMDBs later in the chapter, but suffice to say that things should be automated, persistent, and relevant.

Alongside the CABs and CMDBs, email arose as the most important facilitator of project management and progression. Each of the domain teams leverage email to ensure that there was a written trail leading up to a decision. Teams use email for everything. Simple decisions that could be made in a five-minute face-to-face conversation are relegated to email. Email creates an important contextual history to understand *how* we came to a decision, but it does not enable teams to get the *what* as rapidly as possible. The same five-minute conversation in person could take a day or longer depending on how often resources answer their emails.

The cloud native way

In the earlier chapters, we disassembled the monolith through decoupled, highly available architectures composed of microservices. These services were built in such a way that they could be managed and evolved independently of other components of a system. The technological services underpinning these microservices progressed rapidly, but the organizations that built these systems remained monolithic.

Through painstaking and patient experimentation, companies such as Amazon found that the best way to build systems powered by decoupled microservices was with decoupled micro teams. These teams are the personification of microservice architectures: small, decoupled, and autonomous. Amazon calls these teams *two-pizza teams*, since the whole team can be fed with two pizzas. We will refer to these as CND teams.

Each CND team comprises all the talent and skills required and the owners needed to design, build, deliver, and operate a service. They are a self-contained organizational unit that can manage the entire life cycle of their particular microservice. They don't need to rely on approval from other product owners, or the approval of VPs to decide which particular set of tools or frameworks is acceptable or whether they can push a new change to production.

The guiding principles of these are two-fold:

1. Everything must be API-driven, and once an API is published to external services, all effort must be made to never change it—*APIs are forever*
2. Each team owns its product from design to run. Teams are incentivized to build stable products that run with minimal human management

These two principles create natural incentives for teams to create stable microservices that mesh well with others across the system landscape. Teams can't push buggy or error-prone code over the fence to operation teams, because they *are* the operations team (this is the root of the term DevOps). Team members must take turns on pager duty on a schedule they all agree, forcing them to feel the pain of a poorly executed build or design. As team members suffer through sleepless nights fixing Severity 1 tickets or re-architecting systems, they will be more inclined to architect HA and anti-fragility into their systems on the next iteration.

This fundamentally shifts the skillset of teams from homogeneous groups of similarly skilled individuals to teams composed of whatever skills it takes to get the job done. Teams develop skills that are multidisciplinary and hire talent that completes the ambitions of the group. Furthermore, all team members develop operation skills, which they use in building more reliable systems. CND teams often comprise frontend and backend developers, database and security specialists, and operations experts, which all help each other build a more stable service.

Since each CND team managing a microservice is small, the number of communication pathways between resources is manageable. These teams could make decisions very quickly without relying on providing a large amount of context for what led to that decision point. This meant that email could be put aside, and chat applications (for example, Slack) could be used to track discussions relevant to the team on a continuous basis. These chat mediums allow teams to rapidly communicate and build consensus within their ranks. Separate #channels are used to split the conversation into rooms relevant to different domains concerning the team.

CND teams focus on building repeatable processes that help them go from design to deployment as quickly as possible. This means building pipelines that automate many of the rote tasks done manually by non cloud native teams. We will cover tools and strategy later in the chapter. The process should be tailored to maximize the amount of small deployments to the production system.

In a cloud native world, CMDBs designed to monitor fairly static physical hardware are doomed to failure. Change and configuration management needs to happen more dynamically, as hundreds of changes could happen within an hour. The shift driven here is to a Continuous Discovery service powered by the following:

- Infrastructure as Code and Machine Images
- Code Repositories storing source code
- Pipelines with gated process steps (manual, if necessary) driving faster deployments
- Team chat applications that have API integrations, which can notify teams of changes, request approvals, and outages
- Native cloud configuration services such as AWS Config, which show configuration history and allow development of rules to evaluate compliance

Governance in cloud native operations becomes more dynamic as well. With a combination of services such as AWS Config and automated code triggers from events, one can create automated governance detection, enforcement, and reporting.

Cloud native development teams

In order to take full advantage of cloud technology as an enabler for the business, teams must be reorganized into autonomous organizations, which we refer to as CND teams. The CND tenets are as follows:

- Complete ownership of their service
- Streamline decision-making within their group (build consensus quickly)
- Rotate operations responsibility (everyone does pager duty)
- Publish and maintain APIs forever
- APIs are the only way to interface with other services
- The right tools are the ones that get the job done (the team determines which language, framework, platform, engine, and so on is right for their service)
- Automation is more important than new features (automation enables the release of more features more quickly in the long run)

In order to maximize the speed at which teams develop, they need to have complete ownership of the design and build decision-making process. They cannot rely on resources or senior management to make decisions. This would introduce a huge delay by necessitate building context for that leader to explain why that decision is necessary.

Teams can decide among themselves how they want to streamline decision-making and which design decisions require a larger team discussion. They can choose their own methodologies for consensus building based on their personnel's strength and weaknesses. In addition to consensus-building, they can decide among themselves how operational oversight of their service will be handled. This utilizes their consensus-building mechanism to create an agreeable arrangement for who has *pager duty* and when.

One may doubt how effective CND teams can be when each service will likely rely on other services or systems managed by other teams. This is not a problem so long as the golden rule is followed: every interaction with the outside services must be API-driven. APIs are published and maintained forever. This ensures that any systems built outside but integrating with the primary service can rely on a steadfast, unchanging program interface. Consequently, this does not mean the primary system is immune to change. In fact, change may occur more rapidly as underlying systems can be swapped (such as DB engines or frameworks), but the program interface (the glue that holds disparate services together) will remain unchanged. This rule comes out of necessity, since changing an API requires the team to capture all downstream effects of that change. If a team had to capture all the possible changes and evaluate downstream effects for a given change, they could not truly be decoupled from other services.

Two-pizza teams

The fundamental issue with large organizations is consensus-building. Consensus is needed to move forward on most projects due to the interdependent nature of how we build our technology systems. Since systems are typically large and span multiple teams, once one team makes changes to their part of the system, it may have upstream and downstream effects that they did not anticipate (on subsystems owned and maintained by other teams). The following are some examples:

- **Upstream effect**: The updated subsystem now operates so quickly that it is straining the data feed with pulls for new data
- **Downstream effect**: The updated subsystem is generating data much more quickly which is overwhelming the ability of the downstream consumer to process the feed

With the broad adoption of decoupled systems and SOAs, we solve this from a technology aspect, but the organization has yet to adapt to this new reality. If we have decoupled systems, why not decoupled organizational units? Enter the two-pizza team. It's been called many different things by different organizations: tiger teams, DevOps teams, build-run teams, black ops teams, and so on. For our purposes, we will refer to them as CND teams.

These teams build, run, and maintain their systems, but why are they referred to as two-pizza teams? They need to be fed by a maximum of two pizzas, meaning that the team can't have more than 8-12 people. Where did this limit come from? Fundamentally, making decisions and coming to a consensus becomes difficult in larger groups. This is caused by the increasing number of communication links required between n number of developers. As n increases, the number of communication pathways scales exponentially:

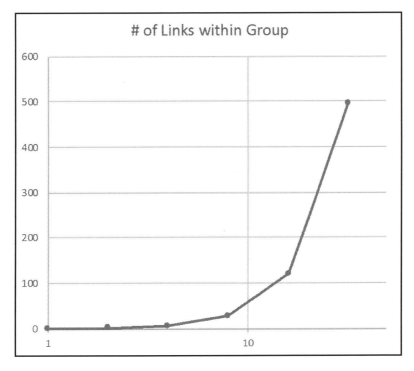

Figure 8.2

Once a team surpasses 10 people, the number of connections between each individual increases exponentially. The trend has been exponential all along, but it becomes much more noticeable. The converse way of making this argument is: **smaller teams can reach consensus more quickly**. This is the origin of the two-pizza limit.

Cloud-managed service providers

Enterprise organizations often partner with Managed Service Providers for the operational management of their cloud environments. The trend has been ongoing with CSPs for quite some time, where the CSP manages the *undifferentiated heavy lifting*—which at first was the physical device management—but has not moved its way up the stack to manage virtual machine clusters for containers, or the management of HA-deployed databases.

These MSPs offer environment management along a wide spectrum of services, which give greater responsibility to the customer on one end, and almost all environment management to the MSP on the other end. MSPs typically offer these services by reducing tooling and framework options for builders. MSPs can require a specific deployment pipeline that needs to be used. They can force container orchestration tools (such as Kubernetes over Mesosphere), force all change requests to come through tools such as Zendesk, and manage identity and access management through Okta.

While MSPs can help rationalize a complex tool environment and reduce operational burdens, we believe MSPs to be a stepping stone to true cloud native architectures along the **Cloud Native Maturity Model (CNMM)**.

MSPs at their heart represent an abdication of responsibility from the technical owner to manage change and evolve their own system. Without thinking about the process of change, along with the purpose/nature of the change itself, a cloud native architecture can be very hard to achieve. This is exemplified in the statement *the path is the way*.

Mature organizations on CNMM Axis-3 have a cloud native way of building and evolving, and it is these systems that produce *cloud native architectures*. One does not simply arrive at the mature end of the model. It is a process that requires organizational and cultural changes to manage and build these types of systems.

Operations with IaC

As with developing code for an application, the process one manages and deploys their code for IaC resembles how developers have been managing their application code.

IaC starts with CND teams storing their IaC in a repo (for example, GitHub, CodeCommit, and BitBucket). Once in a repo, code can be tested, branched, developed, merged, and forked. This enables a larger team to continually work on and develop a stack in isolation without colliding on their contributions.

There exist native cloud services that cover every aspect of the code development process as follows:

Figure 8.3

For the AWS platform, the services that correlate to each of the preceding processes are as follows:

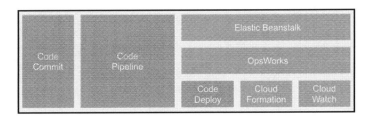

Figure 8.4

A more in-depth example of the AWS coding services is provided in `Chapter 9`, *Amazon Web Services*.

IaC can be validated using SDKs available from the CSPs for common IDEs such as Eclipse. Furthermore, tools such as cfn-nag from Stelligent can be used to automatically catch anti-patterns in your code before deployment. The project can be accessed at `https://github.com/stelligent/cfn_nag`. Cfn-nag can be used at the commit stage, meaning an IaC developer can receive rapid feedback before deployment. This can be inserted in your pipeline and prompt an exit code if any critical faults are found.

Services such as Amazon Code Pipeline provide users with an easy and managed continuous integration and continuous delivery service. Code Pipeline builds, tests, and deploys your code every time there is a new commit on your code repo or a web hook is activated. The deployment is handled by AWS CodeDeploy, which automates software deployment to compute targets available on the platform (such as EC2, AWS Lambda, and even on-premises virtual machines):

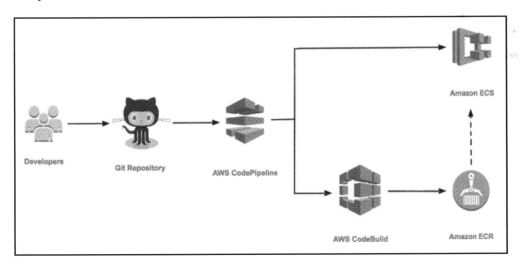

Figure 8.5

A mature cloud native approach for developing code could look like the preceding diagram. Developers create a code repo on Git. Once the code is reviewed, AWS CodePipeline tests and pushes to AWS CodeBuild, which compiles the source code, runs tests, provides software packages, and deploys to Amazon **Elastic Container Registry (ECR)**. ECR then maintains copies of your container-based app, which are deployed to Amazon **Elastic Container Service (ECS)**.

Once your pipeline has completed the process from commit/push to deployment, monitoring and tracking configuration becomes paramount to cloud operations. Creating custom logs and metrics that are pertinent to the particular app, service, or microservice built is key to maintaining stability in the long run:

- For an application, an example may be user request life time (how long have user-based jobs been alive in the queue)
- For a service, an example may be API-driven service requests for a query of how many friends a user has (such as a social network application)
- For a microservice, an example may be how many container requests are coming in from across the enterprise environment for the container orchestration microservice

The cloud native toolKit

The tools for cloud native operations can cover many different areas, and the following list is by no means complete. The list simply reflects some of the most important and pivotal tools the authors have used or encountered in their projects.

Slack

For most developers, the thought of using email or any other chat-based service is a nonstarter. Slack represents a shift in the way teams communicate by bringing together human CND teams and bots to create a unified communications platform for making decisions, sharing progress, and operating systems (https://slack.com/).

Stelligent cfn-nag

The cfn-nag (`https://github.com/stelligent/cfn_nag`) tool looks for patterns in AWS CloudFormation templates that may indicate insecure infrastructure. Roughly speaking, it will look for the following:

- IAM rules that are too permissive (wildcards)
- Security group rules that are too permissive (wildcards)
- Access logs that aren't enabled
- Encryption that isn't enabled

GitHub

GitHub is a development platform that allows you to host and review code, manage projects, and build software. It is by a wide margin the most popular development platform for hosting code, boasting over 28 million developers (`https://github.com/`).

Summary

In this chapter, we discussed the inherent weaknesses of how legacy organizations devote their staff to produce systems. These weaknesses have become increasingly apparent as cloud technology has become a huge enabler to businesses. We then introduced a new model for developing, deploying, and maintaining systems—CND teams.

CND teams are at the heart of building mature cloud native architectures, since they have the agility, freedom, and focus to own their systems all up. They are not strained by CABs or oversight, as long as they maintain their APIs and SLAs advertised to other systems and teams.

We discussed the use of Cloud-Managed Service Providers, and how a Cloud MSP can be a stepping stone to greater cloud maturity. Furthermore, central to cloud native operations are building with IaC. We introduced examples of how to build, test, deploy, and maintain systems with IaC. Finally, we concluded with cloud native tools popular in the marketplace today to enable cloud native operations.

In the next chapter, we will discuss the unique differentiators of Amazon Web Services.

Amazon Web Services

9

Amazon Web Services (**AWS**) is the pioneer in the cloud computing space. It started offering IT infrastructure services in 2006, when the term cloud computing hadn't even been coined! The first few services that AWS launched were Amazon **Simple Queue Service (SQS)**, Amazon **Simple Storage Service (S3)**, and Amazon **Elastic Compute Cloud (EC2)**, and ever since there's been no stopping. Today, AWS is probably one of the most advanced and mature public cloud providers, with presence across 18 geographic regions, 130+ services, and has already announced plans to launch many more in the days ahead. Over a period of time, AWS has also diversified into various new technology and solutions spaces, that has even blurred the typical definitions of IaaS, PaaS, and SaaS. In this chapter, we will discuss some of these differentiators and new architectural patterns which can help you with a mature cloud-native experience by leveraging multiple AWS services. The following are some of the specific topics that you will learn about in this chapter:

- AWS' cloud-native services, strengths, and differentiators around CI/CD, serverless, containers, and microservices concepts, and covering the following services:
    - AWS CodeCommit
    - AWS CodePipeline
    - AWS CodeBuild
    - AWS CodeDeploy
    - Amazon EC2 Container Service
    - AWS Lambda
    - Amazon API Gateway

- Management and monitoring capabilities for AWS cloud-native application architectures
- Patterns for moving off monolithic application architectures to AWS native architectures
- Sample reference architectures and code snippets for CI/CD, serverless, and microservices application architectures

To keep yourself updated on the latest AWS announcements and service launches news, subscribe to the following resources:

- What's new page (`https://aws.amazon.com/new`)
- AWS blog (`https://aws.amazon.com/blogs/aws`)

AWS' cloud native services (CNMM Axis-1)

As a start, let's look at the core services that AWS has to offer, which will be relevant to creating your applications in a cloud-native way.

Introduction

AWS offers a very rich portfolio of services that includes core components around infrastructure capabilities, such as Amazon EC2 (virtual servers in the cloud), Amazon EBS (block storage for EC2), Amazon S3 (cloud-based object storage), and Amazon VPC (isolated cloud resources using virtualized networks). These services have existed for multiple years now and are pretty mature for an enterprise-scale deployment level as well. Apart from scale, these services have very deep feature sets that provide ample options to the end customers to pick and choose configurations as per their specific business requirements. As an example, Amazon EC2 offers more than 50 different types of instances to cater to various possible workloads and use cases. So, if a customer to host a **high-performance computing** (HPC) workload, then there's an option to use *compute optimized* instances, whereas if you have a NoSQL database that is hungry for high IOPS with low storage latency, then *storage optimized* instances come in handy.

In fact, AWS has been adding newer instances types as well as updating to newer, faster processors with larger memory footprints every year, which makes it easier for the customers to leverage the latest and greatest compute configurations without having to worry about typical data center procurement and upgrade cycles. Likewise, on the storage and networking front, Amazon EBS, Amazon S3, and Amazon VPC provide multiple configuration options that can provide flexibility when required.

Couple of the biggest benefits that cloud provides are Elasticity and Agility, which basically means that you can spin up and down your infrastructure in lines with your application's needs. This is very different from the traditional data center approach, where everything had to provisioned for peaks, because of which the infrastructure resources were either way too underutilized or were not scalable for some unpredictable peaks. This has radically changed with the cloud, where providers such as AWS have come up with innovative services such as Auto Scaling, wherein you can automatically change your compute fleet size based on certain application behaviors, such as increased CPU utilization or even custom application monitoring metrics. Apart from triggers based on scaling, you can also autoscale the compute capacity based on time-based usage patterns, for example, hourly, daily, or weekly variability in usage. Very similar to compute autoscaling, AWS also offers Elastic EBS volumes, wherein you can increase volume size, adjust performance, or change the volume type while the volume is in use. These types of services and capabilities are definitely differentiators for the cloud and have in fact become the new normal to build web-scale applications. However, in order to use some of these autoscaling features, applications also need to be ready from an architecture standpoint. As an example, if you want to use autoscaling capabilities for your web server fleet to accommodate increased load on your website, then one of the core changes needed from an application standpoint is that you should not have session state information stored locally on any web server. The same should be externalized in a cache (such as Amazon ElastiCache) or even a database (such as Amazon DynamoDB), so that you can seamlessly scale up or down your webservers fleet without having to worry about a users' session disruption because of that.

The following is a sample architecture that AWS publishes for auto-scalable web applications using various core services:

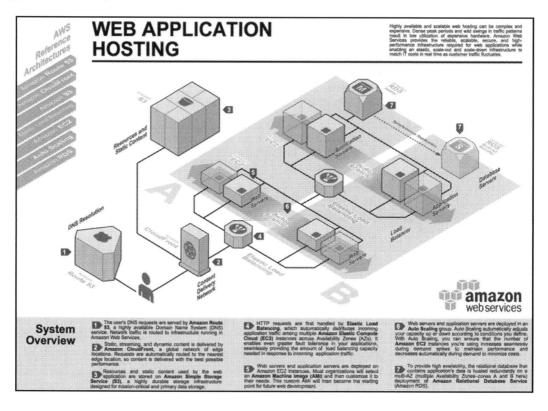

Web application hosting setup (Source – http://media.amazonwebservices.com/architecturecenter/AWS_ac_ra_web_01.pdf)

Now, over and above the core building blocks, such as the ones mentioned in the preceding diagram, AWS offers various higher-level managed services that make it easier for the end user to quickly start deploying their applications without having to worry too much about the underlying infrastructure. As an example, there's Amazon RDS, which is a managed relational database service for MySQL, PostgreSQL, Oracle, SQL Server, and MariaDB. Amazon RDS provides flexibility to set up and operate a relational database while automating time-consuming administration tasks, such as hardware provisioning, database setup, patching, and backups. So, by using this service, you can quickly get started with your database deployments without requiring any specific database administrator level skills. Apart from this, AWS also offers many other services, such as AWS Elastic Beanstalk (to run and manage web apps) and Amazon OpsWorks (to automate operations with Chef), which are like higher-level services in the category of PaaS.

Using these services, you can quickly get your applications running on AWS without getting into the nitty-gritty of the underlying infrastructure. With Amazon OpsWorks, you get an extra set of controls as well, wherein if you want to automate a specific application setup/launch procedure, then you have the capabilities to do that using your own custom Chef recipes.

Other than the preceding points, AWS also offers PaaS services in the big data / analytics and AI space, such as Amazon EMR (hosted Hadoop framework), Amazon Kinesis (works with real-time streaming data), Amazon Lex (builds voice and text chatbots), Amazon Rekognition (searches and analyzes images), and Amazon Polly (turns text into lifelike speech). Using these types of service, developers and data architects can easily create their applications by focusing more on the business logic than the underlying infrastructure management aspects.

Over the last few years, AWS has aggressively moved much further in terms of offering totally newer types of services, which are closer to SaaS. These are mainly the services as part of its business productivity category, such as Amazon Chime (a managed service for video calls and chat), Amazon WorkDocs (enterprise storage and sharing service), and Amazon Connect (managed contact center service). This is a fairly new area for AWS as well, but as these services along with the ecosystem matures, it will create new possibilities for end users to look at the cloud, not just from an infrastructure or platform perspective, but to also utilize productivity software in a pay-as-you-go model.

AWS platform – differentiators

As mentioned in `Chapter 1`, *Introducing Cloud Native Architecture*, CNMM is a maturity model wherein if you are using only core building blocks from the cloud (such as, infrastructure components), then you are also cloud-native, but might be less mature than someone else who might be using services higher up the stack to actually get the full benefits of Cloud. So, based on this concept, if you have to truly leverage the power of AWS cloud, then you should focus on a few of the areas that are talked about in the following sections.

KRADL services

As mentioned in the previous section, AWS has many innovative services that can help architect a multitude of use cases and business problems. However, there are few services that are like AWS differentiators, and so AWS highly recommends that you utilize those instead of trying to build your own comparative capabilities, which may not be as scalable, feature rich, or robust such as AWS offerings.

These services together are known as **KRADL**, and what each letter represents is as follows:

- **K**: Amazon Kinesis
- **R**: Amazon Redshift
- **A**: Amazon Aurora
- **D**: Amazon DynamoDB
- **L**: AWS Lambda

Let's analyze the preceding points in a little detail, based on AWS' definition of these services.

Amazon Kinesis: Amazon Kinesis makes it easy to collect, process, and analyze real-time streaming data so that you can get timely insights and react quickly to new information. With Amazon Kinesis, you can ingest real-time data such as application logs, website clickstreams, IoT telemetry data, and more into your databases, data lakes, and data warehouses, or build your own real-time applications using this data. Amazon Kinesis enables you to process and analyze data as it arrives and respond in real-time instead of having to wait until all of your data is collected before the processing can begin. More details are available at https://aws.amazon.com/kinesis/.

Amazon Redshift: Amazon Redshift is a fast, fully managed data warehouse that makes it simple and cost-effective to analyze all your data using standard SQL and your existing **business intelligence (BI)** tools. It allows you to run complex analytic queries against petabytes of structured data, using sophisticated query optimization, columnar storage on high-performance local disks, and massively parallel query execution. More details are available at https://aws.amazon.com/redshift/.

Amazon Aurora: Amazon Aurora is a MySQL and PostgreSQL-compatible relational database engine that combines the speed and availability of high-end commercial databases with the simplicity and cost-effectiveness of open source databases. It provides up to five times better performance than MySQL with the security, availability, and reliability of a commercial database at one tenth of the cost. Amazon Aurora is a managed database service, built on a fully distributed and self-healing storage system that keeps your data safe. More details are available at https://aws.amazon.com/rds/aurora/.

Amazon DynamoDB: Amazon DynamoDB is a fast and flexible NoSQL database service for all applications that need consistent, single-digit millisecond latency at any scale. It is a fully managed cloud database and supports both document and key-value store models. Its flexible data model, reliable performance, and automatic scaling of throughput capacity, makes it a great fit for mobile, web, gaming, ad tech, IoT, and many other applications. More details are available at https://aws.amazon.com/dynamodb/.

AWS Lambda: AWS Lambda lets you run code without provisioning or managing servers. You only pay for the compute time you consume – there is no charge when your code is not running. With Lambda, you can run code for virtually any type of application or backend service – all with zero administration. Just upload your code and Lambda takes care of everything required to run and scale your code with high availability. You can set up your code to automatically trigger from other AWS services or call it directly from any web or mobile app. More details are available at `https://aws.amazon.com/lambda/`.

Most of the preceding services are Amazon proprietary, so sometimes, end users become conscious about the fear of lock-in. However, the reality is that even in an on-premises world, customers make use of so many different packaged applications (such as databases and ERPs), which themselves are hard to get away with. So, it's more of a perception of lock-in than reality when the same logic is applied to these cloud-native services. In fact, if we take a deeper look, services such as Amazon Aurora and Amazon Redshift offer the same PostgreSQL/SQL interface, so that creates an easily portable mechanism for the applications to be rewired to another platform, if need be. Another perspective to it is that if the customer wants to create similar services on their own, then it will probably take quite a bit of time and effort to not just create but to operate as well as iterate on new features, like AWS does. So, at the end of the day, it's always beneficial to focus on your core business and rather consume these higher-level services from AWS.

Another angle to look at here is that the KRADL services are very unique to AWS platform compared to other cloud providers. For some of these, other cloud providers have come up with comparative offerings, but as AWS was first in the space with many of these and has been iterating regularly on new features ever since, they have the most mature offerings.

 Take a look at this interesting infographic from 2ndWatch, an AWS Consulting Partner, around their analysis of AWS' cloud-native services: `http://2ndwatch.com/wp-content/uploads/2017/05/Cloud-Native-Services.pdf`.

AWS native security services

One of the aspects that's key for any customer in a public cloud is to have the right security posture as per workloads and corporate governance policies. At times, it can be hard to map the controls from an on-premise environment to cloud, as it's not an apple to apple type of comparison. However, in recent times, AWS has innovated on many new services specifically in the security space, which aims to bring down this gap between on-premise controls to native AWS capabilities.

AWS has had the Amazon **identity and access management (IAM)** service for multiple years, using which you can manage your cloud-based users and groups and their access permissions on various AWS resources. With this service, you can enable fine-grained access controls (like, say, apply restrictions to specific API calls in your environment being allowed from specific IP address ranges), integrate with corporate directory to grant federated access, and even enable only **multi-factor authentication (MFA)** based actions on any service.

Now, IAM is a must-have service in order to operate in the AWS environment. However, a couple of other cloud-native services that are often missed but are highly useful for any type of environment are as follows:

- **AWS Key Management Service**: AWS **Key Management Service (KMS)** is a managed service that makes it easy for you to create and control the encryption keys used to encrypt your data, and uses **hardware security modules (HSMs)** to protect the security of your keys. AWS Key Management Service is integrated with several other AWS services to help you protect the data you store with these services. More details are available at `https://aws.amazon.com/kms/`.

- **AWS CloudTrail**: AWS CloudTrail is a service that enables governance, compliance, operational auditing, and risk auditing of your AWS account. With CloudTrail, you can log, continuously monitor, and retain events related to API calls across your AWS infrastructure. CloudTrail provides a history of AWS API calls for your account, including API calls made through the AWS Management Console, AWS SDKs, command-line tools, and other AWS services. More details are available at `https://aws.amazon.com/Cloudtrail/`.

Both of the preceding services are fully managed, integrated with various other AWS services, and super easy to use. In fact, with these type of easy to use and configurable services, the level of controls that any startup customer gets is the same as any enterprise customer using the AWS platform. This is the true power of democratization that cloud previous, wherein all the services or features are available to everyone, thereby making it a level playing field for innovation and new application models.

As a result of these cloud-native services, customers don't need to procure expensive key management appliances, buy, or build custom software packages to perform these must-enable functionalities for your deployments. Having said that, some of these services are only limited to cloud-based environments, so if you have a hybrid environment that includes on-premise infrastructure components, then having a single pane of glass to manage or monitor everything using these services becomes a little challenging.

Apart from the core capabilities that these services provide in terms of functionality, using advanced architectural patterns, one can also create self-learning or self-adapting security models as well. As an example, if you have enabled CloudTrail logging for your account, then based on the API activity logs that the service delivers in your Amazon S3 buckets, you may select to perform some specific actions dynamically if you find any unexpected activity or malicious usage of your AWS account resources. To orchestrate this entire use case, AWS Lambda can be pretty handy, wherein you can define your custom logic to not just detect but even react based on certain conditions. This can be further clubbed with advanced techniques such as machine learning or deep learning wherein instead of just reacting to specific conditions, you can actually build a model to train itself and pre-empt any conditions, even before they occur. Of course, this requires additional effort and greater expertise to create these types of self-adapting security systems, but with the type of service and building block that the cloud now provides, it's definitely possible to move in that direction.

Apart from AWS KMS and AWS CloudTrail, AWS has many other new security services that further help address specific use-cases:

- **Amazon Inspector**: Amazon Inspector is an automated security assessment service that helps improve the security and compliance of applications deployed on AWS. Amazon Inspector automatically assesses applications for vulnerabilities or deviations from best practices. After performing an assessment, Amazon Inspector produces a detailed list of security findings prioritized by level of severity. These findings can be reviewed directly or as part of detailed assessment reports that are available via the Amazon Inspector console or API. More details are available at `https://aws.amazon.com/inspector/`.

- **AWS Certificate Manager**: AWS Certificate Manager is a service that lets you easily provision, manage, and deploy **Secure Sockets Layer (SSL) / Transport Layer Security (TLS)** certificates for use with AWS services. SSL/TLS certificates are used to secure network communications and establish the identity of websites over the internet. AWS Certificate Manager removes the time-consuming manual process of purchasing, uploading, and renewing SSL/TLS certificates.

- **AWS WAF**: AWS WAF is a web application firewall that helps protect your web applications from common web exploits that could affect application availability, compromise security, or consume excessive resources. AWS WAF gives you control over which traffic to allow or block your web applications by defining customizable web security rules. You can use AWS WAF to create custom rules that block common attack patterns, such as SQL injection or cross-site scripting, and rules that are designed for your specific application. More details are available at `https://aws.amazon.com/waf/`.

- **AWS Shield**: AWS Shield is a managed **distributed denial of service (DDoS)** protection service that safeguards web applications running on AWS. AWS Shield provides always-on detection and automatic inline mitigations that minimize application downtime and latency, so there is no need to engage AWS Support to benefit from DDoS protection. More details are available at `https://aws.amazon.com/shield/`.

- **Amazon GuardDuty**: Amazon GuardDuty is a managed threat detection service that provides you with a more accurate and easy way to continuously monitor and protect your AWS accounts and workloads. More details are available at `https://aws.amazon.com/guardduty/`.

- **Amazon Macie**: Amazon Macie is a machine learning-powered security service to discover, classify, and protect sensitive data. More details are available at `https://aws.amazon.com/macie/`.

The biggest benefit of all of the previously mentioned cloud-native services is that you can start to utilize them at any point in time, without having to worry about license procurement, complex configuration, and so on. However, as these services are still new as compared to some of the enterprise ISV software packages with comparable functionalities, for more complex use cases or deeper feature/functionalities, they may not fully meet the needs. For those kind of scenarios, AWS also offers an AWS Marketplace, where multiple ISV partners have cloud-optimized software packages available, which are quick and easy to deploy in the AWS environment. So, depending on the use cases as well as feature set requirements, it's always advised to first evaluate these AWS cloud-native services and then, if need be, look at other ISV solutions.

Machine Learning/Artificial Intelligence

In the last couple of years, AWS has shown a serious commitment to take their offerings in machine-learning/artificial intelligence space to a completely different levels. During its annual developer conference (AWS re:Invent) in 2017, AWS made some big announcements on its ML/AI offerings, which have also gained immense popularity since then. The following are some of the services, which are key from AWS' ML/AI portfolio perspective:

- **Amazon SageMaker**: This enables data scientists and developers to quickly and easily build, train, and deploy machine learning models with high-performance machine learning algorithms, broad framework support, and one-click training, tuning, and inference. Amazon SageMaker has a modular architecture so that you can use any or all of its capabilities in your existing machine learning workflows. For more information, you can refer to `https://aws.amazon.com/sagemaker/`.

- **Amazon Rekognition**: This is a service that makes it easy to add powerful visual analysis to your applications. Rekognition Image lets you easily build powerful applications to search, verify, and organize millions of images. Rekognition Video lets you extract motion-based context from stored or live stream videos and helps you analyze them. For more information, you can refer to `https://aws.amazon.com/rekognition`.

- **Amazon Lex**: This is a service for building conversational interfaces using voice and text. Powered by the same conversational engine as Alexa, Amazon Lex provides high quality speech recognition and language understanding capabilities, enabling an addition of sophisticated, natural language chatbots to new and existing applications. For more information, you can refer to `https://aws.amazon.com/lex`.

- **Amazon Polly**: This is a service that turns text into life-like speech. It enables existing applications to speak as a first-class feature and creates the opportunity for entirely new categories of speech-enabled products, from mobile apps and cars, to devices and appliances. For more information, you can refer to `https://aws.amazon.com/polly`.

Other than the preceding services, AWS also supports many of the popular machine learning frameworks and libraries, which are used by data scientists and developers on a regular basis, including Apache MXNet, TensorFlow, PyTorch, the Microsoft **Cognitive Toolkit (CNTK)**, Caffe, Caffe2, Theano, Torch, Gluon, and Keras. These are offered as an **Amazon Machine Image (AMI)**, so it is pretty easy to get started with just a few clicks. This clubbed with the GPU compute instances and instances with **field programmable gate arrays (FPGAs)** make the processing of complex algorithms and models much faster and easier, thereby ensuring that the overall platform is comprehensive to address any kind of ML/AI use cases.

Object storage (S3, Glacier, ecosystem)

AWS offers multiple different types of storage services, such as for block storage, file storage, object storage, and archive storage. Although all of these services are independent of each other and can be used individually, for various use cases, customers make use of multiples of these services together to also provide various storage tiering options. As an example, Amazon EBS is the block storage that's attached to the Amazon EC2 instances for local data persistence as well as processing. Whenever data needed to be shared between multiple EC2 instances as file shares, Amazon EFS comes in handy as the same EFS share can be attached to EC2 instances using the NFS v4.1 interface.

Now, when data needs to be backed up, a long-term, more durable storage, then Amazon S3 comes into the picture, where not just raw data but even EBS volume snapshots are stored redundantly across various Availability Zones. For long term archival, data can be moved from Amazon S3 to Amazon Glacier. So, using this mechanism, a complete life cycle of data management can be created using multiple storage services.

Other than Amazon EBS, **Amazon Machine Images** (AMI) using which Amazon EC2 instances can be spun up, are also by default stored in Amazon S3. Likewise, all the logs, such as Amazon CloudTrail logs or Amazon CloudWatch logs, are also persisted in Amazon S3. Even AWS migration services such as AWS Snowball, AWS Database Migration Service, and AWS Server Migration Service all have integrations with Amazon S3. Likewise, for any big data architecture involving Amazon EMR, Amazon Redshift, or even Amazon Athena, Amazon S3 is a key component in the overall system. It acts either as a source or/and a target during the life cycle of data being sliced and diced for various analytical problems. Similarly, many other AWS services behind the scenes make use of Amazon S3 for object storage or even backup purposes.

As a result of all these different scenarios, Amazon S3 is one of the key AWS services that should be part of any cloud-native deployment on AWS. In fact, apart from integrations with various other AWS services, Amazon S3 also has deep feature set, which provides flexibility for various application needs. For example, within Amazon S3 there are multiple different storage classes, so depending on your object access patterns, durability, and availability requirements, any of these options can be utilized:

Storage Class	Durability (designed for)	Availability (designed for)	Use case
STANDARD	99.999999999%	99.99%	Ideal for performance-sensitive use cases and frequently accessed data
STANDARD_IA	99.999999999%	99.9%	Optimized for long-lived and less frequently accessed data, for example, backups and older data where frequency of access has diminished, but the use case still demands high performance
Reduced Redundancy Storage (RRS)	99.99%	99.99%	Meant for non-critical, reproducible data that's stored at lower levels of redundancy than the STANDARD storage class

Amazon S3 also has multiple security-related functionalities, like encryption options (server side or client side encryption), versioning of objects to retain history, and MFA protection on object deletion.

Amazon S3 also has a rich ecosystem of ISV partners that either integrate directly with Amazon S3 APIs or use it as a source or a target for multiple storage related use cases. You should look at Amazon's Storage partner solutions at `https://aws.amazon.com/backup-recovery/partner-solutions/` to understand the current ISVs that support Amazon S3 (and other storage services) as part of their solutions.

Based on the preceding points, Amazon S3 is clearly a service that is central to many architectures and is definitely a service that cannot and should not be ignored for any cloud-native deployments. Some sample cloud-native use cases that might be applicable for multiple users are as follows:

- **Web applications**: Amazon S3 can be used as a storage for static content, such as videos, images, HTML pages, CSS and other client-side scripts. So, if you have a totally static website, then there's no need of any web server; just use Amazon S3! If you have global user base and want to cache frequently accessed content in locations closer to your users, then Amazon S3 along with Amazon CloudFront can be a great combination.

- **Logs storage**: For an end-to-end system, there are multiple logs that are generated by various applications and even infrastructure components. These can be persisted locally on disks and analyzed by solutions such as **Elasticsearch, Logstash, and Kibana (ELK)**. However, at scale, lots of customers use Amazon S3 as a sink for all the logs wherein log data from various sources can be streamed to S3 using either open source options such as Fluentd (`https://www.fluentd.org/`), AWS Services (such as CloudWatch Logs or Amazon Kinesis), or commercial ISV offerings (such as Sumologic) that are there in the AWS Marketplace as well. Irrespective of the solution to stream the data or analyze it, Amazon S3 is good candidate for any type of log. In fact, as logs get older, they can be either purged or even transitioned to a less expensive storage (Amazon S3-IA or Amazon Glacier) by using life cycle policies.

- **Data lakes** - Amazon S3 is a great service that can be used to create very highly scalable data lakes, where pre-processed, processed, or even intermediate data can be stored throughout the data processing pipeline. AWS has a reference architecture and an automated deployment module, which further showcases the use of Amazon S3 as a central service in this scenario. You can read about it at `http://docs.aws.amazon.com/solutions/latest/data-lake-solution/welcome.html`.

- **Event-driven architectures** - APIs and loosely coupled architectures are a common pattern these days. Along with APIs comes in a paradigm of having event driven architectures, wherein with a simple API invocation, you can trigger a series of workflows of backend processing. Now, although there are multiple components involved in this type of architectural pattern, from a storage perspective, Amazon S3 can be a pivotal component for a couple of use cases:

  - Suppose you have an API/event-driven architecture to kick-start a media processing pipeline, so for that all the raw media mezzanine objects can be stored in Amazon S3. Likewise, post processing the final video/audio/image output can be put in S3 to be delivered using Amazon CloudFront.

  - Coordination between various services can happen using Amazon S3 as a storage and trigger mechanism. As an example, let's consider there's a Service-A, which starts processing objects in Bucket-A. After it's done, it writes the object in Bucket-B, which then sends an event notification for, say, an `s3:ObjectCreated:*` event, which can be handled by Amazon Lambda functions to trigger on the next step in the workflow. So, this can continue to create a loosely coupled pipeline that is based off S3 as a coordination mechanism.

- **Batch processing** - AWS launched a service for batch computing use cases, called AWS Batch. Although this service can be used for multiple use cases, however, big data/analytics types of use cases are the most common. As a result, Amazon S3 becomes a key service here with its ability to store and process objects at scale. As an example, the following diagram from the AWS website demonstrates batch computing use case from a Financial Services industry wherein data from various sources is collected at the end of the day to run reports and view market performance. So, as is evident, Amazon S3 becomes a sort of master storage for various processing layers down the line:

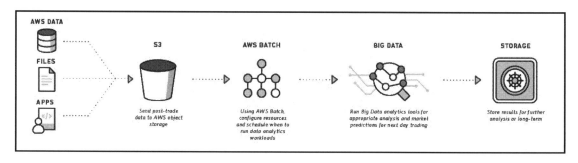

Processing layers (Source – https://aws.amazon.com/batch/use-cases/#financial-services)

Application centric design (CNMM Axis-2)

In the previous section, we saw some of the key cloud-native services that AWS has to offer. Now, in this section, we will look at the second axis of CNMM on how to create AWS native architectures. Although there are multiple different architectures and approaches, we will focus on two key patterns – serverless and microservices. In fact, these two patterns are related as well since the services that help us create a serverless pattern are also applicable to creating smaller, single functionality, fine-grained services in a system. So, let's explore more about how to create a microservice that is also serverless in nature in the next section.

Serverless microservice

The core concept around a serverless microservice is a three-step pipeline, such as the one shown in the following diagram:

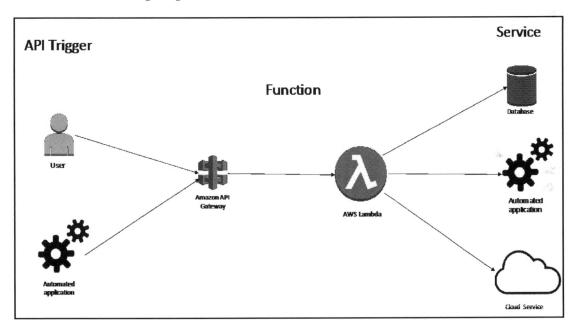

Three-step pipeline

Let's discuss these steps in detail.

API trigger

The microservice can be invoked in two ways as follows:

- An end user who's directly interacting with a web-based portal (or even CLI commands)
- An automated application or another microservice that invokes this service in the chain of an orchestrated workflow

The APIs can also be invoked with some system events, which can then be used to trigger an API with a scripted mechanism.

Function

Once the API is invoked by the *Trigger* layer, it's received by the Amazon API Gateway, which can perform traffic management, authorization and access control, validation, transformation, and monitoring followed by invoking the backend, which in this case would be hosted in AWS Lambda.

AWS Lambda is a serverless compute environment, wherein you simply upload your code (Node.js, Python, Java, or C#), define the trigger, and the rest is handled by the service. So, as in the preceding sample architecture, API Gateway will invoke the Lambda function to execute the business logic there. Within that business logic, you can perform any type of action, which is also detailed in the following section.

Service

Within the AWS Lambda function, although you can perform any backend action, the following are the most common ones that most customers perform:

- Do the entire processing within the AWS Lambda function, which may involve data processing to transformation, local scripts execution, and so on, and finally the result is stored in a data store for long-term persistence. A perfect choice for lots of customers in this scenario is Amazon DynamoDB, which again extends the serverless architecture with no host to manage and is easy to integrate with AWS Lambda with API/SDKs.
- For interacting with another third-party external service or even another microservice within the same environment, many customers use AWS Lambda to invoke those other services. These invocations can be synchronous or asynchronous, depending on the use case.

- Another possibility here is to integrate with other cloud services to perform some other actions. As an example, suppose you want to trigger a LAMP stack creation using an API, so in this case you could invoke CloudFormation from your Lambda code to bring up a new LAMP stack environment.

These are just examples on how to create serverless microservices in AWS, but generally the possibilities are infinite.

Serverless microservice – sample walkthrough

Now that we have covered the basics of a serverless microservice in AWS, let's do some hands-on exercises with a sample application using multiple AWS services.

So, let's create an actual microservice to retrieve weather information for any location. For this, we will use the following architectural components:

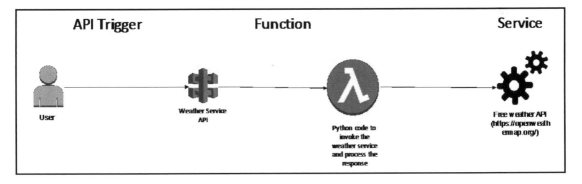

Architectural components

AWS Lambda function creation and configuration

Sign in to the AWS console and select the **Lambda** from the under the **Compute** services. Then, follow these instructions to create a Lambda function:

1. Click on the **Create a function** button.
2. Select the **Blueprint** option, and choose the **microservice-http-endpoint-python3** blueprint.

3. Click on the **Configure** option, and then specify the following values. The following values will be used to configure the Amazon API Gateway endpoint for this microservice:

   1. Set **API Name** to `Serverless Weather Service`.

   2. Set **Deployment Stage** to `prod`.

   3. For **Security**, set it to **Open**. Using this as the option, we will be able to access our API without any credentials (for production workloads, it's always recommended to enable API security with either the **AWS IAM** or **Open with** access key options).

4. In **Create function**, specify the following values:

   1. Basic information section:

      1. Enter a function name (for example, `WeatherServiceFunction`).

      2. Select **Python 3.6** from the **Runtime** list.

      3. For **Description**, use **cloud-native - Serverless Weather Service**.

   2. Lambda function code:

      1. In the **Code Entry Type** field, select the **Upload a .zip file** option. Get the sample Python code ZIP file, `Cloudnative-weather-service.zip`, from the `https://github.com/PacktPublishing/Cloud-Native-Architectures` GitHub location and upload it.

   3. Lambda function handler and role:

      1. For the handler, specify the value as `lambda_function.lambda_handler`.

      2. For the **Role**, select the option **Create new role from template(s)**.

      3. For the **Role Name**, specify **WeatherServiceLambdaRole**.

      4. In the **Policy Templates** option, select the dropdown with the value **Simple Microservice Permissions**.

   4. Tags:

      1. Specify **Key** as `Name` and **Value** as `Serverless Weather Microservice`.

2. Advanced settings:
   1. Set the **Memory** selection to **128 MB**.
   2. Set **Timeout** value as 0 minutes and 30 seconds.
   3. Leave the rest of the settings with the default value.

5. After the preceding configurations are done, review the settings on the final screen and hit **Create function**. In a matter of a few minutes, your Lambda function will be created and you should be able to view it on the **Functions** list, as follows:

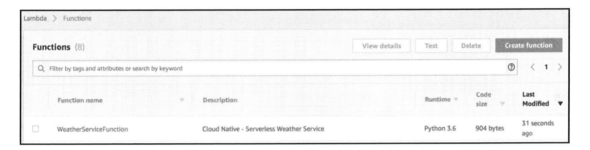

As for the logic, within the Lambda code, it's a simple code that does three things:

- Retrieves the `zip` and `appid` parameters from the received request.
- Invokes the `GET` operation on OpenWeatherMap's API with the `zip` and `appid` parameters as inputs.
- Receives the response and sends it back to the API Gateway to be returned to the end user.

The code is as follows:

```
import boto3
import json
from urllib.request import Request, urlopen
from urllib.error import URLError, HTTPError

print('Loading function')

def respond(err, res=None):
    return {
        'statusCode': '400' if err else '200',
        'body': err if err else res,
        'headers': {
            'Content-Type': 'application/json',
        },
```

```
    }

def lambda_handler(event, context):
    '''Demonstrates a simple HTTP endpoint using API Gateway. You have full
access to the request and response payload, including headers andstatus
code.'''
    print("Received event: " + json.dumps(event, indent=2))

    zip = event['queryStringParameters']['zip']
    print('ZIP -->' + zip)
    appid = event['queryStringParameters']['appid']
    print('Appid -->>' + appid)
    baseUrl = 'http://api.openweathermap.org/data/2.5/weather'
    completeUrl = baseUrl + '?zip=' + zip + '&appid=' + appid
    print('Request URL--> ' + completeUrl)

    req = Request(completeUrl)
    try:
        apiresponse = urlopen(completeUrl)
    except HTTPError as e:
        print('The server couldn\'t fulfill the request.')
        print('Error code: ', e.code)
        errorResponse = '{Error:The server couldn\'t fulfill the request: '
+ e.reason +'}'
        return respond(errorResponse, e.code)
    except URLError as e:
        print('We failed to reach a server.')
        print('Reason: ', e.reason)
        errorResponse = '{Error:We failed to reach a server: ' + e.reason
+'}'
        return respond(e, e.code)
    else:
        headers = apiresponse.info()
        print('DATE    :', headers['date'])
        print('HEADERS :')
        print('---------')
        print(headers)
        print('DATA :')
        print('---------')
        decodedresponse = apiresponse.read().decode('utf-8')
        print(decodedresponse)
        return respond(None, decodedresponse)
```

Configuring the Amazon API Gateway

After performing the preceding steps, go to the **Amazon API Gateway** service in the **AWS Console** and you should see an API like the following already created:

Now, let's configure this API to match our needs:

1. Click on the API's name, **Serverless Weather Service**, to drill down into its configuration.
2. Select the **Resources** option on the left-hand side and then on the right-hand side, expand the resources to show `/WeatherServiceFunction/ANY` and you should see its details as follows:

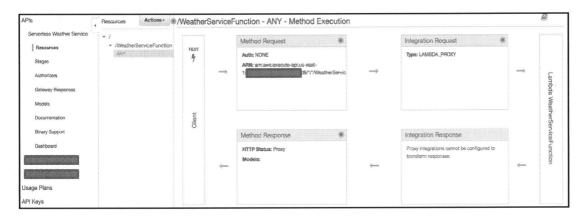

The Resources option view

3. Click on **Method Request** and expand the **URL Query String Parameters** option. Under that, use the **Add query string** button to add the following parameters:
   1. Set the name to `zip` and check the **Required** checkbox.
   2. Add another parameter, set the name to `appid`, and check the **Required** checkbox.

4. In the preceding pane, select the **Request Validator** option and set its value to **Validate body, query string parameters, and headers**.

5. After completing the preceding settings, your **Method Execution** screen should look as follows:

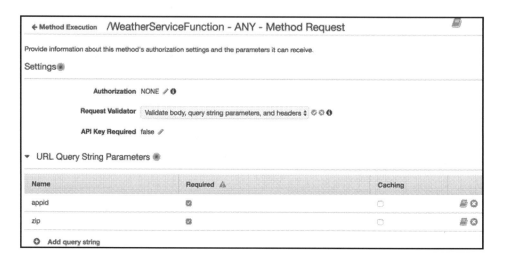

Setting up a Weather Service Account

In order to get the latest weather information, our microservice will invoke APIs from a third-party weather service, OpenWeatherMap (`https://openweathermap.org`). So, go to the URL and create a new, free account. Once you have created an account, go to your account settings and note down the API key from the following option:

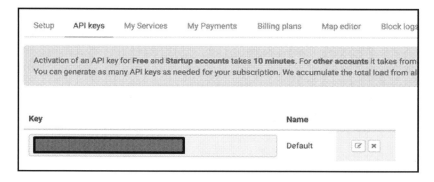

The API keys tab

This key will be used to authenticate our API calls to the OpenWeatherMap service.

Testing the service

Now that we have all the necessary pieces set up, let's go back to the Amazon API Console and try testing the service. For that, follow these steps:

1. Open the `/WeatherServiceFunction/ANY` file under the Resources option, and hit the **Test** option.
2. Under the method, select **Get** as the option.
3. For the query string, we need two inputs: the ZIP code of the city for which you want to query the current weather and the OpenWeatherMap's API key. To do this, create a query string such as `zip=<<zip-value>>&appid=<<app-id>>`. In this, replace the italicized values with actual inputs and form a string such as `zip=10001&appid=abcdefgh9876543qwerty`.
4. Hit the **Test** button at the bottom of the screen to invoke the API and the Lambda function.
5. If the test is successful, you will see a response with **Status: 200**, and in the response body, you will get the weather information in a JSON format, as follows:

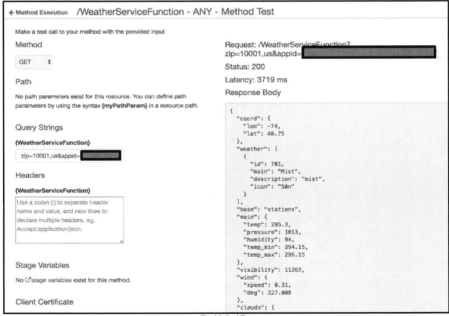

The Method Test

If there's an error in test execution, check the logs in the bottom half of the screen to debug the issue.

Deploying the API

After successfully testing the API, we have to deploy the API as well so that it can be active in the **prod** environment. For that, select the **Deploy API** option from the **Actions** drop-down menu within the API configuration screen, as follows:

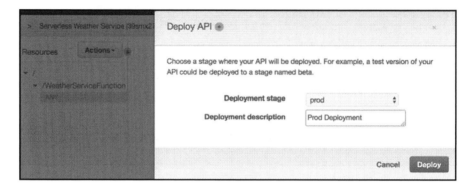

Once the API is deployed, you can go to the **Stages** option on the left-hand side, select the **prod** stage, and under that, **GET** the HTTP method, as follows:

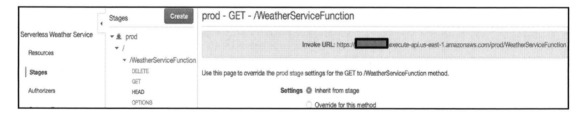

The Stages option

You can copy the deployed API's URL and try accessing it by providing the `zip` and the `appid` parameters as part of the URL as follows:

```
https://asdfgh.execute-api.us-east-1.amazonaws.com/prod/WeatherServiceFunct
ion?zip=10001,us&appid=qwertyasdfg98765zxcv
```

 Note: Please replace the highlighted text with your environment's specific values.

To make the testing process of the deployed API easier, you can also use the sample HTML page, which is available at the `https://github.com/PacktPublishing/Cloud-Native-Architectures` GitHub link, as follows:

1. Download the HTML page, edit the source to update your API endpoint on *line 28*, and save it:

```
<form method="get" action="https://<<updated-
endpoint>>>/Prod/weatherservice">
```

2. Open the web page in a browser, supply the required field values, and hit the **Get Weather** button to retrieve the weather for that location:

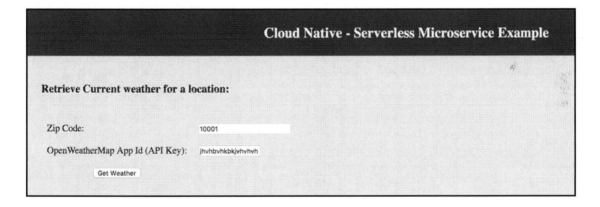

Serverless microservice automation using AWS SAM

As we learned in the previous section, it's very easy to build a simple serverless microservice from the AWS console. However, if you have to do the same using an automated and scripted way, then there are other mechanisms to achieve it. One of the most popular ways in the AWS environment is to use AWS CloudFormation, wherein you can create your own templates to describe the AWS resources, and any associated dependencies or runtime parameters, required to run your application. You can also visualize your templates as diagrams and edit them using a drag-and-drop interface, or even use the AWS command-line interface or APIs to manage the infrastructure components. Since everything you do in CloudFormation is using JSON or YAML formatted text files, as a result you are effectively managing your infrastructure as code.

Using AWS CloudFormation, you can create and update AWS Lambda, API Gateway, and various other services, which might compose your serverless microservice. Now, although this is easy to do, sometimes you have a simple application and rather than writing a pretty long and elaborate CloudFormation, it's better to use some other mechanisms. For the same reason, Amazon created the AWS **Serverless Application Model** (**SAM**), which is natively supported by AWS CloudFormation and provides a simplified way of defining the Amazon API Gateway APIs, AWS Lambda functions, and Amazon DynamoDB tables needed by your serverless application.

AWS SAM is a powerful way to create your serverless applications quickly as it requires significantly less code and configurations as compared to CloudFormation. To use SAM to create your applications, you primarily need three things:

- A SAM YAML template with configurations of your resources (Lambda function, API Gateway, and DynamoDB tables)
- An AWS Lambda function code `.zip` file
- An API Gateway's API definition in a Swagger format

 You can find more information on AWS SAM at the following GitHub repository: `https://github.com/awslabs/serverless-application-model/`.

Now, in order to create the same weather serverless microservice example using AWS SAM, let's look at the steps and code snippets.

SAM YAML template

The following is the SAM YAML template for the Weather Service example. It broadly consists of three components:

- An API Gateway definition that points to the Swagger file for detailed configuration.
- An AWS Lambda function configuration with a link to code the .zip file, handler name, and runtime environment. In order to link this Lambda function with the API gateway instance, it also has details on the REST API methods and the URI paths, which will be used as triggers to the Lambda function.
- The final section is around output, which is basically the URI of the API endpoint once the entire stack has been created by SAM:

```
AWSTemplateFormatVersion: '2010-09-09'
Transform: AWS::Serverless-2016-10-31
Description: A simple cloud-native Microservice sample, including
an AWS SAM template with API defined in an external Swagger file
along with Lambda integrations and CORS configurations

Resources:
  ApiGatewayApi:
    Type: AWS::Serverless::Api
    Properties:
      DefinitionUri: ./cloud-native-api-swagger.yaml
      StageName: Prod

Variables:
        # NOTE: Before using this template, replace the <<region>>
and <<account>> fields
        # in Lambda integration URI in the swagger file to region
and accountId
        # you are deploying to
        LambdaFunctionName: !Ref LambdaFunction

  LambdaFunction:
    Type: AWS::Serverless::Function
    Properties:
      CodeUri: ./Cloudnative-weather-service.zip
      Handler: lambda_function.lambda_handler
      Runtime: python3.6
      Events:
        ProxyApiRoot:
          Type: Api
          Properties:
            RestApiId: !Ref ApiGatewayApi
```

```
            Path: /weatherservice
            Method: get
      ProxyApiGreedy:
        Type: Api
        Properties:
          RestApiId: !Ref ApiGatewayApi
          Path: /weatherservice
          Method: options
```

The output from the preceding code is as follows:

```
ApiUrl:
  Description: URL of your API endpoint
  Value: !Join
    - ''
    - - https://
        - !Ref ApiGatewayApi
        - '.execute-api.'
        - !Ref 'AWS::Region'
        - '.amazonaws.com/Prod'
        - '/weatherservice'
```

API definition Swagger file

APIs are everywhere these days, including in packaged applications, cloud services, custom applications, and devices. However, it can be a nightmare for different applications to integrate with each other if everyone used their own standards and mechanisms to define and declare their API interfaces. So, to help with the standardization process and bring some structure to the world of REST APIs, the OpenAPI initiative was created. More details can be found at `https://www.openapis.org/`.

In order to create APIs that are compliant with **OpenAPI Specification (OAS)**, Swagger (`https://swagger.io/`) provides various tools that help enable development across the entire API life cycle, from design and documentation to test and deployment.

The AWS API Gateway supports importing or exporting API definitions from the Swagger API format, which is YAML based. To better integrate with the AWS API Gateway, there are additional elements that can be added to the Swagger definition, and the following is a sample YAML for the serverless weather microservice, which has both standard Swagger elements with AWS API Gateway-specific configuration parameters.

In order to use this sample in your environment, please update the region and AWS account number parameters as per your AWS account settings in the following template:

```yaml
swagger: "2.0"
info:
  title: "Weather Service API"
basePath: "/prod"
schemes:
- "https"
paths:
  /weatherservice:
    get:
      produces:
      - "application/json"
      parameters:
      - name: "appid"
        in: "query"
        required: true
        type: "string"
      - name: "zip"
        in: "query"
        required: true
        type: "string"
      responses:
        200:
          description: "200 response"
          schema:
            $ref: "#/definitions/Empty"
      x-amazon-apigateway-request-validator: "Validate body, query string
parameters,\
          \ and headers"
      x-amazon-apigateway-integration:
        responses:
          default:
            statusCode: "200"
        uri: arn:aws:apigateway:us-
east-1:lambda:path/2015-03-31/functions/arn:aws:lambda:region:account-
number:function:${stageVariables.LambdaFunctionName}/invocations
        passthroughBehavior: "when_no_match"
        httpMethod: "POST"
        contentHandling: "CONVERT_TO_TEXT"
        type: "aws_proxy"
    options:
      consumes:
      - "application/json"
      produces:
      - "application/json"
      responses:
```

```
        200:
          description: "200 response"
          schema:
            $ref: "#/definitions/Empty"
          headers:
            Access-Control-Allow-Origin:
              type: "string"
            Access-Control-Allow-Methods:
              type: "string"
            Access-Control-Allow-Headers:
              type: "string"
      x-amazon-apigateway-integration:
        responses:
          default:
            statusCode: "200"
            responseParameters:
              method.response.header.Access-Control-Allow-Methods:
  "'DELETE,GET,HEAD,OPTIONS,PATCH,POST,PUT'"
              method.response.header.Access-Control-Allow-Headers:
  "'Content-Type,Authorization,X-Amz-Date,X-Api-Key,X-Amz-Security-Token'"
              method.response.header.Access-Control-Allow-Origin: "'*'"
          requestTemplates:
            application/json: "{\"statusCode\": 200}"
          passthroughBehavior: "when_no_match"
          type: "mock"
definitions:
  Empty:
    type: "object"
    title: "Empty Schema"
x-amazon-apigateway-request-validators:
  Validate body, query string parameters, and headers:
    validateRequestParameters: true
    validateRequestBody: true
```

AWS Lambda code

The Python-based Lambda code for this application is the same as it was in an earlier section. You can download the ZIP file from the `https://github.com/PacktPublishing/Cloud-Native-Architectures` GitHub location.

AWS SAM usage

Behind the scenes, AWS SAM uses AWS CloudFormation's change sets functionality (`http://docs.aws.amazon.com/AWSCloudFormation/latest/UserGuide/using-cfn-updating-stacks-changesets.html`). In order to create our serverless weather microservice example using SAM, follow these steps:

1. Download the SAM YAML template, API Gateway Swagger file, and AWS Lambda code `.zip` file in a single directory.

2. Create an Amazon S3 bucket (from the AWS console or the API) with any available name, such as `CloudNative-WeatherService`.

3. Now, it's time to upload the Lambda code and Swagger API file definition to the S3 bucket you created in the previous step and then update the SAM YAML file with their S3 locations. To do this, you can use the following AWS CLI command, which automatically handles all of this and creates a resultant SAM YAML file, which can be used in successive steps:

   ```
   aws Cloudformation package \
   --template-file ./Cloudnative-weather-microservice.yaml\
   --s3-bucket CloudNative-WeatherService \
   --output-template-file Cloudnative-weather-microservice-
   packaged.yaml
   ```

    If you don't have AWS CLI already installed and configured, then please refer the AWS documentation at `http://docs.aws.amazon.com/cli/latest/userguide/installing.html`.

4. Once the packaging command is completed successfully, the next step is to start with the actual deployment. For this, use the following command, specifying the packaged YAML file from the previous step and the name of the stack that you are about to create:

   ```
   aws Cloudformation deploy \
   --template-file ./Cloudnative-weather-microservice=-packaged.yaml\
   --stack-name weather-service-stack \
   --capabilities CAPABILITY_IAM
   ```

5. Once the preceding command completes successfully, you can go to the AWS CloudFormation console to see the stack status there. From the Outputs tab of the completed CloudFormation stack, you will see a parameter called **ApiURL** with a value of your API Gateway's Weather Service API endpoint. With that, your API is all set and you can test the same using the procedure which was explained in previous sections.

Automation in AWS (CNMM Axis-3)

Amazon has had a long-time culture of having smaller teams that are self-contained, fully responsible for an end-to-end execution from planning to operations. These teams are nimble, have different roles (product management, developer, QA engineer, infra/tooling engineers, and so on) to manage all aspects of the software delivery cycle, but the team is big enough to be fed by two pizzas!

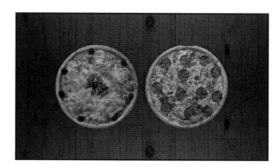

The whole concept around the two-pizza team is to keep them independent, fast moving, and better collaborating to avoid any overheads in terms of communication and processes. This is also an ideal setup from a DevOps perspective, where the team is responsible for a complete release life cycle, which also includes deploying to production environments and infrastructure management.

The other benefit that this setup provides is that each team is responsible for a specific piece of business functionality that often integrates with other components in the system using simple APIs that are REST/HTTP-based. This is essentially the core concept around a microservice, which further brings in agility and loosely connected components to bring in greater resilience and scalability to the overall system.

Amazon has multiple different businesses and teams internally that follow these principles and provide everyone with a common scalable software deployment platform, called **Apollo**. This deployment service has been used by thousands of developers across Amazon over multiple years, so it has been iterated upon and made robust for enterprise grade standards.

If you are interested in learning more about the story of Apollo, then refer this blog post by Werner Vogels, the Amazon CTO: http://www.allthingsdistributed.com/2014/11/apollo-amazon-deployment-engine.html.

Based on this internal experience, Amazon has created many of the AWS capabilities as well. They range from simple APIs, SDKs, and CLI support, to fully-fledged services to enable source code management, continuous integration, and continuous delivery/deployment to software pipeline management. We will explore more of these in the next section.

Infrastructure as code

One of the core benefits of the cloud is the capabilities it provides for infrastructure automation and treating everything like code. Though AWS has REST APIs for all the services offers and also supports various Software development kits for various popular programming languages (such as Java, .NET, Python, Android, and iOS), over and above these is one of the most powerful services it has: AWS CloudFormation.

AWS CloudFormation gives developers and systems administrators an easy way to create and manage a collection of related AWS resources, provisioning and updating them in an orderly and predictable fashion. The following is a sample CloudFormation Designer depiction of a simple deployment, which has an EC2 instance with one EBS volume and an Elastic IP address:

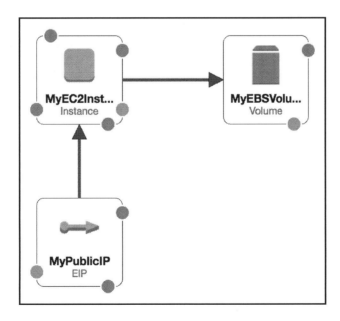

Now, when this simple deployment is turned into a YAML CloudFormation template, it looks like the following:

```yaml
AWSTemplateFormatVersion: 2010-09-09
Resources:
  MyEC2Instance:
    Type: 'AWS::EC2::Instance'
    Properties:
      ImageId: ami-2f712546
      InstanceType: t2.micro
      Volumes:
        - VolumeId: !Ref EC2V7IM1
  MyPublicIP:
    Type: 'AWS::EC2::EIP'
    Properties:
      InstanceId: !Ref MyEC2Instance
  EIPAssociation:
    Type: 'AWS::EC2::EIPAssociation'
    Properties:
      AllocationId: !Ref EC2EIP567DU
      InstanceId: !Ref EC2I41BQT
  MyEBSVolume:
    Type: 'AWS::EC2::Volume'
    Properties:
      VolumeType: io1
      Iops: '200'
      DeleteOnTermination: 'false'
      VolumeSize: '20'
  EC2VA2D4YR:
    Type: 'AWS::EC2::VolumeAttachment'
    Properties:
      VolumeId: !Ref EC2V7IM1
      InstanceId: !Ref EC2I41BQT
  EC2VA20786:
    Type: 'AWS::EC2::VolumeAttachment'
    Properties:
      InstanceId: !Ref MyEC2Instance
      VolumeId: !Ref MyEBSVolume
```

Now that your core infrastructure components have been turned into a scripted fashion, it's very easy to manage them like any other application code, which can be checked in to a code repository, changes can be tracked at the time of committing, and can be reviewed before deployment to the production environment. This whole concept is known as **Infrastructure-as-Code**, and helps not just with routine automation but also enables deeper DevOps practices in any environment.

Apart from AWS' services, there are many popular third-party tools such as Chef, Puppet, Ansible, and Terraform, which further help operating infrastructure components in a scripted, code-like manner.

CI/CD for applications on Amazon EC2, Amazon Elastic Beanstalk

AWS provides a bunch of services to create your application's Continuous Integration and Continuous Deployment pipelines natively on AWS. There are also many popular tools, such as Jenkins, Bamboo, TeamCity, and Git, that can either be independently set up on AWS or even integrated with the CI/CD services that AWS offers. As a whole, there are plenty of options and users can pick and choose the right ones as per their needs:

Capability	AWS Service	Other tools
Source code repository, version control, branching, tagging, and so on	AWS CodeCommit	Git, **Apache Subversion (SVN)**, Mercurial
Compiles source code and produces software packages that are ready to deploy	AWS CodeBuild	Jenkins, CloudBees, Solano CI, TeamCity
Tests automation covering functionality, security, performance, or compliance	No direct AWS services, but AWS CodeBuild can integrate with various testing tools	Apica, Blazemeter, Runscope, Ghost Inspector
Automated code deployments to any instance	AWS CodeDeploy	XebiaLabs

Apart from the preceding services, AWS also offers two other services that help in DevOps-related implementations:

AWS CodePipeline: This helps you fully model and automate your software release processes in the form of pipelines. A pipeline defines your release process workflow, and describes how a new code change progresses through your release process. A pipeline comprises a series of stages (for example, build, test, and deploy), which act as logical divisions in your workflow.

The following is a sample CodePipeline based CI/CD pipeline and uses various other services like AWS CodeCommit, AWS CodeBuild, AWS Lambda, Amazon SNS, and AWS CodeDeploy to orchestrate the entire process. As CodePipeline integrates with AWS Lambda, it also gives you additional options to customize actions and workflows in line with your CI/CD process requirements:

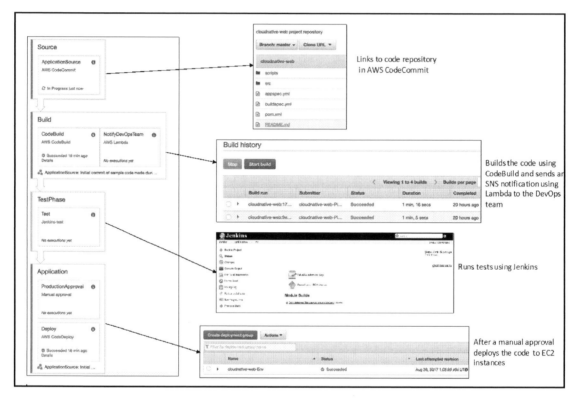

A sample CodePipeline based CI/CD pipeline

Using the previously mentioned CI/CD process, you can either have in-place updates, which is code being deployed to the same EC2 instances, or have a new fleet of instances to perform Blue/Green deployment, in which Blue is the current environment and Green is the new environment with the latest code changes. The concept of Blue/Green deployments is also based on the cloud best practices of *immutable infrastructure*, wherein your instances and environment are totally replaced rather than being updated in case of any new configuration or code release. This is analogous to the immutable variables in many programming constructs where you instantiate them once and they can never be updated, which makes the process of any changes easy and consistent, avoiding any conflicts, as it's always a new variable or instance.

The main benefits of performing **Blue/Green** deployments are as follows:

- You don't touch an existing environment, thereby making the application updates less risky
- You can gradually roll over to the new (**Green**) environment and can easily roll back over to the previous (**Blue**) deployment if there are any issues
- You treat the infrastructure as code, baking the entire process of creating **Blue/Green** deployments within your application deployment scripts and processes

The following is a sample **Blue/Green** deployment using AWS CodeDeploy, where you replace an autoscaled set of EC2 instances behind an ELB (**Blue** environment), to a new set of autoscaled instances (**Green** environment). You can find more details on the process in the AWS documentation at `http://docs.aws.amazon.com/codedeploy/latest/userguide/welcome.html#welcome-deployment-overview-blue-green`:

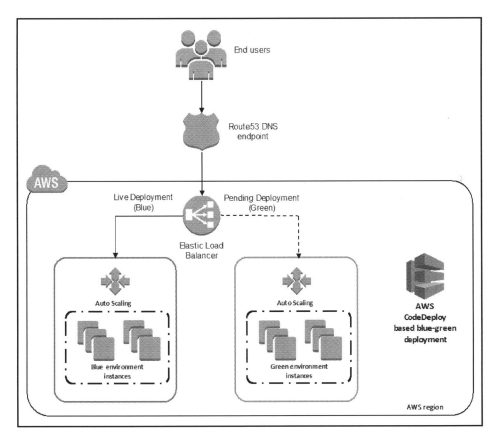

In order to quickly use and integrate the various AWS DevOps oriented services, AWS has another service called AWS CodeStar. This service provides a unified user interface and a project management dashboard, including an integrated issue tracking capability, enabling you to easily manage your software development activities in one place. This service also offers various templates of sample applications that can deployed to Amazon EC2, AWS Elastic Beanstalk, and AWS Lambda, and managed using various DevOps services. The following is a screenshot of the AWS CodeStar dashboard for one of the provided sample applications:

AWS CodeStar dashboard

CI/CD for serverless applications

The process to manage the CI/CD pipelines is very similar to the process described in the previous section around managing application environments in Amazon EC2. The main steps involved for automating this process for a serverless application are as follows:

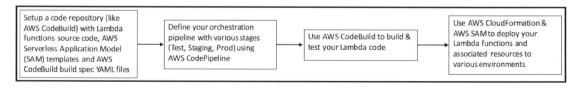

CI/CD for Amazon ECS (Docker containers)

Containers have revolutionized the software packaging aspects, by enabling the creation of lightweight, standalone, and executable packages of a piece of software that includes everything needed to run it: code, runtime, system tools, system libraries, and settings that can be deployed on various computing environments. Although there are multiple different types of container platforms, one of the most popular ones is Docker containers. Amazon offers the Amazon **EC2 Container Service** (**ECS**) and Amazon **Elastic Container Service for Kubernetes** (**EKS**) to deploy and manage Docker containers at scale and in a reliable fashion. Amazon ECS and Amazon EKS also integrate with various other AWS services such as Elastic Load Balancing, EBS volumes, and IAM roles to make the process of deploying various container-based applications even easier. Along with Amazon ECS and Amazon EKS, AWS also offers an Amazon **EC2 Container Registry** (**ECR**) to store, manage, and deploy Docker container images to an Amazon ECS-based environment.

In order to build a CI/CD workflow to deploy various application versions on to Amazon ECS, the following is a high-level workflow using services such as AWS CodePipeline, AWS CodeBuild, AWS CloudFormation, and Amazon ECR:

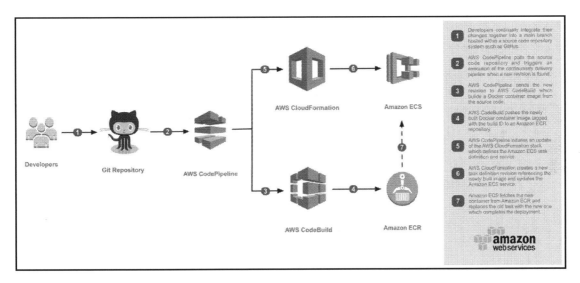

Workflow using different services

CI/CD for security services – DevSecOps

As discussed in the previous section, AWS has multiple cloud-native AWS services and most of them have SDKs, APIs that make it easier to integrate them with other applications and processes. Another key theme we just discussed is DevOps, which is basically a combination of cultural philosophies, practices, and tools that increase an organization's ability to deliver applications and services at high velocity. Now, if applications are being rapidly delivered at a high velocity to various environments and security organization's policy-related checks that are not integrated in those processes, then it can create a nightmare for the organization, wherein some controls might be left unattended for being exploited. As a result, having security woven into DevOps is a must and it's also called DevSecOps (or SecDevOps).

The core way to achieve this is to treat the security components and services in an infrastructure-as-code fashion and integrate them with the existing DevOps practices. As an example, if the Corporate Security team of an organization has defined standards around how VPCs should be set up for any environment, which NACL rules should be applied and how IAM users and their policies should be created, then those should be documented in CloudFormation templates, which the application teams just refer to and reuse by applying the capability of nested CloudFormation stacks. This way, the security team focuses on creating and updating the security and networking components that lie in their area of responsibility and the application team focuses on the code, the testing process, and deployment across the fleet of servers as per the environment.

Other than infrastructure provisioning aspects, this practice can be taken to the next level by also involving security checks along the entire software development pipeline, by including tests for areas such as the following:

- Ensuring that code analysis tools are integrated and security-related findings are addressed before pushing to production
- Enabling audit logs, including services such as AWS CloudTrail logging, apart from standard application logging

- Running various security tests, including virus/malware scans and penetration testing, which might be required for compliance-sensitive workloads
- Checking databases and various other static configuration and binary files, and that PHI/PII data (such as credit card numbers, social security numbers, and health records) is either encrypted or obfuscated and not available in plain text for any possible exploits

Many customers also make use of custom logic and applications to automate various stages of the preceding pipeline using AWS Lambda. These functions can not just be executed proactively, but also can be triggered by various reactive means such as event triggers from sources such as CloudWatch monitoring, CloudWatch Events, and SNS alerts.

A couple of other services that help in an effective DevSecOps implementation are AWS Config and Amazon Inspector. AWS Config can help assess, audit, and evaluate the configurations of your AWS resources, whereas using Amazon Inspector you can automatically assesses applications for vulnerabilities or deviations from best practices, thereby providing the base rules and frameworks out of the box, which can be augmented with your custom policies and checks using Amazon Lambda-based definitions.

Patterns for moving off monolithic application architectures to AWS native architectures

In the earlier sections, we discussed multiple options to create greenfield cloud-native applications using various AWS services. That part is a little easy, as you are starting fresh and so you can use various cloud services as you architect your solutions. However, if you have a huge technical debt in an on-premise environment and want to reduce that by moving over to a cloud platform such as AWS, then it takes more effort and planning.

In recent years, AWS has matured its migration services, methodology, and messaging to make it easier for organizations to not just think of greenfield but even plan for brownfield implementations in AWS. They have a methodology of the **6Rs**, which possibly covers every scenario for any workload migration to AWS. The 6Rs that AWS has are Rehosting, Replatforming, Repurchasing, Refactoring/Re-Architecting, Retire, and Retain.

The following is a snapshot of this methodology:

(Source - https://medium.com/aws-enterprise-collection/6-strategies-for-migrating-applications-to-the-Cloud-eb4e85c412b4)

In order to develop the partner ecosystem with the 6Rs aligned methodology, AWS has a **Migration Acceleration Program** (**MAP**), which is now the backbone of its entire enterprise segment migration strategy. More details on the program is available at `https://aws.amazon.com/migration-acceleration-program/`.

Apart from the this, AWS has a more holistic framework for any organization that's planning to start their cloud journey, and it's called AWS **Cloud Adoption Framework** (**CAF**). This is a detailed framework covering six different perspectives oriented towards Business and Technology stakeholders in any organization:

- Business
- People
- Governance
- Platform
- Security
- Operations

More details on AWS CAF are available at the following link: `https://aws.amazon.com/professional-services/CAF/`.

Summary

In this chapter, we focused on AWS and its capabilities based on the CNMM described earlier. So, in line with that, we focused on understanding the core AWS capabilities around building cloud-native architectures and effectively operating in your applications in that environment. We then dived deep into a sample serverless microservice application, leveraging various key AWS services and frameworks. Finally, we understood the principles around DevOps and DevSecOps and how those translated to various different application architectures ranging from deploying on Amazon EC2, Amazon Elastic Beanstalk, AWS Lambda, and the Amazon EC2 Container Service. Finally, we looked at migration patterns to move your applications to AWS and the concept of the 6Rs and the AWS CAF.

In the next chapter, we will focus on trying to understand the capabilities of the Microsoft Azure cloud platform and how it compares to AWS.

10
Microsoft Azure

Microsoft Azure had a very different start compared to AWS. It was originally launched in 2009 as the Windows Azure platform, where the focus was on developers and **Platform-as-a-Service (PaaS)** components. The initial set of services that were launched were Windows Server AppFabric and ASP.NET MVC2 to help developers build applications using the frameworks and services in the cloud. The only infrastructure components at that time were Windows Server virtual machines to enable hybrid use cases, but the overall strategy was still geared towards developer community, which was radically different from AWS, who had more infrastructure components around that time being offered apart from some basic application-centric services. With this foray into the cloud, Azure continued the push towards application aspects until 2014, when it changed the whole strategy to go into the IaaS space as well and also rebranded the platform to Microsoft Azure.

 Refer to this first blog post, announcing the launch of Windows Azure: `https://news.microsoft.com/2009/11/17/microsoft-cloud-services-vision-becomes-reality-with-launch-of-windows-azure-platform/`.

Since the time Microsoft entered the cloud IaaS market with the launch of Azure Virtual Machines in June 2012 (with general availability in April 2013), Azure has grown dramatically in terms of its global presence as well as the services it has to offer. At the time of writing this book, Microsoft Azure has 36 regions globally, with plans for six additional regions to come online in the near future. One point to consider here is that there's a subtle difference in the way AWS describes its regions versus Microsoft Azure. For AWS, it's a cluster of **Availability Zones (AZs)** that make up a region, and an AZ can comprise one or more data centers in itself, whereas for Microsoft Azure, a region is a geographic location where it has a data center. Microsoft recently announced that it will also now offer AZs like AWS, however that feature is still in beta and will take some time to roll out globally. So, for users who are looking for high availability deployments in Microsoft Azure in the interim, there's another option called Availability Sets (details are available at `https://docs.microsoft.com/en-us/azure/virtual-machines/windows/manage-availability?toc=%2Fazure%2Fvirtual-machines%2Fwindows%2Ftoc.json#configure-multiple-virtual-machines-in-an-availability-set-for-redundancy`).

Another important aspect of Microsoft's cloud business is that apart from Microsoft Azure, it also has services around Microsoft Office 365 and Microsoft Dynamics 365 CRM, which are included in there.

To keep yourself updated on the latest Microsoft Azure announcements and service launches news, subscribe to the following resources:

- Azure Updates page: `https://azure.microsoft.com/en-us/updates/`
- Microsoft Azure Blog: `https://azure.microsoft.com/en-us/blog/`

In this chapter, we will cover the following topics:

- Microsoft Azure's cloud native services, strengths, and differentiators around CI/CD, serverless, containers, and microservices concepts, covering the following services:
  - Azure functions
  - Visual Studio team services
  - Azure container service
  - Azure IoT
  - Azure machine learning studio
  - Office 365
- Understanding cloud native database capabilities:
  - Azure Cosmos DB
- Management and monitoring capabilities for Microsoft Azure native application architectures
- Patterns for moving off monolithic application architectures to Microsoft Azure native architectures
- Sample reference architectures and code snippets for CI/CD, serverless, containers, and microservices application architectures

Azure's Cloud Native Services (CNMM Axis-1)

As discussed in Chapter 1, *Introducing the Cloud Native Architecture*, the first and foremost aspect in being cloud native is to understand and utilize the cloud provider's services, which can help differentiate beyond the core infrastructure layer.

As per various independent analyst reports and analysis, Azure is the only cloud provider that's close to AWS in terms of its cloud services and ability to execute. So, in lines with that, Azure has multiple offerings that not just cover the core aspects such as compute, storage, networking, and databases, but multiple higher services in the space of data/analytics, AI/cognitive, IoT, web/mobile, and enterprise integration. In the next subsection, we will focus on some of these higher-level applications and managed services that can help anyone be more cloud native and harness the full power of the platform, so let's dive right into it.

Microsoft Azure platform – differentiators

In a very similar vein as the previous chapter on AWS, where we discussed some of the differentiating services from Amazon, let's look at some of the Azure services that are its core differentiators and are recommended to build effective cloud native application architectures. These services also greatly improve the productivity of the teams developing the applications as they can now focus on the core business logic rather than having to worry about stitching together basic capabilities on their own, which often is not as scalable and fault-tolerant compared to what the cloud providers can offer with their years of experience operating those components across global and multi-customer environments. So, let's dive into a few key Azure services that can further accelerate your cloud native journey.

Azure IoT

Microsoft Azure has a set of services that help us build connected platforms and solutions, which help us ingest massive amounts of data from devices (or things), applying rules on the fly to filter data, analyzing in real-time, and persisting to various data stores for creating different types of views and solutions on top of it. One of the main services that Azure has in this space is Microsoft Azure IoT Hub, which has multiple features that you can use to connect, manage, and operate a connected device's environment. Although it has multiple features, some of the specific ones are as follows:

- **Device registration, authentication, and authorization**: One of most important aspects in an IoT scenario is ensuring that devices are properly provisioned and securely connecting to the backend. To enable this, Azure IoT provides options through the portal and the API to create individual devices, which provides an individual device endpoint within the cloud. This method of individually adding the devices using the portal is viable only when you have limited devices and so you can add them one by one. However, if you have thousands of devices that you would like to register, then Azure IoT Hub provides a separate `ImportDevicesAsync` method that you can use to bulk upload, delete, or even apply status changes to thousands of devices in one API call. Likewise, if you want to bulk export registered devices information, then the `ExportDevicesAsync` method can help. Once the devices have been created, apart from the endpoint, a symmetric X.509 key is also created, which helps with device authentication. This, clubbed with policy-based access controls and a secure communication channel (TLS-based encryption), make it secure for the devices to connect and exchange information with the IoT Hub. The following is a high-level breakdown of these controls:

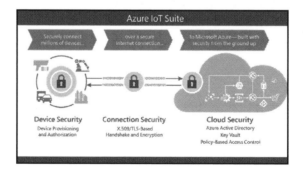

Azure IoT Suite (Source – `https://docs.microsoft.com/en-us/azure/iot-hub/iot-hub-security-ground-up`)

- **Communication protocols**: Different devices have different types of protocol and integration support. However, in most IoT scenarios, MQTT, AMQP, and HTTPS are the protocols that most of the devices support. Azure IoT Hub also supports all of these protocols, making it thereby easier to connect the majority of the devices out of the box, without any major configuration requirements. However, sometimes, some devices have different types of protocols and communication mechanisms that do not fall under this supported protocols set. So, for such scenarios, there's a Microsoft Azure IoT Protocol Gateway (`https://github.com/Azure/azure-iot-protocol-gateway/blob/master/README.md`), which the customers can fork from GitHub, make any changes as per translation requirements, and deploy it on Azure VM instances. This makes it easier to cater to a variety of devices so that they can be connected and be managed using the Azure IoT Hub service:

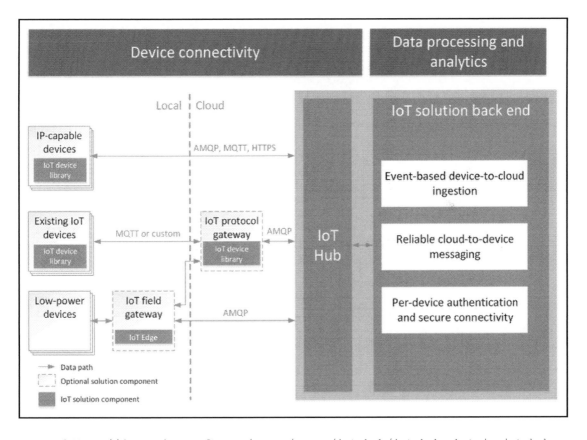

(Source - `https://docs.microsoft.com/en-us/azure/iot-hub/iot-hub-what-is-iot-hub`)

- **Device Twins**: Devices are not always connected to the backend IoT Hub, but your backend application often needs to query the last known status of the device or even wants to set a particular status as soon as the device connects to the backend using IoT Hub, so for such device state synchronization-related operations, Azure IoT Hub provides device twins functionality. These device twins are JSON documents that have tags (device metadata), and properties (desired and reported), using which you can create your desired application logic to communicate and update the devices:

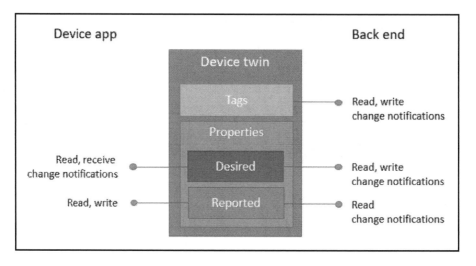

(Ref-https://docs.microsoft.com/en-us/azure/iot-hub/iot-hub-node-node-twin-getstarted)

- **Azure IoT Edge**: Sometimes, instead of sending over the data from devices to the cloud, it's easier to perform analytics or a simple computation at the edge itself. A typical scenario of this would be a use case, wherein the devices are in a remote location and the network connection might be flaky or expensive, so for those scenarios, edge analytics makes sense. To enable this aspect, Azure has a capability called IoT Edge, where you can run your code and logic closer to the devices itself using multiple SDKs (C, Node.js, Java, Microsoft .NET, and Python) that Azure offers. This enables a seamless hybrid cloud architecture, where some logic is executable at the edge, and more complex processing data is transmitted to the cloud, with various services helping with the scalable processing there.

Apart from Azure IoT Hub, Azure also offers out of the box industry and use case-specific solution offerings that customers can directly deploy with a click and scale to production grade architecture as per their specific requirements. Behind the scenes, these solutions make use of multiple Azure services, such as Azure IoT Hub, Azure Events Hub, Azure Stream Analytics, Azure Machine Learning, and Azure Storage. This is a differentiator for the Azure IoT service, as other cloud providers only offer core building blocks for the connected devices and IoT use cases, whereas Azure also offers out-of-the-box, ready-to-use solutions.

Here is a snapshot of the solutions that the Azure IoT Suite offers currently:

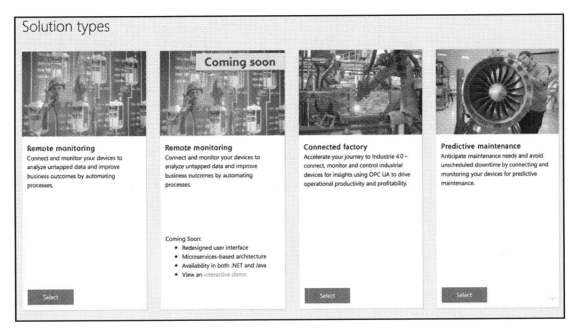

Azure Cosmos DB

Azure Cosmos DB is Microsoft's globally distributed, multi-model database. Azure Cosmos DB enables you to elastically and independently scale throughput and storage across any number of Azure's geographic regions. Azure Cosmos DB guarantees single-digit-millisecond latencies at the 99th percentile anywhere in the world, offers multiple well-defined consistency models to fine-tune performance, and guarantees high availability with multi-homing capabilities (more details are available here: `https://azure.microsoft.com/en-us/services/cosmos-db/`).

Azure Cosmos DB was launched in May 2017, however it's not really a brand-new offering per se. It actually inherited lots of functionality from its predecessor, Azure DocumentDB, which was launched a couple of years prior to it, and was more focused on the NoSQL-based architectural pattern. However, Azure CosmosDB is just not a simple reincarnation of Azure DocumentDB with a new name; it actually introduced multiple new functionalities and capabilities which were not there before. The three important differentiators that new Cosmos DB brings in are:

- **Globally distributed deployment model**: Azure has multiple regions, and if you want to deploy an application that spans many of those regions with a shared database, then CosmosDB allows that with a global deployment model. You can select the regions where your DB instance is replicated either during the time of creation of your database, or you can do that later too when the database is active. You can also define which region is *read* or *write*, or *read/write*, as per your requirements. Along with that, you can also define the failover priorities for each of the regions to handle any large scale regional events and issues.

For some use cases, you may want to restrict the data to a specific location or region (like for data sovereignty, privacy, or in-country data residency regulations), and then to meet those needs you can control this using policies that are controlled using the metadata of your Azure subscription:

Click on a location to add or remove regions from your Azure Cosmos DB account.

* Each region is billable based on the throughput and storage for the account. Learn more

WRITE REGION

East US

READ REGIONS

Central US

West Central US

Canada East

Canada Central

- **Multi-model APIs**: This is one of the biggest differences from the earlier version of Azure DocumentDB, as now it supports various other models:
  - **Graph database** - This is the model in which data has multiple vertices and edges. Each vertex defines a unique object in the data (such as a person or device) and it can be connected to n-number of other vertices using edges, which define a relationship between them. To query Azure Cosmos DB, you can use the Apache TinkerPop graph traversal language, Gremlin, or other TinkerPop-compatible graph systems, such as Apache Spark GraphX.
  - **Table** - This is based on the Azure table storage, which is basically a NoSQL key-value approach to storing massive amounts of semi-structured datasets. Cosmos DB adds the global distribution capabilities here on top of Azure Table Storage APIs.
  - **JSON documents** - Cosmos DB also provides the option to store JSON documents in your database, which can either be accessed using existing DocumentDB APIs or newer MongoDB APIs.
  - **SQL** - Cosmos DB also supports some basic SQL functions using the existing DocumentDB API. However, this is not as full-fledged as the Azure SQL database, so if advanced SQL operations are required, then Cosmos DB might not be a fit for that.
- **Consistency models**: Normally, other cloud databases provided limited options in terms of how the data is replicated across different partitioned nodes and geographies. The most common options in distributed computing are as follows:
  - **Strong Consistency**, where the response is only returned after the commit is successful across different replicas and so read after write would ensure that you have the latest value
  - **Eventual Consistency**, where the response after a commit is immediately returned and various nodes synchronize the data eventually, thereby leading to a scenario wherein immediate read after write may give a stale value

However, Cosmos DB has taken it to the next level. It has introduced various other consistency models (bounded staleness, session, and consistent prefix) that lie between strong and eventual consistency models, as follows:

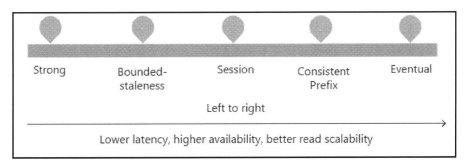

The following is a screenshot from the Azure CosmosDB portal, which shows these consistency model settings:

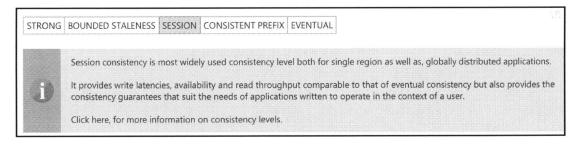

As a result of all of these differentiating capabilities, Azure Cosmos DB is a great choice for multiple cloud native scenarios such as shared databases for globally distributed application architectures, telemetry, and the state information store for connected platforms/IoT and backend persistence for serverless applications.

Azure machine learning studio

Microsoft initially launched the service under the name of Azure Machine Learning; however, they later changed it to Azure Machine Learning Studio in line with its core capabilities of being able to manage the entire process using the Studio itself (Visual Workbench). It's a managed service that you can use to create, test, operate, and manage predictive analytic solutions in the cloud. The core value proposition of this service is that you do not necessarily need to be a data scientist in order to build machine learning models as it provides multiple sample datasets and analysis modules, which can be used together to create your machine learning experiment. Once you have tried, tested, and trained your experiment, you can use it to start generating predictive analysis for your actual data and expose them as web services as well. The following diagram summarizes these core concepts in a concise manner:

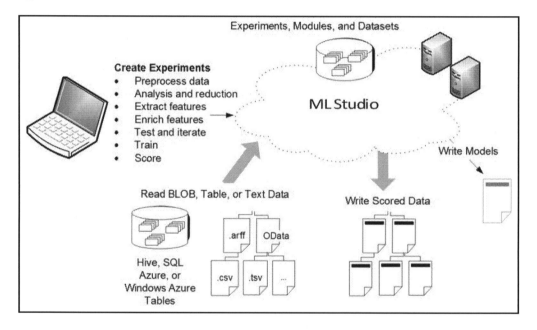

(Source-https://docs.microsoft.com/en-us/azure/machine-learning/studio/what-is-ml-studio)

One of the biggest benefits of Azure Machine Learning Studio is that there are multiple algorithms that are available out of the box as follows:

- **Anomaly Detection**: Identifies and predicts rare or unusual data points, such as predicting a credit risk or detecting a fraudulent activity.
- **Classification**: Identifies what category new information belongs to. It could be a simple yes/no or true/false categorization, or a complex one such as the sentiment analysis of a social media post.
- **Clustering**: Separates similar data points into intuitive groups, such as predicting customer taste or the level of interest in a particular item.
- **Recommendation**: Predicts the likelihood that a user would prefer an item based on a previous user interaction. This is typical in online shopping portals, where additional product options are provided based on your past browsing history.
- **Regression**: Forecasts the future by estimating the relationship between variables, such as predicting car sales figures for the next few months.
- **Statistical Functions**: Mathematical computations on column values, calculating correlations, z scores, probability scores, and so on.
- **Text Analytics**: Works with both structured and unstructured text to detect the language of input text, creates n-gram dictionaries, and extracts the names of people, places, and organizations from unstructured text.
- **Computer Vision**: Image processing and image recognition tasks to detect faces, image tagging, color analysis, and so on.

> To learn more about Azure Machine Learning algorithms, refer to the cheat sheet at the following link: `https://docs.microsoft.com/en-us/azure/machine-learning/studio/algorithm-cheat-sheets`.

As you can see, there are multiple algorithms already available; however, developers/data scientists often need to extend or modify some of the functionalities, so also possible to use R or Python script modules and Jupyter notebooks.

In terms of execution, as we mentioned previously, you can expose your machine learning workflow to external applications using REST web services. In this, there are two broader options based on the type of execution models as follows:

- **Request Response Service (RRS)**: For stateless, synchronous execution
- **Batch Execution Service (BES)**: Batch processing in an asynchronous way

Visual Studio Team Services

As we discussed in the previous chapter, AWS offers multiple services that enable successful DevOps practices in any organization. Likewise, Azure has a set of services/features DevOps that help developers build applications leveraging CI/CD principles and processes. In fact, even before Microsoft had cloud-based services in this space, it had an on-premises platform called Team Foundation Services (TFS), which developers and teams could make use of to deliver quality products. With an increased emphasis and focus on the cloud, Microsoft launched a cloud-based service called Visual Studio Team Services (VSTS), which is like a *cloudified* version of the pre-existing TFS. The biggest benefit for VSTS is, of course, that it is a managed platform. Azure does lots of heavy lifting on behalf of the customer so that they can focus on their core business of developing applications with proper collaboration and practices. Also, since TFS has been in existence for quite some time, VSTS is also a rich platform with multiple inbuilt capabilities and third-party integrations.

To understand the differences between VSTS and TFS, refer to the following link:
https://docs.microsoft.com/en-us/vsts/user-guide/about-vsts-tfs

Since our focus here is on cloud native capabilities, let's dive deeper into VSTS and discuss a few of the main functionalities that it provides:

- The first and the foremost is the ability to manage code, various versions, and branches. For the same, VSTS provides a couple of options, including Git (distributed) or Team Foundation Version Control (TFVC), and a centralized, client-server system. For using Git-based repositories, developers can make use of variety of IDEs, including Visual Studio, Eclipse, Xcode, and IntelliJ. Likewise, for TFVC, you may use Visual Studio, Eclipse, and Xcode. The VSTS cloud-based UI also provides various options to explore the code files in the project, and look at push/pull and commits-related details from there itself.

- The other important aspect is the ability to have continuous integration and continuous deployment, which is central to any successful DevOps practice. So, again, VSTS enables this by using various functionalities that includes being able to create build and release definitions, creating libraries of build variables that may vary as per environment, as well as the definition of deployment groups where you can define target instances that are Windows, Ubuntu, or RHEL.

- In order to implement DevOps, many teams also make use of Scrum, which are Kanban software development methodologies. So, it's important to integrate these processes with the code development practices, and that's what VSTS also helps with by providing project dashboards, sprint backlogs, task dashboards, and related visualizations to enable closer planning and collaboration. It not only helps project managers to evaluate the overall status, but even product managers to write stories, developers to link their tasks/bug fixes/checkins to respective stories, and QA teams to write their test cases and record results, thereby providing an end to end platform.

- Apart from core service capabilities, another key aspect is to have ecosystem partner integrations available in an out-of-the-box or easy to use manner. That's exactly what Visual Studio Marketplace offers. You can select multiple plugins, including for work item visualization, code searching, slack integration, and more. Refer to the following link for more details of the available software and integrations: `https://marketplace.visualstudio.com/vsts`

 Interestingly, VSTS Marketplace also has a plugin to manage and integrate with AWS services such as Amazon S3, AWS Elastic Beanstalk, AWS CodeDeploy, AWS Lambda, and AWS CloudFormation: `https://marketplace.visualstudio.com/items?itemName=AmazonWebServices.aws-vsts-tools.`

Office 365

One of the most popular products that Microsoft has had for multiple years is Microsoft Office. With the advent of cloud, Microsoft started a SaaS offering of the same set of applications under the umbrella of Office 365. So, with that, anyone (home, business, or education users) could go online, get a subscription of the Office 365 suite, and start using it directly from the browser of their choice. Now, although this is a cloud-based offering from Microsoft, it technically doesn't fall under the Azure umbrella as Azure is more infrastructure and platform services oriented. However, we still wanted to cover it here, as Office 365 is an important piece to Microsoft's overall cloud business and many enterprises while making a move to cloud also factor in Office 365 as one of the core applications to migrate to in that transformation journey. The following are the applications that Microsoft offers as part of Office 365:

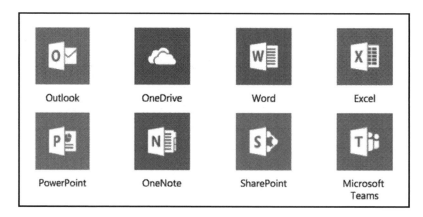

As we discussed previously, there's a close link between Azure and Office 365, and one of the main areas of integrations is authentication. What this means is that behind the scenes, Office 365 uses Azure AD to manage user identities. The other benefit of this linkage is that if a customer is using Active Directory on-premises for their user identities, then they can sync the passwords from there to Azure AD and set up single sign-on as well. This makes it easier for the end users as they don't have to remember additional credentials other than their corporate identities, and the experience of logging into Office 365 is also seamless.

One another reason that Office 365 is important is because of competitive reasons with other cloud providers. So, although AWS offers a set of business applications (such as Amazon Workdocs and Amazon Chime), and likewise Google has G Suite, from an enterprise adoption perspective, Microsoft has had the lead for multiple years. Office has been the de facto collaboration and productivity platform. So, for this reason as well, it makes it easier for customers to migrate and adopt Office 365 with minimal disruption to their business.

Application Centric Design (CNMM Axis-2)

As discussed in the previous chapter, creating serverless and microservice-based applications is a key cloud native way to differentiate as compared to pre-cloud era design patterns. So, let's look at how can we design such applications in Microsoft Azure cloud using multiple key services.

Serverless microservice

In this section, we are going to create a serverless microservice application on Microsoft Azure. In order for you to easily compare and learn capabilities across cloud providers, we will use the same example of creating a Weather Services application, which we discussed in the previous chapter on AWS. So, as a refresher, the overall application will have three main parts:

- An API trigger to invoke the application.
- A function that is written in Azure Functions.
- An external weather service to which we will pass some parameters and get results:

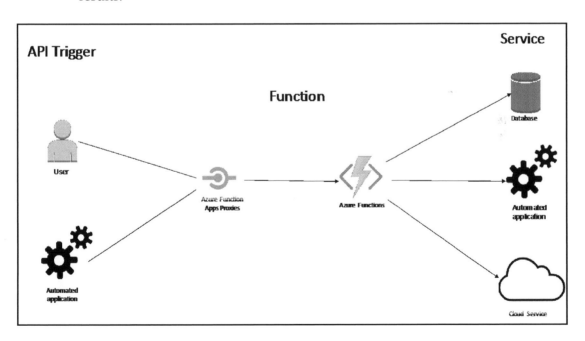

The main parts of a Weather Services application

Serverless microservice – walkthrough

In order to create the previously mentioned service, follow these steps in Azure portal:

1. Click the Create a resource button found on the upper left-hand corner of the Azure portal, and then select **Compute** | **Function App.**

2. Create the **Function App**, as per the settings in the following screenshot (some settings might vary as per your account and existing resources):

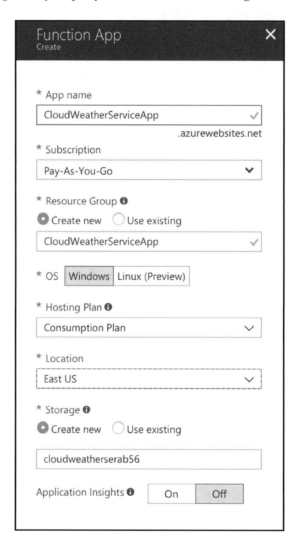

3. Once the **Functions App** is created, it's time to create our core business logic in the form of an Azure function. So, for that, expand your new function app, then click the **+** button next to **Functions**, and create a new **HTTP trigger** function as follows:

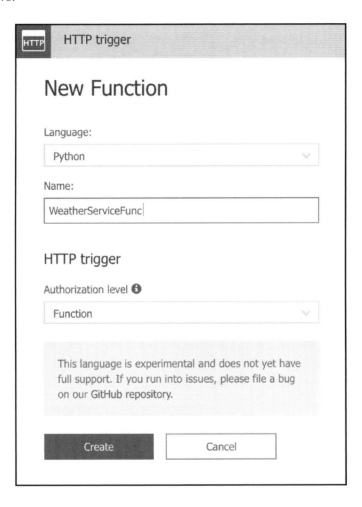

4. Once the function is created, edit the inline code and use the following Python-based logic:

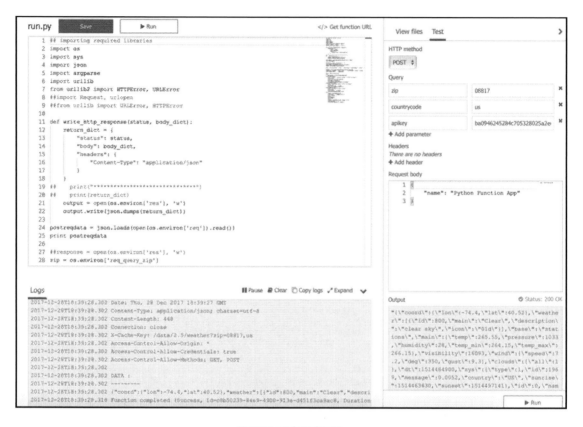

The Python code for the function

```
## importing required libraries
import os
import sys
import json
import argparse
import urllib
from urllib2 import HTTPError, URLError
```

```
## response construction and return
def write_http_response(status, body_dict):
    return_dict = {
        "status": status,
        "body": body_dict,
        "headers": {
            "Content-Type": "application/json"
        }
    }
    output = open(os.environ['res'], 'w')
    output.write(json.dumps(return_dict))

## extract input parameter values
zip = os.environ['req_query_zip']
countrycode = os.environ['req_query_countrycode']
apikey = os.environ['req_query_apikey']

print ("zip code value::" + zip + ", countrycode:" + countrycode + ",
apikey::" + apikey)

## construct full URL to invoke OpenWeatherMap service with proper inputs
baseUrl = 'http://api.openweathermap.org/data/2.5/weather'
completeUrl = baseUrl + '?zip=' + zip + ',' + countrycode + '&appid=' +
apikey
print('Request URL--> ' + completeUrl)

## Invoke OpenWeatherMap API and parse response with proper exception
handling
try:
    apiresponse = urllib.urlopen(completeUrl)
except IOError as e:
    error = "IOError - The server couldn't fulfill the request."
    print(error)
    print("I/O error: {0}".format(e))
    errorcode = format(e[1])
    errorreason = format(e[2])
    write_http_response(errorcode, errorreason)
except HTTPError as e:
    error = "The server couldn't fulfill the request."
    print(error)
    print('Error code: ', e.code)
    write_http_response(e.code, error)
except URLError as e:
    error = "We failed to reach a server."
    print(error)
    print('Reason: ', e.reason)
    write_http_response(e.code, error)
```

```
else:
    headers = apiresponse.info()
    print('DATE :', headers['date'])
    print('HEADERS :')
    print('---------')
    print(headers)
    print('DATA :')
    print('---------')
    response = apiresponse.read().decode('utf-8')
    print(response)
    write_http_response(200, response)
```

5. Save the function, add sample query parameters (as shown in the preceding screenshot), and test your function. To look at all the function execution logs and results, you can go to the **Monitor** option under your function name and see the details as follows:

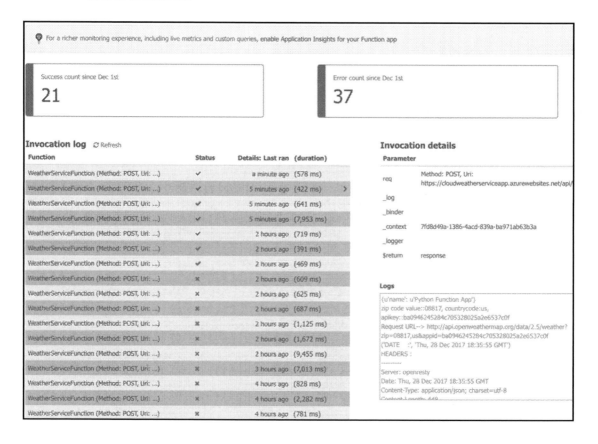

6. Once you have unit tested the Azure Function from the portal, go to the **Integrate** option under your function and ensure that the HTTP GET method is enabled, apart from the other settings, as follows:

7. Now, it's time to create an external facing API interface using proxies. To do that, you must first retrieve your Azure function URL from the top-right corner of your function definition, as follows:

Retrieving Azure function

8. To expose this Azure function using an API, create a new proxy by pressing the + sign against the **Proxies** option. Ensure that it has the settings, like in the following screenshot. In the backend URL field, put the URL of your Azure function that you copied in the previous screenshot:

With this, your serverless microservice is now ready and you can test it using a web browser or CLI, which is detailed in the following subsection.

Browser-based testing

You can copy the deployed API's URL from the Proxy URL field and then try accessing it by providing the zip, countrycode, and the appid parameters as part of the URL, as follows:

```
https://asdfqwert.azurewebsites.net/?zip=10001&countrycode=us&apikey=qwerty
asdfg98765zxcv
```

Note: Please replace the highlighted text with your environment's specific values.

Command-line-based testing

For this, you need to run the following commands:

```
$ curl -X GET
'https://asdfqwert.azurewebsites.net/?zip=10001&countrycode=us&apikey=qwert
yasdfg98765zxcv
"{"coord":{"lon":-74,"lat":40.75},"weather":[{"id":802,"main":"Clouds","des
cription":"scattered
clouds","icon":"03d"}],"base":"stations","main":{"temp":266.73,"pressure":1
024,"humidity":44,"temp_min":266.15,"temp_max":267.15},"visibility":16093,"
wind":{"speed":3.1,"deg":320},"clouds":{"all":40},"dt":1514582100,"sys":{"t
ype":1,"id":1969,"message":0.004,"country":"US","sunrise":1514549991,"sunse
t":1514583454},"id":0,"name":"New York","cod":200}"
```

Automation in Azure (CNMM Axis-3)

The entire concept of the public cloud is based on the premise that you can easily utilize and integrate the cloud services using APIs, SDKs, and REST web services. Another layer to this paradigm is the higher-level automation and orchestration services that cloud providers have created, which make it even easier to leverage the true power of cloud with less human intervention and thereby enable self-healing, autoscalable applications. Apart from this, developers can now assume greater responsibility to manage the full stack of their application environment on their own rather than have a separate ops team that they had to rely on earlier. This enables rapid releases, faster time to market, and increased agility in the application development lifecycle. As we discussed in the previous chapter, AWS offers services such as Amazon CloudFormation, AWS CodePipeline, AWS CodeBuild, and AWS CodeDeploy to enable these practices and culture, so in a very similar way, Azure has a whole bunch of services that can be used to enable DevOps, automation, and more cloud native application development practices. So, let's explore more around these concepts in the following sections.

Infrastructure as code

As discussed in the previous chapter as well, one of the key cloud automation techniques is to manage infrastructure-as-code, so that effective DevOps practices can be implemented. Like AWS offers Amazon CloudFormation, in a very similar manner, Azure has a service called **Azure Resource Manager (ARM)** Templates. Using this service, users can create standardized, repeatable JSON-based templates, which can be used to provision entire application stacks as a single entity to a resource group. The Azure portal provides an interface to directly author/edit the template there, or if users prefer an IDE-based development, then Visual Studio Code also offers extensions using which makes it easy to author ARM templates. The visual editor in the Azure portal also helps detect any JSON syntactical errors (such as missing commas curly braces, and so on), but semantic validations are not supported. Once you have finalized the template, you can deploy it either directly using the Azure portal, or even use CLI, PowerShell, SDKs, and so on to create your application environments. If there's any error during the template deployment phase, ARM provides debugging as well as output details, which comes in handy for evaluating progress and correcting any issues. Unlike AWS CloudFormation, ARM templates don't support YAML, which is more human-readable and generally more concise than JSON.

 In order to effectively use Visual Studio Code to develop ARM templates, refer to the following blog post: `https://blogs.msdn.microsoft.com/azuredev/2017/04/08/iac-on-azure-developing-arm-template-using-vscode-efficiently/`.

One differentiating feature for Azure Resource Manager is around subscription governance, wherein the account owner can register for a resource provider to be configured with your subscription. Some resource providers are registered by default, whereas for the majority, the user has to opt for them using a PowerShell command such as the following:

```
Register-AzureRmResourceProvider -ProviderNamespace Microsoft.Batch
```

Azure team has a GitHub repository where it hosts hundreds of sample templates for ARM. So, taking a basic example of a LAMP stack from there, it can be easily used to create a new template in ARM from the Azure portal, as follows:

GitHub – https://github.com/Azure/azure-quickstart-templates/

A snippet of that same LAMP stack template is as follows, and the complete template is available at: `https://github.com/Azure/azure-quickstart-templates/tree/master/lamp-app`:

```
{
  "$schema":
"https://schema.management.azure.com/schemas/2015-01-01/deploymentTemplate.
json#",
  "contentVersion": "1.0.0.0",
  "parameters": {
    "storageAccountNamePrefix": {
      "type": "string",
      "maxLength": 11,
      "metadata": {
        "description": "Name prefix of the Storage Account"
      }
    },
```

```
    "adminUsername": {
      "type": "string",
      "metadata": {
        "description": "User name for the Virtual Machine."
      }
    },
    ......
    ......
    ......
    ......

    {
      "type": "Microsoft.Compute/virtualMachines/extensions",
      "name": "[concat(variables('vmName'),'/newuserscript')]",
      "apiVersion": "2015-06-15",
      "location": "[resourceGroup().location]",
      "dependsOn": [
        "[concat('Microsoft.Compute/virtualMachines/',
variables('vmName'))]"
      ],
      "properties": {
        "publisher": "Microsoft.Azure.Extensions",
        "type": "CustomScript",
        "typeHandlerVersion": "2.0",
        "autoUpgradeMinorVersion": true,
        "settings": {
          "fileUris": [
"https://raw.githubusercontent.com/Azure/azure-quickstart-templates/master/
lamp-app/install_lamp.sh"
          ]
        },
        "protectedSettings": {
          "commandToExecute": "[concat('sh install_lamp.sh ',
parameters('mySqlPassword'))]"
        }
      }
    }
  ]
}
```

Unlike Amazon CloudFormation, ARM doesn't provide a visualization option natively, but there are tools available online that can help. The following is one such visualization of the LAMP stack template that's generated using `http://armviz.io/editor/4`:

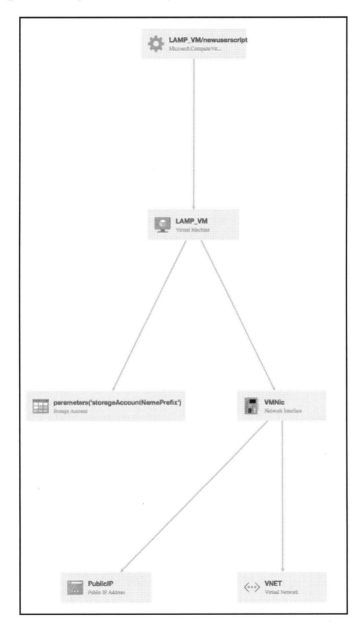

LAMP stack template

Now, as described previously, you can easily define an entire stack in an ARM template, but you often need more elaborate, step-by-step (sequential or parallel) orchestration across different systems and services. Sometimes, you also want to trigger that workflow, based on some events, such as code changes in GitHub. So, for those comprehensive types of orchestration tasks, Azure has a service called Azure Automation. Using this service, you can create either a textual runbook where you directly write a PowerShell or Python script/module that defines your business logic, or if you don't want to directly interact with the code that much, then there's a graphical runbook mode as well. In the latter, you have a canvas in the Azure Automation portal, where you can create various individual activities from a broad variety of library items, define configuration for all the activities, and link them together to run a complete workflow. Before actually deploying that workflow, you can also test it there itself and debug or modify it based on results and logging output.

The following is a sample graphical runbook that's available in the Azure Automation Gallery, which connects to Azure using an Automation Run As account and starts all V2 VMs in an Azure subscription, in a resource group, or a single named V2 VM. As you can see in the following screenshot, on the left-hand side are PowerShell cmdlets, other runbooks, and assets (credentials, variables, connections, and certificates), which can be added to the canvas in the center to modify the workflow. On the right-hand side is the configuration screen, where settings for each of the activities can be updated and their behavior defined as per the required business logic:

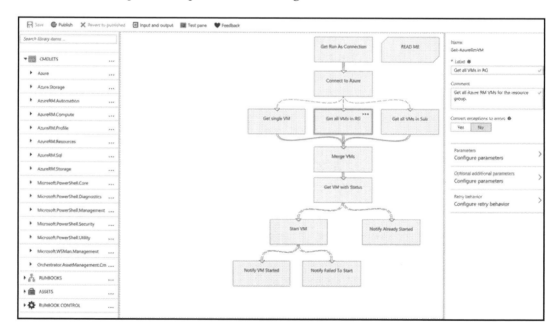

A sample graphical runbook

CI/CD for serverless applications

As discussed in the earlier section of this chapter, you can easily create serverless applications using Azure functions. It's easy to develop and deploy your Azure functions directly from the portal itself, however that's neither efficient from a team collaboration perspective and nor does it offer the possibility to automate the processes in-line with DevOps methodologies. So, to address that, Microsoft has a set of tools, specifically around VSTS integration with Azure functions, which makes it easy to orchestrate the entire CI/CD pipeline. There are more options as well from a deployment sources standpoint, such as Bitbucket, Dropbox, OneDrive and so on, but in this section we will focus more on VSTS, which is one of the most common methods.

> Go to the following link for more details on Visual Studio tools for Azure Functions: `https://blogs.msdn.microsoft.com/webdev/2016/12/01/visual-studio-tools-for-azure-functions/`

Now, in order to effectively deploy the same Azure function to different types of environments, it's of utmost importance to separate out the core logic from the environment-specific configuration details. In order to do that, you can create an Azure functions type of a project from Visual Studio which has your core business logic in one or more functions. To manage environment-specific configuration aspects, these can be woven together in ARM templates. This also helps deploy stage-specific Azure functions in their own resource groups, which again brings a clear separation that's needed to meaningfully implement CI/CD processes.

The following is a high-level architecture diagram explaining the overall process:

The steps of continuos integration process

As shown in the preceding diagram, in terms of the continuous integration process, there are three main steps such as are common for most projects, though these can be custom tailored as per individual requirements:

1. Build the code.
2. Run unit tests and ensure that everything looks good.
3. Create the solution package that can be deployed to the respective environments.

Once the CI process is complete, it's time to move to the continuous deployment phase. Usually, most customers have different phases in the pipeline, Dev, Test, UAT, and finally Production. All of these can be orchestrated using Visual Studio Team Services, where you can define the deployment process, which includes environment-specific configurations as well as the approval process. For lower-level environments, such as Dev and Test, most customers usually follow an automatic deployment process based on unit testing results, but for higher-level environments such as UAT and Production, it's a common practice to include a manual approval process to control gating procedures based on lower environments test results. To complete the DevOps loop, the final deployments are monitored using Azure Application Insights, which help with further refinement and application updates to improve application functionality across environments.

CI/CD for Azure container service (Docker containers)

Microsoft offers a managed Docker container service, **Azure Container Service** (**AKS**), using which customers can easily deploy scalable, open source APIs-based container deployed applications. The most important aspect that AKS provides is the orchestration and placement-related aspects for the containers, so that the end users can focus on their core applications rather than having to worry about launching and scaling applications manually. For the orchestration aspects, AKS offers a few options, such as Docker, Swarm, Kubernetes, and Mesosphere DC/OS, which are shown in the following screenshot:

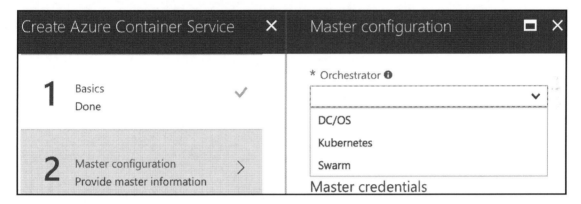

Another important aspect for any managed container platform is the functionality of a container registry where you can store master copies of different container images based on application stacks and configuration. For this, Azure offers **Azure Container Registry** (**ACR**), which is private registry for you to tag and upload images there.

Container-based applications often need to access and persist data in an external data volume. Azure files can be used as this external data store. Refer to the following link for more details: `https://docs.microsoft.com/en-us/azure/aks/azure-files`.

Now, in order to enable CI/CD practices with the Azure Container Service, the steps are very similar to the ones described in the previous section around enabling CI/CD for Azure functions. At a high level, the following are the key steps and the flow to enable these practices:

1. Store your application code in a code repository such as the Visual Studio Team Services Git repository. Apart from the core application code, this may also include Docker files and compose and deployment files, which will be needed to create Docker images and enable deployment as per various environment-specific requirements.

2. Any time a code change is committed to the code repository, it triggers a continuous integration build process in VSTS and creates new Docker images, which are then stored in the Azure Container Registry.

3. Once the new Docker images are released to the registry, it triggers a new release using VSTS, which can be gradually promoted from Dev, Test, UAT, and then Production.

4. This release process is integrated with different orchestrators supported by AKS, which pull the latest Docker image from the container registry and push it out the running instances to bring up the latest version of the application.

As part of the preceding process, multiple customizations can be performed, like being able to run particular types of tests or integration with other systems, which can be again easily managed using VSTS-based CI/CD pipelines.

The Kubernetes extension for VSTS is available on the Visual Studio Marketplace: `https://marketplace.visualstudio.com/items?itemName=tsuyoshiushio.k8s-endpoint`.

Patterns for moving from monolithic application architectures to Azure native architectures

Although cloud migrations have common patterns and methodologies, every cloud provider brings in a different flavor to it with their services and overall messaging. So, like we discussed earlier, AWS has a 6Rs migration methodology, but when it comes to Azure's methodology, it's pretty simplistic. As per https://azure.microsoft.com/en-us/migration/, it mainly categorizes migration into three parts:

- **Discover**: In this phase, you assess the current state of virtual machines, databases, and applications in an on-premises environment and evaluate their migration path and priority.
- **Migrate**: This is the actual process of moving your applications, databases, and VMs to the Azure cloud by using cloud native or third-party tools, which help you transfer the bits by means of replication.
- **Optimize**: Once your applications and data is in the Azure cloud, you can further fine-tune for costs, performance, security, and management by leveraging better architectures and more cloud native services. Also, this phase is more like an iterative one, as optimization has to be done regularly and repeatedly based on changing applications needs and newer cloud services.

For the preceding three phases, Azure has a set of cloud native services along with a few key partners that it recommends as alternatives. The following is a table that summarizes a few of those options. For the latest information, it's recommended to check out https://azure.microsoft.com/en-us/migrate/partners/:

Phase	Azure Native Tools/Services	Partner Tools/Services
Discover	Azure Migrate (VM assessment), Data Migration Assistant (database assessment)	Cloudamize, Movere, TSO Logic, CloudPhysics
Migrate	Azure Site Recovery (VM migration), Azure Database Migration Service (Database migrations)	Cloudendure, Velostrata
Optimize	Cloudyn (now part of Microsoft)	N/A

Apart from the preceding tools, Azure also offers a different messaging service compared to AWS when it comes to hybrid cloud computing aspects. AWS focuses more on its cloud native services and how they can be leveraged or extended to manage resources, even in private on-premises environments, thereby bridging the gap between the private and public cloud to enable hybrid computing environments. When it comes to Azure, it takes it a step further with the notion of enabling a hybrid cloud with a key service in that space called Azure Stack. The way Azure defines this service is as follows:

> *"Azure Stack is an extension of Azure, bringing the agility and fast-paced innovation of cloud computing to on-premises environments. Only Azure Stack lets you deliver Azure services from your organization's datacenter, while balancing the right amount of flexibility and control-for truly-consistent hybrid cloud deployments."*

> *-Source -* https://azure.microsoft.com/en-us/overview/azure-stack/

The key use cases that Azure Stack tries to address are as follows:

- Edge and disconnected
- Cloud applications to meet varied regulations
- Cloud application model on-premises

Now, even though the preceding points may seem compelling to enable a hybrid cloud environment with a singular set of management tools and DevOps processes across the Azure public cloud and Azure Stack, there are some key cons as well, which the users have to be aware of in this approach. One of the main challenges here is that Azure Stack takes the user back to the days of managing servers and data centers, where you again have to do the heavy lifting around racking, stacking the Azure Stack boxes, and then of course manage the cooling, power-related operational aspects to keep it up and running. So, net-net, although Azure Stack enables deploying containers, microservices, and PaaS environments locally, since you still have to manage the underlying infrastructure, it is not a truly *cloud native* type of architectural pattern.

Summary

In this chapter, we focused on the Microsoft Azure cloud platform in line with the CNMM model we described earlier. We started with the basics of Microsoft Azure, its brief history, and then deep into a few of its differentiating services and offerings. We then looked at the same sample serverless microservice application that we used in Chapter 9, *Amazon Web Services*, as well, and deployed it on Azure using Azure functions and proxies. After that, we focused on DevOps and CI/CD patterns and how those relate to both serverless and Docker container-based application models. Finally, we looked at Azure's cloud migration guidance, how it differentiates from AWS' messaging, followed by Azure Stack-related hybrid cloud aspects.

In the next chapter, we will focus on trying to understand the capabilities of Google Cloud compare and contrast it with AWS and Azure.

11
Google Cloud Platform

As per various analyst reports, the third most significant public cloud provider is Google with their **Google Cloud Platform** (**GCP**). The origins of GCP can be tracked back to 2008 when Google launched the Google App engine to focus on the developer community with its foray into **platform as a service** (**PaaS**) types of offerings. Slowly and gradually, Google has expanded the set of services that it offers and it was really around 2012 that Google started to step up the focus around the pace of releases and geo expansion, which gradually made it one of the dominant players in this space. Since then, GCP has expanded into multiple different spaces ranging from core services like compute, storage, networking, and databases to many higher-level application services in the space of big data, IoT, **artificial intelligence** (**AI**), and API platforms and ecosystems.

 To keep yourself updated on the latest GCP announcements and service launches news, subscribe to the following GCP blog: `https://cloud.google.com/blog/`.

In this chapter, we will focus on the following:

- Google Cloud Platform's cloud-native services, strengths, and differentiators around CI/CD, serverless, containers, and microservices concepts, covering the following services:
    - Google Kubernetes Engine
    - Google Cloud Functions
    - Cloud AI
- Management and monitoring capabilities for GCP native application architectures
- Patterns for moving off monolithic application architectures to Google Cloud Platform native architectures

- APIs, SDKs, open source frameworks, and partner ecosystem support to build cloud-native applications
- Sample reference architectures and code snippets for CI/CD, serverless microservices application architectures

GCP's cloud-native services (CNMM Axis-1)

As discussed in earlier chapters, let's first understand what type of cloud-native services Google Cloud offers that can help the end users and benefit businesses from the true power of various services and platforms.

Introduction

Google was a little bit of a late entrant to the public cloud space, but in the last few years it has really picked up pace in terms of its services coverage as well as customer adoption. As per various analyst reports, it ranks third as a cloud provider (after AWS and MS Azure) based on overall vision and its ability to execute, making it a promising candidate for any kind of cloud-native application's development and deployment. So, let's look at some of the services that it offers in that space and how it can potentially help you adopt them effectively.

Google Cloud Platform – differentiators

Google has many interesting services in the space of **machine learning (ML) / artificial intelligence (AI)**, application containerization, and collaboration, which we will focus on in this section. In fact, many of these services are a result of Google creating them for their internal usage or even for the consumer business, which are now being productized and available under the Google Cloud umbrella. So, let's dive in a bit and understand a few key concepts, which are very popular with customers.

Cloud AI

Google was one of the first cloud providers to offer services in the Artificial Intelligence and machine learning space, with a multitude of services in this domain catering to different types of users from developers to data scientists. Also, most of these services/APIs have originated from Google's internal usage and existing product offerings, which have now been exposed as APIs/services under the Google cloud umbrella. These services cover a variety of AI/ML use cases, like the following:

- **Image and Video Analysis**: One of the common requirements for most of the organizations starting with their AI/ML journey is to classify and understand the context and metadata around their images and video streams. In the image analysis space, Google offers a Cloud Vision API (`https://cloud.google.com/vision/`), which can help classify images into thousands of categories, detect individual objects and faces within images, and find and read printed words contained within images. You can also detect any explicit content, identify logos, landmarks, or even search the web for similar images. Similarly, for video analysis, Google offers Cloud Video Intelligence (`https://cloud.google.com/video-intelligence/`), which can search every moment of every video file in your catalog, quickly annotates videos stored in Google Cloud Storage, and helps identify key entities within your video and when they occur within the video. Using this video analytics, you can generate appropriate content recommendations for end users and even show more contextual advertisements in lines with the content itself.

- **Speech and text-related AI services**: There are multiple AI-related aspects when it comes to text and speech analysis as well as conversions between one form to another. For the same reason, Google offers the Cloud Speech API (`https://cloud.google.com/speech/`), which can convert audio to text and can recognize over 110 languages and variants and thereby help transcribe audio content. Likewise, to convert written text-to-speech, Google offers the Cloud Text-To-Speech API (`https://cloud.google.com/text-to-speech/`) to synthesize natural-sounding speech with 30 voices, which is available in multiple languages and variants. Apart from this, Google also offers a service to detect a particular language in the text and also to convert text from one language to another using the Cloud Translation API (`https://cloud.google.com/translate/`). Another service which Google offers in this space is for the deep analysis of text by extracting information about people, places, events, and much more, which is mentioned in text documents, news articles, or blog posts. This service is a Cloud Natural Language (`https://cloud.google.com/natural-language/`), which can help understand the sentiment and intent (like positive or negative reviews) from social media content or customer conversations in call center type of text message exchanges.

- **Chatbots**: One of the most common uses of AI these days is to create conversational interfaces (or chatbots) for websites, mobile applications, messaging platforms, and IoT devices, that are capable of natural and rich interactions between users and your business. These chatbots can understand the intent and context of conversation to provide highly efficient and accurate responses. For this, Google has a service called DialogFlow Enterprise Edition (`https://cloud.google.com/dialogflow-enterprise/`), which has multiple out-of-the box templates and supports 20+ languages and integration with 14 different platforms to provide rich experience to the end users.

- **Custom Machine Learning**: In most cases, advanced users (such as data scientists) like to have more control of their algorithms, ML models, and the way the system generates results. So, for such scenarios, services like the ones discussed previously don't provide that level of deeper control and configurability, and that's why Google offers a set of services like Cloud AutoML (`https://cloud.google.com/automl/`) and Cloud Machine Learning Engine (`https://cloud.google.com/ml-engine/`), which provide greater options. As an example, if a retailer would like to classify images of various dresses as per their colors, shape, and design, then they can use Cloud AutoML to feed some sample data to train custom ML models, which can then be used to generate image recognition for actual images. Likewise, if data scientists would like to create their own custom models to perform predictive analytics, then they can use a framework like TensorFlow along with a managed service like the Cloud Machine Learning Engine, which is already integrated with many other Google services and also provides a familiar interface like Jupyter notebooks to create custom models. These services, clubbed with Cloud TPUs (TensorFlow Processing Unit, `https://cloud.google.com/tpu/`), provide up to 180 teraflops of performance, providing the computational power to train and run cutting-edge machine learning models at scale.

In order to stay up to date on the latest Google Cloud big data and machine learning-related announcements, you can subscribe to the following blog: `https://cloud.google.com/blog/big-data/`.

Kubernetes Engine

In the last few years, the developer community has embraced the use of containers (like Docker) to deploy applications in the form of images that are lightweight, stand alone, and include everything needed to run it: code, runtime, system tools, system libraries, and settings. Now, to effectively run containers at scale, you need an orchestration engine which can help in operational aspects like the autoscaling of the cluster in lines with load, auto-healing of impaired nodes, setting, and managing resources limits (such as, CPU and RAM), providing integrated monitoring and logging capabilities—which is where Kubernetes (popularly known as K8s) comes into the picture. Google is the original creator of Kubernetes and has also been using it internally for container-based production deployments for multiple years before making it open source and making it part of the Cloud Native Computing Foundation.

If you love reading comics, then this Kubernetes Engine comic is not to be missed: `https://cloud.google.com/kubernetes-engine/kubernetes-comic/`.

Kubernetes draws on the same design principles that run popular Google services and provides the same benefits—automatic management, monitoring and liveness probes for application containers, automatic scaling, rolling updates, and more.

You can quickly get started using the Google Cloud console or APIs/CLIs and deploy your first cluster, like we did in the following screenshot. You can also use the Google Cloud Shell to deploy a sample application to test out the cluster features:

Apart from the Kubernetes Engine, Google also offers a Container Builder (`https://cloud.google.com/container-builder/`) service, using which you can bundle up your applications and other artefacts into Docker containers for deployment. As the service also supports automated triggers from source code repositories (such as GitHub, Bitbucket, and Google Cloud Source repositories), you can create fully automated CI/CD pipelines which can be initiated as soon as there's a new code check in. Another service which is related to this container ecosystem is the Container Registry (`https://cloud.google.com/container-registry/`) so that you can store your private container images and allow push, pull, and management of images from any system, VM instance, or your own hardware.

G Suite

Google has been offering online collaboration and productivity applications for independent users for quite some time. However, to make its mark in the enterprise space, Google launched G Suite (`https://gsuite.google.com/`) under its cloud business and since then has acquired multiple marquee customers:

Image showing the Google G Suite (source – `https://gsuite.google.com/features/`)

Broadly speaking, G Suite offers services in primarily four different categories, as follows:

- **Connect**: These are the set of services like Gmail, calendaring, Google+, and Hangouts, which enable better connections across the organization
- **Create**: In order to enable better collaboration, Google offers services like Docs, Sheets, Forms, Slides, Sites, and Jamboard, that can be used to create and share content between users
- **Access**: Lots of times, users want to back up and share files, videos, and other media using secure cloud storage, so for the same, Google Drive and Cloud Search come in handy
- **Control**: A final set of services are in the administration space so that enterprise controls like user management, security policies, backup and retention, and mobile devices management can be handled from a central place

 G Suite has an official blog to keep its users up to date on announcements and new features: `https://gsuiteupdates.googleblog.com/`.

Application Centric Design (CNMM Axis-2)

Now that we have explored a few interesting cloud-native services from Google Cloud, let's dive into the next topic of actually building some cloud-native application architectures and the best practices around those.

Serverless microservice

Similar to the approach we took in our previous chapters around AWS and MS Azure, we will look at creating a serverless microservice using a few Google Cloud services. In fact, before we even dive in there, it's interesting to note the way Google defines its serverless services portfolio, which can be seen in the following diagram, wherein even some early services including App Engine are included, apart from the latest ones that include Cloud Functions and the Cloud Machine Learning Engine. For more details, please refer to the whitepapers and content on the Google Cloud portal:

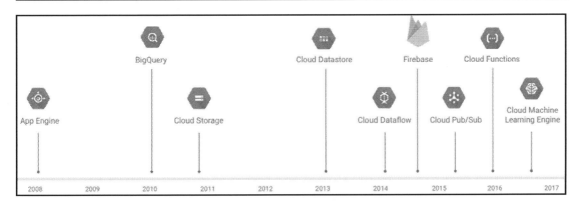

Image source – https://cloud.google.com/serverless/whitepaper/

As for the actual application, we will again use the same sample of building a serverless weather service application, which behind the scenes will invoke the OpenWeatherMap API. Like we did in previous chapters, we will use the cloud functions capability of Google cloud, however won't be able to use Google Cloud Endpoints (managed API service) as at the time of writing this book, there's no direct integration between the two services. Also, the Google Cloud functions currently only support JavaScript and execute in Node.js runtime, so we will convert the business logic of our earlier written functions to JavaScript to demonstrate this sample use case. As a result, we will use the following reference architecture to build the sample application:

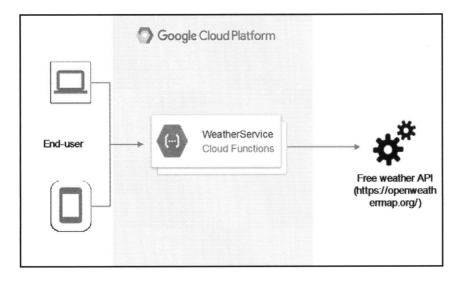

Serverless microservice – sample walkthrough

As in previous chapters, we will create a serverless microservice using Google Cloud Functions, so let's follow these to create a working example:

1. Go to Google Cloud Console and locate **Cloud Functions**, as follows:

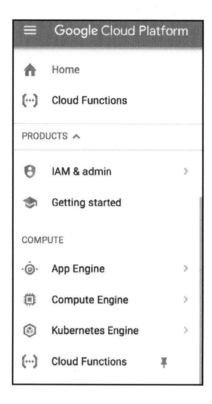

2. Click on the **Create Functions** option and start the process of defining an HTTP trigger function, as follows:

3. Use the following code in the **index.js** section to handle the main business logic of our serverless microservice. Also, please note that just below the code in the console, the value of the **Function to execute** option should be set to weatherService:

```
function handlePUT(req, res) {
 // Return Forbidden message for POST Request
 res.status(403).send('Forbidden!');
 }

function handleGET(req, res) {
 // Retrieve URL query parameters
 var zip = req.query.zip;
 var countrycode = req.query.countrycode;
 var apikey = req.query.apikey;

// Create complete OpenWeatherMap URL using user-provided
parameters
 var baseUrl = 'http://api.openweathermap.org/data/2.5/weather';
 var completeUrl = baseUrl + "?zip=" + zip + "," + countrycode +
"&appid=" + apikey;
 console.log("Request URL--> " + completeUrl)

// Import the sync-request module to invoke HTTP request
 var weatherServiceRequest = require('sync-request');

// Invoke OpenWeatherMap API
 var weatherServiceResponse = weatherServiceRequest('GET',
completeUrl);
 var statusCode = weatherServiceResponse.statusCode;
 console.log("RESPONSE STATUS -->" + statusCode);

// Check if response was error or success response
 if (statusCode < 300) {
 console.log("JSON BODY DATA --->>" +
weatherServiceResponse.getBody());
 // For Success response, return back appropriate status code,
content-type and body
 console.log("Setting response content type to json");
 res.setHeader('Content-Type', 'application/json');
 res.status(statusCode);
 res.send(weatherServiceResponse.getBody());
 } else {
```

```
console.log("ERROR RESPONSE -->" + statusCode);
//For Error response send back appropriate error details
res.status(statusCode);
res.send(statusCode);
}
}

/**
 * Responds to a GET request with Weather Information. Forbids a
PUT request.
 *
 * @param {Object} req Cloud Function request context.
 * @param {Object} res Cloud Function response context.
 */
exports.weatherService = (req, res) => {
switch (req.method) {
case 'GET':
handleGET(req, res);
break;
case 'PUT':
handlePUT(req, res);
break;
default:
res.status(500).send({
error: 'Something blew up!'
});
break;
}
};
```

4. Now, click on the **package.json** option and edit it to include our code-specific dependencies, as follows:

Here's the code snippet to put in the **package.json** window:

```
{
"name": "sample-http",
"version": "0.0.1",
"dependencies": {
"sync-request": "^2.0"
}
}
```

5. Click the **Create** button once you have verified that all of the settings and code are in line with the previously mentioned steps. In a few minutes, the function will be created and active in the console.

6. Now, it's time to test the function and for the same, go to your function details page and under the **Tigger** option, you will find the HTTPS endpoint for your function which can be used to invoke and test the microservice. Copy this URL which will then be used in the next step:

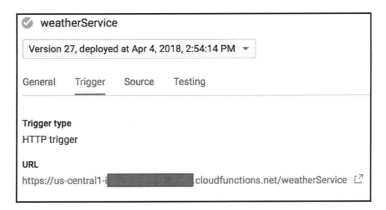

7. Now, append the following parameters to the preceding URL: `zip`, `countrycode`, and `apikey`, as follows:

```
https://us-central1-abcdef-43256.cloudfunctions.net/weatherService/
?zip=10011&countrycode=us&apikey=vjhvjvjhvjhv765675652hhjvjsdjysfyd
fjy
```

Now, use any internet browser of your choice and go to this URL and see the magic for yourself! If the function executes successfully, then you should be able to see a JSON response with weather information for the location you specified in the parameters.

8. You can also test the same using the command line by using the `curl` command as follows:

```
$ curl -X GET
'https://us-central1-idyllic-coder-198914.cloudfunctions.net/weathe
rService/?zip=10001&countrycode=us&apikey=098172635437y363535'
{"coord":{"lon":-73.99,"lat":40.73},"weather":[{"id":500,"main":"Ra
in","description":"light
rain","icon":"10d"}],"base":"stations","main":{"temp":285.07,"press
ure":998,"humidity":87,"temp_min":284.15,"temp_max":286.15},"visibi
lity":16093,"wind":{"speed":10.8,"deg":290,"gust":14.9},"clouds":{"
all":90},"dt":1522869300,"sys":{"type":1,"id":1969,"message":0.0059
,"country":"US","sunrise":1522837997,"sunset":1522884283},"id":4200
27013,"name":"New York","cod":200}
```

9. Once you have tested the function, you can also monitor it from the console, under the **General** tab of the function details. There are multiple different views available, like those based on *invocations*, *memory usage*, and *execution time*, as follows:

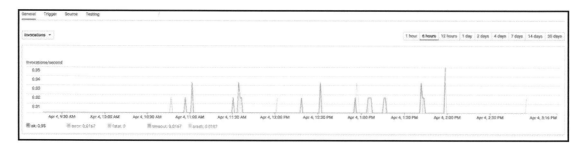

Invocation/sec view

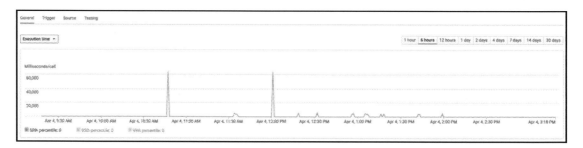

Execution time (Milliseconds/call) view

10. Another important aspect of managing your Google Function is the Stackdriver **Logs** option, which can provide you with details of backend debugging from the code and function execution, as follows:

Screenshot showing the **Logs** option

So with this, we have completed an end-to-end demo of how to design a serverless microservice using Google functions.

Automation in the Google Cloud Platform (CNMM Axis-3)

As discussed in previous chapters as well, automation is one of the key aspects when looking at optimally deploying and managing your applications in cloud. So in line with this, Google Cloud apart from offering many services which help automate processes and workflows, also has a rich set of APIs and SDKs. In fact, based on developer's individual preferences there are multiple options for SDK client libraries, including Java, Python, NodeJS, Ruby, Go, .Net and PHP, that provide flexibility and ease of automation and integration. So in the upcoming section, let's explore this further and look at various options for automation and DevOps implementations.

Infrastructure as code

Google Cloud offers a service that is very similar to AWS CloudFormation, called Google Cloud Deployment Manager, using which infrastructure components can be easily authored in a declarative fashion (YAML) to automate various provisioning and automation-related tasks. Therefore, using this, service you can create templates which can have multiple components of the application provisioned and deployed using a template.

For example, if you had a three-tier web application which is autoscaled and has load balancers in front of it, with a database for persistence, then instead of creating that manually every time you want to launch a new instance of the application, you could possibly write a YAML Cloud Deployment Manager template which can automate the entire process. To make it dynamic, you can also use template properties and environment variables in the template which can be supplied based on different individual launches. Test/Dev environments may have smaller fleet size, compared to production which has to be fully scalable.

There are a couple of other interesting features around template modules and composite types, which can help extend the functionality of Deployment Manager greatly. As part of the template modules, you can write helper files in Python or Jinja to perform specific functions, like generating unique resources names, and make your templates even more sophisticated. Using the same mechanism of leveraging Jinja or Python-based logic, you can create composite types, which is basically the ability to have one or more templates that are preconfigured to work together. As an example of a Composite type, you can create a type which is basically a specific configuration of a VPC network, which can be reused whenever you are creating a new set of application environments.

 Refer to the following link for the latest supported resources with Cloud Deployment Manager: https://cloud.google.com/deployment-manager/docs/configuration/supported-resource-types.

Now, let's take a look at an actual sample and how that can be used to create resources in Google Cloud. To make it easy to get started, Google offers samples on GitHub and so we use a sample from there only to quickly get started and demonstrate the concepts. The following is the link to this sample, which basically creates a virtual machine in a specific Google Cloud project: https://github.com/GoogleCloudPlatform/deploymentmanager-samples/blob/master/examples/v2/quick_start/vm.yaml.

As also mentioned in the notes of this template, remember to update the placeholders for your project id will be MY_PROJECT, as well as instance family name: FAMILY_NAME, to properly provision sample instance using Deployment Manager.

One of the quickest ways to do this is by using Google Cloud Shell, which comes with **pre-installed gcloud (CLI)** and so requires minimal configuration. As in the following screenshot, we used the sample template to provision the resources and the command was completed successfully:

```
cloudnativearchitectures@dyllic-coder-198914:~$ gcloud deployment-manager deployments create simple-deployment --config vm.yaml
The fingerprint of the deployment is 7y7p0qjcFEg7CpiDsqiphQ==
Waiting for create [operation-1525443310211-56b61f2a14fb8-7a136a28-a6aa7aa5b]...done.
Create operation operation-1525443310211-56b61f2a14fb8-7a136a28-aaa7aa5b completed successfully.
NAME                       TYPE                  STATE       ERRORS  INTENT
quickstart-deployment-vm   compute.v1.instance   COMPLETED   []
```

Post the successful creation of your resources, you can also use the gcloud CLI to describe the created resources, as follows:

```
cloudnativearchitectures@idyllic-coder-198914:~$ gcloud deployment-manager deployments describe simple-deployment
---
fingerprint: 7y7pOqjcF6g7Cp1OeqlphQ==
id: '6126455663787889665'
insertTime: '2018-05-04T07:15:10.302-07:00'
manifest: manifest-1525443310334
name: simple-deployment
operation:
  endTime: '2018-05-04T07:15:46.580-07:00'
  name: operation-1525443310211-56b61f2s14fb8-7a136a28-eaa7aa5b
  operationType: insert
  progress: 100
  startTime: '2018-05-04T07:15:10.880-07:00'
  status: DONE
  user: cloudnativearchitectures@gmail.com
NAME                        TYPE                  STATE        INTENT
quickstart-deployment-vm   compute.v1.instance   COMPLETED
```

Apart from using the gcloud CLI, you can also use the Google Cloud Console and go to the Cloud Deployment Manager section and look at the same deployment to get more details by clicking on various sections and links, as follows:

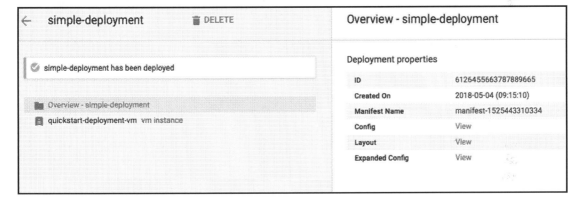

CI/CD for serverless microservices

Google Cloud is still in its early stages when it comes to CI/CD-related aspects for serverless microservices. Although for source code management Google offers a service called Cloud Source Repositories (https://cloud.google.com/source-repositories/), which can also be used to manage the code for Cloud functions, beyond that, native capabilities to create a fully-fledged CI/CD environment are limited at the time of writing this book.

One of the options which helps in this process is the serverless framework, which has a plugin for Google Cloud Functions and helps create, install, package, and deploy functions related to business logic easily. More details can be found at the following link: `https://github.com/serverless/serverless-google-cloudfunctions`.

There's also an example, which can help you quickly get started: `https://serverless.com/framework/docs/providers/google/examples/`.

CI/CD for container-based applications

One of the most popular ways to deploy container-based applications on Google Cloud is by using Kubernetes. In fact, as discussed earlier, Kubernetes originated from Google's internal technologies, invented to solve problems exactly like continuous code integration and deployment. That's why if you are looking to implement CI/CD patterns in such an environment, then it's easy to do so.

It's pretty straightforward to implement release management aspects if you are using Kubernetes CLI/API as it has actions which can implement updating resources with the latest version of application code by using the latest container images. You can do this by using the rolling updates mechanism, or if during the update process there are some issues that have been discovered, then you can also abort the process or roll back to previous versions. More details on the Kubernetes CLI update operations can be found at the following link: `https://kubernetes.io/docs/reference/kubectl/cheatsheet/#updating-resources`.

Google Cloud has an interesting comic that can help you learn the CI/CD options with Kubernetes in a fun manner: `https://cloud.google.com/kubernetes-engine/kubernetes-comic/`.

Another mechanism to implement CI/CD in the Kubernetes environment is by using Jenkins, which is an open source automation server that lets you flexibly orchestrate your build, test, and deployment pipelines. In order to do that, you need to deploy Jenkins on the Kubernetes Engine (a Google Cloud hosted version of Kubernetes) and install Kubernetes plugins for Jenkins, setting up proper configuration to orchestrate the entire deployment process. The following diagram shows the entire setup and different steps, as per the Google Cloud documentation:

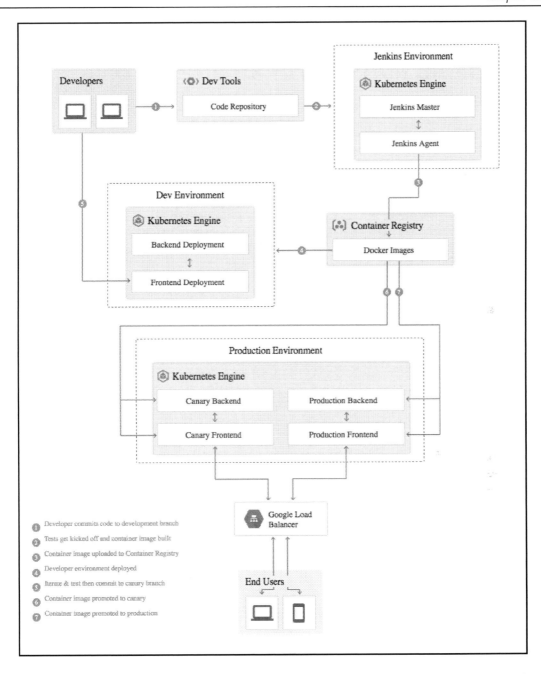

Image showing how to set up a continuous delivery pipeline using Jenkins and Kubernetes Engine (source – https://cloud.google.com/solutions/continuous-delivery-jenkins-kubernetes-engine)

Patterns for moving off from monolithic application architectures to Google cloud native architectures

As discussed in earlier sections, originally, our focus was mainly on greenfield applications and how to leverage cloud-native capabilities like serverless, containers, microservices architectures, CI/CD patterns, and so on. However, in typical enterprise environments, most customers already have significant investment in their existing on-premise or colocation environments, so those workloads also need to be moved to the cloud to benefit holistically. To enable the same, Google Cloud offers some native services as well as partner offerings which can be leveraged across various stages of migration. Broadly speaking, Google suggests four different phases in any migration project, which includes *assessment*, *planning*, *network configuration*, and *replication*.

For most the part, during the assessment and network configuration phases, the onus is on the customer to look at the appropriate tooling, developing automation that can enable the discovery of existing workloads in on-premise environments as well as the creation of matching the network config on cloud, which can enable a seamless migration path.

For the planning phase, Google has a set of recommended partners, such as Cloudamize, CloudPhysics, and ATADATA, which can be leveraged to inspect the current on-premises environment and accordingly map them to the correct cloud services as well as right-sized instance types for best performance.

 Refer to the following link for the latest set of Google Cloud recommended migration partners: https://cloud.google.com/migrate/.

Similarly, for the actual VM migration phase, Google has a set of recommended partners, like CloudEndure, Velostrata, and ATADATA, which can again help replicate on-premise virtual machines directly to the cloud. Apart from these partner offerings, Google Cloud also offers an option to directly import the virtual disks using its native service capability, however that's not an optimal option for large scale migrations and partner products offer better capabilities there. You can find more details on the VM Migration aspects at the following link: https://cloud.google.com/compute/docs/vm-migration/.

Other than VM migrations, another very important aspect to consider in large scale migrations is around data migration. To do that, there are a few different options, as follows:

- **Cloud Storage Transfer Service**: This service helps you transfer data from other clouds (like AWS) to Google Cloud storage buckets using HTTP/HTTPS-based interfaces. You could do this directly using the Google Cloud Console, REST APIs, or even using Google Cloud Client API libraries. More details can be found at `https://cloud.google.com/storage/transfer/`.

- **Google Transfer Appliance**: Like the AWS Snowball service, Google Cloud also offers a physical appliance which you can lease from Google to transfer large amounts of data to the cloud. At present, it's available in 2 different sizes – 100 TB and 480 TB – which you can request for a few days to connect to your local storage systems, transfer data, and then ship back to Google to transfer it in one of your cloud storage buckets. Before being stored on the Transfer Appliance, all captured data is deduplicated, compressed, and encrypted with an industry standard AES 256 algorithm using a password and passphrase that you specify. With this service, you save on both cost and time, as this helps you quickly migrate the data without using your internet bandwidth. More details can be found at `https://cloud.google.com/transfer-appliance/docs/introduction`.

- **Google BigQuery Data Transfer Service**: In most cases, customers are also using many SaaS applications, like Adwords, DoubleClick Campaign Manager, DoubleClick for Publishers, and YouTube. In order to analyze the data from these services, customers can use the BigQuery Data Transfer Service to directly transfer their data to BigQuery and build a data warehouse to run analytical queries. This service ensures continuous data replication at scale, and to visualize the trends, customers can use ISV offerings like Tableau, Looker, and ZoomData, on top of the BigQuery instance. More details can be found at `https://cloud.google.com/bigquery/transfer/`.

To understand which service is better suited for your migration projects, look at the *Choose the Right service matrix* published at `https://cloud.google.com/products/data-transfer/`.

Summary

In this chapter, we dove deep into the third significant cloud provider, Google Cloud Platform, and after understanding its origins and evolution, we focused on differentiating services like Cloud AI, Kubernetes Engine, and G Suite. Post that, we understood the concepts around serverless microservices and actually created a sample weather service application, leveraging Google Cloud functions. That led us to the next section, which focused on automation and how Google Cloud Deployment Manager can be used to create repeatable templates for treating infrastructure as code. We also looked at options for implementing CI/CD patterns in serverless environments as well as Kubernetes-based containerized deployments. Finally, we explored various options to migrate existing on-premise applications and workloads using various Google Cloud Native services as well as partner offerings. With all of the aforementioned concepts, we have completed exploring the top three public cloud providers and their capabilities to build more cloud-native architectures.

In the next and final chapter, we will bring all the concepts together and look at some of the evolving technology trends and predications based on those, so that you are ready to brace for the continuous change in this arena!

12
What's Next? Cloud Native Application Architecture Trends

In the previous chapters, we learned about multiple different aspects, starting from the core definition of the **Cloud Native Maturity Model (CNMM)**, then peeling back different layers, and finally trying out various cloud providers hands-on. In this chapter, we are going to focus on a bunch of newer things, including looking at the future and talking about a few predictions!

Here are some of the areas we will focus on:

- Top seven predictions for the next three years – what to expect in terms of the evolution of cloud native architectures
- The future of enterprises on the cloud
- New IT roles that will possibly evolve (such as an AI Officer)

These topics will help you learn the following skills:

- Understanding the trends to future-proof your strategies and architectures
- Areas of growth and evolution in your personal career

So, let's dive right in!

Predictions for the next three years – what to expect in terms of cloud native architecture evolution

Although the cloud has already become mainstream for all types of applications and use cases, if we look at the overall market potential, it's still in its very early stages. That, coupled with the trends and advancements we are seeing, let's look at the top seven predictions that will promote the cloud native adoption in the coming three years.

Open source frameworks and platforms

Many customers are worried about lock-in aspects in the public cloud. However, this fear is totally unfounded as every piece of software and application has some vendor-specific intellectual aspects which provide value to the customer, so they shouldn't just be viewed from a lock-in perspective. As an example, for, say, word processing, many of the customers make use of Microsoft Word, so if you use that to create a document, in a way you are tied to the application, but that doesn't imply that you are locked in. However, in many of the enterprise scenarios, there are certain COTS applications which can be replaced by other open source options which both helps bring down costs and reduces dependency on a specific vendor. As a classic example of this, many of the enterprise customers who have been using Oracle databases for years have now started to go down the path to re-platform those databases to open source options like PostgreSQL or MySQL.

In the same spirit, nowadays there's a need for cloud providers to demonstrate their alignment to open source software standards, and so they have also released multiple frameworks and packages on GitHub that can be forked by anyone. A popular example of such an open source platform is Kubernetes (an open source system for managing containerized applications), which is available under the Apache-2.0 license and can be cloned or downloaded from GitHub (`https://github.com/kubernetes/kubernetes`).

Another major step in this direction to make microservice-based cloud architectures open and community led was the launch of the **Cloud Native Computing Foundation (CNCF)** (`https://www.cncf.io/`) in 2017. As this was announced, a few of the very first Platinum members were all hyper-scale cloud providers like Amazon Web Services, Microsoft Azure, and Google Cloud. Since its launch, many organizations have now become a part of this community and they continue to lead the mission of keeping the software for container-based microservices ecosystems active and open source.

 To learn more about CNCF's charter, review the following link: `https://www.cncf.io/about/charter/`.

Other than efforts around CNCF, all the public cloud providers are, in general, also making an effort to stay open and developer-friendly. The following are links to the top three cloud provider's open source microsites:

- Open source at AWS: `https://aws.github.io/`
- Open source software on Azure: `https://azure.microsoft.com/en-us/overview/open-source/`
- Open source on Google Cloud: `https://github.com/GoogleCloudPlatform`

Future trend #1

Open Source software and frameworks will continue to increase and make cloud native architectures even more developer friendly.

Increased abstraction from infrastructure services

A few years back, when the public cloud started to gain traction, the main emphasis was on the core infrastructure blocks covering Compute, Storage, Networking, Databases, and so on. However, as various cloud providers started to introduce newer services, that trend changed rapidly as the services were more higher level and abstracted the underlying infrastructure aspects greatly. As an example, we have seen services like Amazon Connect, which is a cloud-based contact center offering from AWS, and the end user doesn't have to bother about the underlying infrastructure at all and can quickly get started in a matter of minutes, focusing on their core business aspects, call routing logic, and so on.

Another aspect from an application deployment perspective we have seen is that rather than using native virtualized cloud-based instances, developers are moving towards container-based deployments or even serverless approaches using services like AWS Lambda. These techniques further abstract the user from the underlying infrastructure and let them focus on core application and business logic. In fact, this trend is not just visible in the compute layer, but even the databases (like Amazon's serverless Aurora), messaging (Amazon SQS), analytics (Amazon Athena), and so on.

As a result of the aforementioned shift, we will continue to see application deployment models change, which will be less dependent on the infrastructure specifications, as that will be automatically handled by the services itself. Another side effect of such changes will be that lines between the typical **Infrastructure-as-a-Service (IaaS)**, **Platform-as-a-Service (PaaS)**, and **Software-as-a-Service (SaaS)** aspects will continue to be blurry and everything will become cloud or cloud native, to be more accurate. We are already seeing some variations of this, even currently, where new terms like **Functions-as-a-Service (FaaS)** or **Anything-as-a-Service (XaaS)** are being used in multiple contexts.

Future trend #2

Cloud services will be more application and software oriented by changing the deployment models to be agnostic to underlying infrastructure. Also, lines between IaaS/PaaS/SaaS will become even more blurry with a greater number of cloud native services being introduced.

Systems will become smarter and AI/ML driven, starting with DevOps and moving on to NoOps

With the advent of the public cloud, we saw new types of infrastructure management patterns, which included autoscaling as well as self-healing-based techniques, making the application scaling and fault recovery process as automated as possible. During the next wave of automation, we saw DevOps become more mainstream, which was also a result of blurring lines between true developer and system operations roles due to abstracted cloud services. As a result, we saw faster and frequent deployments, easy rollback mechanisms in the case of issues, and better tools and services, which made the entire process easier and integrated. However, even with these type of advanced automation techniques, there's a need for operations and updates at certain operating system and application level aspects, which is still mostly a manual effort. Newer services like Amazon Lambda and Amazon serverless Aurora are taking that kind of heavy lifting away from the customers' hands, but still, there's a long way to go until the systems are truly smarter and can handle most of the ops-related aspects on their own. This may also mean that systems will have to be smarter, where instead of reactively responding to a situation they will proactively predict possible failures scenarios and the need for any changes, thereby reducing the need to manually correct anything or even build sophisticated automations, which may not even be needed!

To enable the aforementioned transition, technologies like Artificial Intelligence and Machine Learning will play a big role. In fact, in part, that has already started to happen, where many cloud providers' services are powered by predictive modelling techniques behind the scenes. As an example, Amazon Macie uses Machine Learning to automatically discover, classify, and protect sensitive data in AWS. Likewise, Amazon GuardDuty identifies suspected attackers through integrated threat intelligence feeds and uses Machine Learning to detect anomalies in account and workload activity. These are great examples of Machine Learning being used in the space of security, however, as we progress, the same principles and mechanisms will become more mainstream for application deployment and management models, where typical operations will change greatly.

 Refer to this interesting blog post where Amazon details the mathematical and Machine Learning-based tools it has created to handle security-related aspects in many of its services: `https://aws.amazon.com/blogs/security/protect-sensitive-data-in-the-cloud-with-automated-reasoning-zelkova/`.

Future trend #3

Cloud services and systems will be smarter, where typical requirements around infrastructure and application operations will diminish, thereby resulting in newer principles of NoOps.

Developers will natively develop new applications in the cloud, instead of first developing locally

Even though the cloud has become very popular for any type of application deployment, most of an application's development (the actual coding) happens in an offline mode where developers have IDEs on their workstations: they write the code, run the unit tests there, and once everything looks good, it is pushed to the central code repository, which again may or may not be in the cloud. However, once the entire build process runs, the actual deployment of application binaries happens in the cloud most of the time. This is primarily due to a few factors:

- In order to develop in the cloud, they need to be continuously connected to the internet, which may not always be possible.
- The IDEs and tools that the developers are comfortable with using on their workstations have never been designed for cloud-type environments.
- Some customers also fear that their codebase, which is their core IP, may not be safe to be put into the cloud.

I am sure the preceding points are just a sample of possible reasons for developing locally, but most of the preceding fears are totally unfounded. In fact, the cloud has come a long way where if developers are natively developing there, then it not only makes the process easier but also enables them to leverage many cloud services natively in their architectures, which otherwise would need to be coded on their own.

As examples of ongoing improvements in this context, Azure has Visual Studio Code to code for the cloud and likewise Amazon has AWS Cloud9, which helps code with just a browser. In the same spirit, Microsoft also acquired GitHub, which again is focusing on attracting developers and making it easy for them to develop natively in the cloud. In fact, all of this is just the beginning, and with time it will be much easier for developers to natively develop for the cloud, and the entire dev/test experience will be radically different in the future. This will further enable easy global collaboration and have applications created and managed in a decentralized manner.

Future trend #4

Cloud services will enable developers to be first-class citizens by providing multiple different options to effectively develop for the cloud in the cloud.

Voice, chatbots, and AR/VR-based interaction models will become prevalent, mainly powered by the cloud

In the last year or so, we have seen a great deal of conversations and action around Artificial Intelligence/Machine Learning, as well as Augmented Reality/Virtual Reality. Although these technologies have existed for multiple years, for effective AI/ML algorithm creation you need lots of data, and likewise for AR/VR, you need plenty of CPUs/GPUs. Now, as the cloud provides you the underlying infrastructure components at scale, you can virtually store petabytes of data and have thousands of CPUs available to you in no time for bringing your new-age applications to life. Apart from this, we have also seen tons of progress in the services and frameworks in this area, like Apache MXNet (`https://mxnet.apache.org/`), TensorFlow (`https://www.tensorflow.org/`), Caffe (`http://caffe.berkeleyvision.org/`), PyTorch (`https://pytorch.org/`), and so on. Similarly, we have seen major growth in various types of bots, ranging from simple Q&A types of bots to a full-featured bot which can complete a specific use case, like travel bookings. These bots are also becoming mainstream as part of cloud-based contact center implementations wherein, based on the call routing flow, many of the tasks can be fully handled by the bots themselves without any human dependency. These bots also function on AI/ML technologies as behind the scenes they use techniques like **Natural Language Processing (NLP)**, voice-to-text, text-to-voice, image recognition, and **Optical Content Recognition (OCR)**. Likewise, on the AR/VR side, we have seen the use of digital avatars being used for both end user interactions (for example, customers can digitally try dresses online), as well as industrial/enterprise use cases (like detecting problems in heavy machinery through a remote engineer). These trends are further amplified by cloud services like Amazon Sumerian, which can be used to create VR, AR, and 3D experiences that can run on popular hardware such as Oculus Go, Oculus Rift, HTC Vive Google Daydream, and Lenovo Mirage as well as Android and iOS mobile devices.

Take a look at the following Google Duplex Demo from Google IO 2018: `https://www.youtube.com/watch?v=bd1mEm2Fy08`.

Another classic example of voice-based interaction is Amazon Alexa, which is a cloud-based voice service which you can directly interact with using devices like Amazon Echo, Amazon Echo Dot, or you can even integrate in your own devices using the Alexa Voice Service (`https://developer.amazon.com/alexa-voice-service`). As a result of these integrations, and available Alexa skills, you can control your TV, temperature/lights at home, or even do banking operations (like checking a credit card's payment status or initiating a payment).

Earlier, for invoking an application, a user would typically need browser-based access or mobile app and likewise, for system level-integrations, APIs would come in handy. However, with the aforementioned new types of interaction mechanisms of chatbot, voice, or AR/VR-based interfaces, the application development patterns are also changing. In fact, not just for applications, but even for infrastructure management tasks, many organizations have started to create Alexa skills to launch an EC2 instance, get monitoring details, or even delete it. One area which is still nascent as of now is gesture-based (like hand or facial gestures without any applications) interfaces, however that too is a function of time before it becomes mainstream. As a result, in the future, applications will be more interactive, leverage multiple different interfaces, and also have a better user experience.

Future trend #5

Cloud services will enable applications to be more interactive, leveraging techniques like voice, gestures, and virtual reality/augmented reality, thereby reducing the gap between humans and machines.

Cloud native architectures will expand beyond data centers to "things"

Traditionally, applications have been designed for either server-based environments or mobile devices. However, off late, that's changing a bit, where now code and applications are also being written for "things". These *things* could be any physical device, like your light bulb, thermostat, child's toy, or an actual car, which is connected to the internet and controlled that way. As per this article from Gartner (`https://www.gartner.com/newsroom/id/3598917`), an estimated 20.4 billion such devices will be connected to the internet by 2020, thereby greatly changing the way we interact with them. In fact, with so many devices connected to the backend, the application architectures and the amount of data that's transmitted and consumed will greatly change. Again, this wouldn't be possible without the cloud as this will require scalable stream-based data processing techniques, and services like AWS IoT and Amazon Kinesis will become central to implementations. Apart from that, many devices can't also be connected to the internet all the time, as they are in remote locations which have limited internet connectivity (like sensors in oil rigs), so for those scenarios, even *edge computing* will be pretty critical. These kinds of use cases will be supported by services like AWS Greengrass, which lets you run local compute, messaging, and data caching for connected devices in a secure way. For smaller devices like micro-controllers, which again need to support such edge computing scenarios, new kernel services like Amazon FreeRTOS will be pretty critical and enable those deployments.

As the data from these edge devices will be ingested in the cloud, there will be the possibility to perform real-time, batch, or even trend analytics, which will again continue to open new avenues and evolve the architectural patterns.

Future trend #6

Cloud native applications will have an end-to-end impact, right from the edge to the backend applications to the customer facing portals, thereby changing the way applications are created and deployed.

Data will continue to be new "oil"

Data management has always been pivotal to any successful application development and deployment, and with the cloud, this trend continues to grow, as now you can harness new channels of information as well as store petabytes of data easily. In fact, many organizations are now moving to a model where they are creating centralized data lakes, where data is being fed from various different sources, which includes devices connected to the web to social media and business applications, which is then used for analytics purposes and to get deep insights and trends.

 Review these data lake architecture details on AWS and Azure:
https://aws.amazon.com/answers/big-data/data-lake-solution/
https://docs.microsoft.com/en-us/azure/data-lake-store/data-lake-store-overview.

The preceding trend has also been promoted by the fact that there are now better and faster options in order to move the data to the cloud. Until a few years back, it was only possible to transfer the data over the internet/network with options like AWS DirectConnect or by using virtual appliances like AWS Storage Gateway. However, in the last couple of years, all of the cloud providers have created physical appliances, like Amazon Snowball, which can be ordered to your data centers, connected locally to transfer data, and, once done, shipped back to cloud providers for moving data to services like Amazon S3. It's not just these smaller data transfer appliances, as now you can also request a 45-foot long ruggedized shipping container, pulled by a semi-trailer truck, that can transfer 100 PB data per AWS Snowmobile! This is just the beginning of innovation and in the future, transfer to/from the cloud will become even easier and that will further promote collection, aggregation, and analytics from vast sets of data. As data moves to the cloud, applications will follow the trend and that's the reason data will continue to be central in overall cloud adoption.

Future trend #7

Data will be central to any cloud deployment and, as data migration paths to the cloud become easier to use, cloud native architecture adoption will increase dramatically.

The future of enterprises on the cloud

Enterprises are always risk averse and so have always been slow-movers in any technology patterns. The cloud is no different in that respect, as for many years, the enterprises were watching the progress, sitting on the side-lines and waiting for others to be first-movers. It was at the same time that we saw a huge surge of many new start-ups that were all using the cloud and slowly started to disrupt the mainstream, well-established enterprises. As examples, Lyft and Uber challenged the taxi/transportation business, Airbnb disrupted the hospitality industry, and likewise Oscar Insurance radically changed the health insurance sector. These types of successes were never easier earlier, but now with the cloud, everyone has access to same set of services and infrastructure resources which they can scale up/down based on their business needs... and this changes the playing field for everyone.

As a result of the aforementioned effect, many enterprises have realized that before anyone else disrupts their business, they themselves have to do it and ride this wave of innovation with the cloud. Therefore, we have seen many enterprises not just adopt the cloud, but even go all-in in the last few years in an attempt to redefine their operational and business model. Although this list of enterprise customers is continuously increasing, we have seen customers like GE, Capital One, Adobe, Hess, Kellogg's, Novartis, Infor, Suncorp, BestBuy, Philips, Goldman Sachs, and so on have all gone public on their usage of one or the other cloud platforms.

Refer to the following links for case studies from various cloud providers:

- AWS: `https://aws.amazon.com/solutions/case-studies/enterprise/`
- Azure: `https://azure.microsoft.com/en-us/case-studies/`
- Google Cloud: `https://cloud.google.com/customers/`

Other than commercial entities, we have also seen government and public sector entities adopting the cloud in a big way. As a few examples, NASA, FDA, FINRA, the US Department of Homeland Security, Government of Singapore, Transport for London, Government of Ontario, Business Sweden, City of Tel Aviv, the Chilean Ministry of Health, and so on all have some or the other workloads deployed in the cloud and can be seen as public references on various cloud providers' websites.

The change for enterprises is huge, as it's not just a technology upgrade/re-platforming, but it also has many operational and business implications wherein everything is now on-demand/opex oriented versus capex, which is pretty new model for the enterprises. Other than that, in order to move fast and to truly harness the power of the cloud, they also need to have smaller teams (like DevOps, two-pizza teams) who can try out new cloud services and features rapidly and incorporate them in their application architectures. Apart from keeping this agile/innovative culture, enterprises also need to have proper governance and security controls in place so that they can demonstrate the right controls to their auditors and ensure that the laws of the land are being adhered to properly. To make these entire changes smoother, various cloud providers have come up with pretty comprehensive cloud adoption and change management frameworks, which help the enterprise customers' CIO/CTOs and various other stakeholders make the move to cloud in a frictionless and disruption-proof manner.

 Refer to the following AWS Enterprise Strategy blog for interesting nuggets of information: `https://aws.amazon.com/blogs/enterprise-strategy/`

Another change all the enterprise customers have to handle is the training of their staff on the target cloud platform. For this, all cloud providers have comprehensive programs around training and certifications, which can help the customers and employees learn about service functionality, integration techniques, and best practices. However, apart from training their own employees, enterprise customers need experts to be involved in supporting them in critical phases of the project. For the same, all cloud providers have their specialist Professional Services consultants, who can come in and advise the customer on various technical, process, and project delivery aspects. To further help with the setup of **Cloud Centers of Excellence (CCOE)** and delivery teams equipped with the necessary cloud knowledge, in most cases, customers also make use of various consulting partners who specialize in various areas and help make cloud projects successful.

With the previously mentioned ingredients, customers are able to bring about change in their daily work and make their cloud native journey smooth and successful. As a result of these practices, we have seen some very interesting innovations from enterprise customers, as follows:

- Capital One's Amazon Alexa skill: `https://www.capitalone.com/applications/alexa/`
- FINRA Collects, Analyzes Billions of Brokerage Transaction Records Daily Using AWS: `https://youtu.be/rHUQQzYoRtE`

- NASA JPL's presentation on, How the Cloud is Helping Answer Cosmic Questions: `https://youtu.be/8UQfrQNo2nE`
- BMW Supports Model Launch, Develops Prospects with Cloud-Based Social Marketing: `https://customers.microsoft.com/en-us/story/bmw-supports-model-launch-develops-prospects-with-clo2`
- Airbus Defense and Space improves the quality of satellite images using Cloud Machine Learning: `https://cloud.google.com/blog/big-data/2016/09/google-cloud-machine-learning-now-open-to-all-with-new-professional-services-and-education-programs`

New IT roles

One of the long-term impacts of the cloud permeating enterprises is that there are multiple new roles which have evolved. Some of these are already mainstream, whereas with evolving technology trends, some of them are starting to become more popular:

- **Chief Technology & Innovation Officer (CTIO)**: Earlier, organizations had either a CTO or a CIO, but nowadays due to increased focus on innovation, mainly powered by the cloud, a new role of CTIO has started to appear.
- **Cloud Solutions Architect**: Earlier, we used to have Application Architects, System Architects, Integration Architects, and so on, however with the possibilities that have opened up with cloud native architectures, a new role of Cloud Solutions architect has become very popular.
- **Cloud Migration Architect**: As many of enterprises have a huge amount of technical debt which they have to remove to effectively leverage the cloud, a new migration focused on the Cloud Migrations Architect role has started to appear off late.
- **DevOps Professional/Cloud Automation Engineer**: In order to fully leverage the power of the cloud, it is important to focus on automation and orchestration functionalities, which oftentimes requires coding, scripting, and ensuring that the proper operational procedures are in place, for which DevOps Professional/Cloud Automation Engineer roles have become pivotal.
- **Cloud Security Architect**: Security controls and procedures in the cloud are very different compared to an on-premises setup. Therefore, to leverage the cloud's security controls in a proper fashion, ensuring that proper compliance and governance models are being adhered to, the Cloud Security Architect role is being adopted in many organizations.

- **Cloud Economics Professional**: This is a very unique role and still not mainstream, however some organizations have started to hire professionals who focus on cloud usage optimization more from a cost management perspective. They focus more on looking at better financial constructs (like Reserved Instances) or even help with cost segregation within the internal organization by leveraging techniques like tagging.

Along with the preceding roles, there are multiple other roles which have become mainstream because of the growth of big data, analytics, and Machine Learning powered by the cloud. In fact, as AI and ML grow in the years to come, there's already increased discussion on the possible roles which may become important in that area. One such role is a *Chief AI Officer*, who will focus on not just technology aspects of harnessing the power of AI/ML, but also look at its social implications. As an example, when AI/ML becomes smarter and is able to make decisions on its own, like driving a car, then who's responsible when that self-driving car hits a pedestrian? Is it the AI or the developer who built that AI system? It's not an easy problem to solve and that's why new roles like *Chief AI Officer* will actually focus on these types of new society-impacting situations and even work with governments and various regulatory bodies to create proper rules and frameworks to maintain the balance of the society.

So, net-net, along with the aforementioned changes, the enterprises will have to evolve and adapt to stay successful and competitive in this new innovation-led era!

Summary

This brings us to the last section of this book, and we have covered lots of ground right from the beginning. So, let's go back a bit and reflect on what we have learned through, the various chapters.

We started by defining what it actually means to be *cloud native*, as that was the core part of laying the foundation of the entire discussion in the rest of the chapters. So, as a quick refresher, the CNMM revolves around three main axes:

- Cloud Native Service
- Application Centric Designs
- Automation

So, every customer will have a varying degree of maturity of across all of these axes, but essentially, they can still be cloud native:

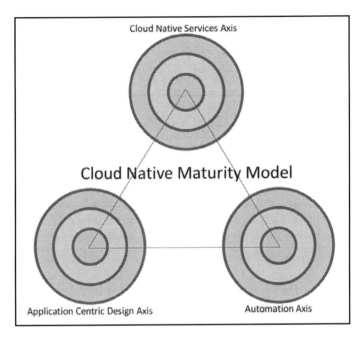

After this, we went into the details of the Cloud Adoption Framework and what it means from multiple different perspectives, including business, people, governance, platform, security, and operations. This eventually led us to the next important set of topics revolving around the essence of microservices, serverless, and how to build applications in the cloud using the 12-factor application framework. We then also looked at the cloud ecosystem, which is comprised of technology and consulting partners, as well as different software licensing and procurement models including marketplaces, bring-your-licenses, and so on. With all of these general concepts clearly understood, we started to take the onion-peeling approach and dived into the specifics of how you think about scalability, availability, security, cost management, and operational excellence, which are very important to understand from a cloud perspective, and how this is similar or different from the existing on-premise models.

After all of these concepts were clear, it was time to get our hands dirty by diving right into the specifics of the top three leading cloud providers, including Amazon WebServices, Microsoft Azure, and Google Cloud Platform. In each of these sections, we looked at their capabilities and differentiation based on the earlier described CNMM model. We looked at every cloud provider's key service offering, based on CNMM axis-1, followed by developing and deploying a serverless microservice based on CNMM axis-2, and finally concluded with automation/DevOps possibilities based on CNMM axis-3. This exercise gave us a deeper insight into the terms of all cloud providers and their relative comparisons as well.

Finally, in this chapter, we looked at a couple of aspects. One of the main was the top seven technology trends, which we can expect to see evolve in the next three years. This will help us look at not just current capabilities, but even plan for the future. After, we dived in to see the impact of the cloud on enterprises and how they are embracing the change. In the same section, we also learned about the new IT roles which we have seen evolve due to the cloud becoming mainstream in enterprises.

With this, we came to a conclusion, and if there's one thing you want to take away from this entire book, then that will be – *"Cloud is the new normal, and if you have to harness the full power of it, then there's no better way than being fully committed and going cloud native!"*

Other Books You May Enjoy

If you enjoyed this book, you may be interested in these other books by Packt:

Cloud Native Development Patterns and Best Practices
John Gilbert

ISBN: 978-1-78847-392-7

- Enable massive scaling by turning your database inside out
- Unleash flexibility via event streaming
- Leverage polyglot persistence and cloud-native databases
- Embrace modern continuous delivery and testing techniques
- Minimize risk by evolving your monoliths to cloud-native
- Apply cloud-native patterns and solve major architectural problems in cloud environment

Cloud Native programming with Golang
Mina Andrawos, Martin Helmich

ISBN: 978-1-78712-598-8

- Understand modern software applications architectures
- Build secure microservices that can effectively communicate with other services
- Get to know about event-driven architectures by diving into message queues such as Kafka, Rabbitmq, and AWS SQS
- Understand key modern database technologies such as MongoDB, and Amazon's DynamoDB
- Leverage the power of containers
- Explore Amazon cloud services fundamentals
- Know how to utilize the power of the Go language to access key services in the Amazon cloud such as S3, SQS, DynamoDB and more.
- Build front-end applications using ReactJS with Go
- Implement CD for modern applications

Leave a review - let other readers know what you think

Please share your thoughts on this book with others by leaving a review on the site that you bought it from. If you purchased the book from Amazon, please leave us an honest review on this book's Amazon page. This is vital so that other potential readers can see and use your unbiased opinion to make purchasing decisions, we can understand what our customers think about our products, and our authors can see your feedback on the title that they have worked with Packt to create. It will only take a few minutes of your time, but is valuable to other potential customers, our authors, and Packt. Thank you!

Index